Space and Place in
The Hunger Games

Space and Place in *The Hunger Games*

New Readings of the Novels

Edited by DEIDRE ANNE EVANS GARRIOTT,
WHITNEY ELAINE JONES *and*
JULIE ELIZABETH TYLER

McFarland & Company, Inc., Publishers
Jefferson, North Carolina

LIBRARY OF CONGRESS CATALOGUING-IN-PUBLICATION DATA

Space and Place in the Hunger Games : New Readings of the
    Novels / edited by Deidre Anne Evans Garriott, Whitney Elaine
    Jones and Julie Elizabeth Tyler.
        p.   cm.
    Includes bibliographical references and index.

    ISBN 978-0-7864-7633-6 (softcover : acid free paper) ∞
    ISBN 978-1-4766-1451-9 (ebook)

    1. Collins, Suzanne. Hunger Games.   2. Place (Philosophy)
in literature.   3. Space and time in literature.   I. Garriott,
Deidre Anne Evans, editor of compilation.   II. Jones, Whitney
Elaine, editor of compilation.   III. Tyler, Julie Elizabeth,
editor of compilation.
PS3603.O4558Z88 2014
813'.6—dc23   2014003626

BRITISH LIBRARY CATALOGUING DATA ARE AVAILABLE

© 2014 Deidre Anne Evans Garriott, Whitney Elaine Jones and
Julie Elizabeth Tyler. All rights reserved

*No part of this book may be reproduced or transmitted in any form
or by any means, electronic or mechanical, including photocopying
or recording, or by any information storage and retrieval system,
without permission in writing from the publisher.*

On the cover: arrow (Stockbyte/Thinkstock); fiery backdrop
(© 2014 Shutterstock)

Manufactured in the United States of America

McFarland & Company, Inc., Publishers
  Box 611, Jefferson, North Carolina 28640
    www.mcfarlandpub.com

To the children who are hungry for food,
for words, for stories, and for a voice.

Acknowledgments

We would like to thank professors and peers at the University of Tennessee for their generous support and guidance. We would also like to thank our families and friends for their encouraging words and enthusiasm about this project. We would like to acknowledge our contributing authors for their hard work and creativity, without which this project would not exist. And finally, we as co-editors would like to thank each other for the unfailing professionalism exhibited at each phase of this project, and most importantly for the loyalty, love, and good humor that comprise a strong and lasting friendship.

Table of Contents

Acknowledgments — vii

Introduction: Taking Up and Entering Critical Space — 1

Part I: Identifying and Challenging Narrative Spaces

Transgressing the Text and Playing Narrative Games: Katniss's Narrative, "Real or Not Real?"
 JULIE ELIZABETH TYLER — 16

Tipping the Odds Ever in Her Favor: An Exploration of Narrative Control and Agency in the Novel and Film
 ANNE M. CANAVAN *and* SARAH N. PETROVIC — 45

Part II: Provoking Change and Creating Radical Spaces

Katniss and Her Boys: Male Readers, the Love Triangle and Identity Formation
 WHITNEY ELAINE JONES — 60

The Making of the Citizen and the Politics of Maturation
 SUSAN SHAU MING TAN — 83

Part III: Experiencing Trauma in Safe Spaces

The Privileged Reader as Capitol and Learning Sympathy through Narrative
 ANN M. M. CHILDS — 102

Recreating the Holocaust: YA Dystopia and the Young Jewish Reader
 ADAM LEVIN — 124

Part IV: Popular Responses in Actual Spaces

"I have a kind of power I never knew I possessed": Transformative Motherhood and Maternal Influence
 KATIE AROSTEGUY — 146

Performing the Capitol in Digital Spaces: The Punitive Gaze of the
Panopticon Among Fans and Critics
   DEIDRE ANNE EVANS GARRIOTT   160
Creating a New Ethics: Student Responses, Reality Television and
Audience Awareness
   LINDA J. RICE *and* KATIE WRABEL   184

Part V: Envisioning Future Spaces

Outside the Seam: The Construction of and Relationship to
Panem's Nature
   CARISSA ANN BAKER   198
Political Muttations: "Real or Not Real?"
   BRUCE MARTIN   220

*Conclusion: Where Can We Go and What Can We Disrupt
   from Here?*   243
About the Contributors   247
Index   249

Introduction: Taking Up and Entering Critical Space

Suzanne Collins's dystopian, young adult (YA) trilogy *The Hunger Games* is not only about Katniss, the Girl on Fire, and her fight against the Capitol. It is not only a story about her romances with Gale, the vengeful rebel, and Peeta, the Boy with the Bread. Nor is it only a story about killing children, the pervasive media, and reality television. It is a novel about all of these things—and about particular encounters with and understandings of *space* and *place*, as contested concepts and phenomena. It is about how places define us and divide us from each other. It is about how space can be used politically and socially to wield power and create social hierarchies. It is about safe places and dangerous places. And it is about how space and place can be conceptualized, carved out, imagined, and used.

The trilogy is sensitive to encounters with and understandings of space and place, as well as of the political ramifications of dividing spaces and turning them into places. Space and place are essential to identity and even identification as a rhetorical process. These words, though closely related, often conflated, and used interchangeably, signify different ideas about landscape and how it is used. In their introduction to *Places of Public Memory: The Rhetoric of Museums and Memorials*, Carole Blair, Greg Dickinson, and Brian L. Ott assert that "place organizes memory" (1). Memory is a way of knowing ourselves, and public memory is a way of knowing each other. If place organizes memory, as Blair, Dickinson, and Ott argue, then it is the methodology of knowing ourselves and each other. However, as these public memory scholars note, place and space are different concepts. Though often used as synonyms, they assert, "a *place* that is bordered, specified, and locatable by being named is seen as different from open, undifferentiated, undesignated *space*" (23). Space becomes place because of human intervention, imposition, and interpretation. Thus, space and place are not binaries but relational: they rely on each other. Space must exist for a place to be imagined and constructed (Blair, Dickinson and Ott 23).

To provide an example, Katniss describes her environment in terms of divided spaces. We can perceive division through space in her earliest description of District 12. As she heads to the woods to hunt, she tells us, "Our part of District 12, nicknamed the Seam, is usually crawling with coal miners heading out to the morning shift at this hour" (THG 4). Before we can fully imagine all of District 12 or the larger political entity to which it belongs, Panem, we are aware that Katniss knows her world through defined places. She claims the Seam as "Our part of District 12." In doing so, we learn that even District 12 is divided between Katniss's "us" and a so-far unseen "them." This identification of "us" and "them" is predicated on identifying the places to which the "us" and "them" belong.

Immediately following this early description of the Seam and District 12, Katniss tells us that District 12 is surrounded and defined by a barbed-wire, supposedly-electrified fence (4). Going beyond the fence to the woods is "trespassing," indicating that this place is unique from District 12 (5). We learn much about Katniss simply because she knows how to negotiate these two places, how to pass through from one to the other unseen. She is clearly brave and daring, because she risks punishment if she is caught and because she trespasses with only a partner, Gale, rather than with an entire community. She is rebellious, as well, because she breaks the law. Thus, Collins uses places and divided spaces to develop her characters as well as her plot.

The most jarring example involves Panem and the districts' disruption of our own sense of place as we learn more about Katniss's world. Through Katniss's description of District 12 as a coal mining region, we imagine mountains surrounded by woods outside of the fenced district. It is not necessarily a place we, the readers, would know or recognize. It is *other*. On her way to the Capitol, however, we learn that "they tell us the Capitol was built in a place once called the Rockies. District 12 was in a region known as Appalachia" (41). This nation of districts, in which children are "reaped" for a gladiator-style fight to the death, invokes the United States. What is striking to us as co-editors of and contributing authors in this text, is that Katniss lives within the very region where we live and are engaging ourselves as scholars. We realize that our own sense of place has been destroyed and remade into a political entity that disgusts us. Some readers have been so taken with the idea that they are living in Panem now—that Panem shares its space with the United States—that they have sought to make maps, tracing Panem over the U.S.'s current political boundaries. Several *Tumblr* sites are devoted to using the trilogy to determine how the U.S.'s landscape has changed and its boundaries redrawn to make up Panem.

In line with the aforedescribed definitions of space and place, several authors in this collection argue that *The Hunger Games* creates "safe space," and thus suggest that this textual site is unbounded and atemporal. It can be manipulated and used for exploring ideas without transgressing the purpose of a specified, locatable place. In fact, we as editors observed that more often than not, both we and the contributors intuitively describe the trilogy as challenging sites of knowledge, such as gender roles, and opening up new ways of thinking about common topics and themes. We argue that *The Hunger Games* reverses the expected chronology of using *space* to create *place* and instead breaks down *place* to create *space*, where traditional ways of thinking our called into question and examined. In other words, just as the trilogy disrupts our sense of place, we argue that the trilogy also disrupts knowledge and place and instead returns us to the freedom and safety of space.

Our earliest conceptions of this project began with the goal of inviting other scholars to discuss the trilogy's consequences in the world outside of the text—in our world. As readers of the novels ourselves, we felt their effects in our lives, starting with our motivation to produce and contribute to this collection of critical essays. Indeed, one editor and contributor, Whitney Elaine Jones, as co-assistant teacher in an upper-level undergraduate literature course, has experienced teaching this trilogy, and has seen how her own students have appropriated symbols from the text, like the Mockingjay pin, and worn them all over campus. We watched as Twitter-users micro-blogged their opinions about how the novels should be adapted to film. We felt that the trilogy also challenges conventions of young adult (YA) fiction and calls into question the authenticity of the adolescent voice in the genre, the authenticity of the narrator, and child's role as a grassroots political activist.

Because of this shared sense of significance that we three felt and observed on our own university campus, we submitted a call-for-papers through an academic listserv. We invited critics from a variety of backgrounds—academic or popular, institutionally-affiliated or independent, graduate student or Ph.D.— to submit abstracts for essays about *The Hunger Games*. Because we were in our first stages of imagining this collection of critical essays and because we were concerned about how the trilogy seemed to affect the readers' world outside of textual space, we asked for submissions to consider the "real world" implications and "real work" of the novels. We received a surprising number of submissions, which we read and vetted, selecting eight authors (not including the three of us) from more than three dozen abstracts to contribute essays to this collection. These eight authors demonstrated creativity in their insight into Collins's work and innovation in their research plans, contributing diversity to existing conversations about the trilogy, while at the same time being relevant to the collection we envisioned.

Aware of the effects of *The Hunger Games* in the world and on us as readers, we took our cues from trilogy's multi-genred appeal—as written texts and produced films that synthesize a variety of narrative, rhetorical, and aesthetic forms—and set out to create a critical space "safe" enough to welcome a range of scholarly conversations, but "radical" in the sense that the collection would challenge and even transgress conventional scholarship. The contributing authors used literary, political, and popular research and theories to inform their critical investigations of the text. This diversity of theoretical approaches and fields reflects our own investment in transgressing, disrupting, and intersecting academic and popular spaces and practices. We committed, also, to putting together a collection that provides intellectual complexity as well as relevance and accessibility to a range of audiences. Through our decidedly interdisciplinary approach to a text that we deem an important and controversial social artifact, we achieved exactly these things.

As our contributors wrote and revised their essays for this text, we realized that this book had evolved from merely analyzing the "real work" of Collins's trilogy. Instead, we found that contributors and co-editors alike shared their enthusiasm for investigating how *The Hunger Games* is a consequential text. We intuited that our contributing authors repeatedly suggest, imply, or directly reference the trilogy's work as producing "space" or "place." At the level of the text, the trilogy's narrative space(s) raise questions about storytelling, narrative agency, and author-ity, as explored in essays by Julie Elizabeth Tyler and Anne M. Canavan and Sarah N. Petrovic. In addition, the trilogy's provision of both radical and safe spaces mean that the trilogy enables readers to choose how they use the trilogy for their own emotional and intellectual needs—perhaps by following their own desires to challenge the status quo, or alternatively by healing from their own traumas and anxieties. On the "safe side," Adam Levin's and Ann M. M. Childs's essays, respectively "Recreating the Holocaust: YA Dystopia and the Young Jewish Reader" and "The Privileged Reader as Capitol and Learning Sympathy through Narrative," assert that the trilogy provides a "safe space" for new, yet specific, discussions. Levin argues that the texts provide new ways for Jewish youths to understand the Holocaust in a secular, safe space. Childs posits the trilogy as a safe place for readers to identify with the Other. On the "radical" side, Whitney Elaine Jones's exploration of gender implies that gender is a space, particularly in *The Hunger Games*, that can be deconstructed and reconfigured.

The Hunger Games also engages with existing spaces, such as the rhetorical and discursive spaces of internet commentary about the trilogy and the more tangible environmental spaces that are in a state of crisis. Because of this engagement, essays in this collection challenge readers and scholars toward an active and nuanced awareness of what is currently happening in the real world, as exemplified by Deidre Anne Evans Garriott's essay "Performing the Capitol in Digital Spaces: The Punitive Gaze of the Panopticon Among Fans and Critics." Garriott's essay argues that readers have used the trilogy to carve a digital panoptic space where they assert their social and political opinions and monitor each other through a variety of online media. And finally *The Hunger Games* trilogy speculates about spaces that may emerge in the future, whether *The Hunger Games* merely predicts these spaces' emergence or whether the trilogy and its surrounding discourse *create* these spaces.

Contributing authors' implicit and explicit dealings with space and place are the most prominent consistencies that emerged in the final phases of editing this collection. Other consistencies among authors go beyond examinations of reality TV, political oppression, and economic disparity, as commonly cited indicators of our world's current status and as fodder for speculating about the world's dystopian future. Authors in this collection consistently attend to the trilogy's more abstract phenomena, such as the symbiotic relationship between the text and readers, and the ontological and epistemological problems of the Epilogue.

Given these consistencies and varieties amidst the scholarship in this collection, we suggest that the collection at large is about how the trilogy is a place and space for multiple discourses—political, social, and literary. Although this collection is not the first piece of scholarship to interrogate the importance of place and space, we argue that the critical space that this book creates is unique and unprecedented. It is among the first publications to examine how *The Hunger Games* creates spaces inside and outside of the text, spaces that are consequential and productive. Through this collection of essays as a "safe space" for varied critical readings, we argue that YA fiction generally and *The Hunger Games* specifically are meaningful texts that have the potential to change our notions about the genre, about literature, about young adults, and about the world. To that end, we have written and collected articles that discuss the ways that Collins's trilogy has already begun to make changes and produce sites of study. With this collection, we are extending the space we create to scholarship and conversations external to the incendiary work that has been accomplished by Collins, her readers, other scholars, and the authors of this collection. While other collections of critical essays on *The Hunger Games* have focused on traditional literary readings and examinations of the trilogy, this collection of essays more assertively places *The Hunger Games* in conversation with the world in which it was written, in which it is read, in which it is adapted, and in which it produces other texts. This collection provides a different and engaging way of thinking about texts as the productive and consequential artifacts that we believe them to be.

In response to these interests in spaces and places and other consistencies among contributing authors' work, this book organizes the individual essays into five parts: I. Identifying and Challenging Narrative Spaces, II. Provoking Change and Creating Radical Spaces, III. Experiencing Trauma in Safe Spaces,

IV. Popular Responses in Actual Spaces, and V. Envisioning Future Spaces. The following paragraphs summarize each essay's argument and contributions to the varied and emerging critical conversations about Collins's work.

In Identifying and Challenging Narrative Spaces, Julie Elizabeth Tyler's essay "Transgressing the Text and Playing Narrative Games: Katniss's Narrative, 'Real or Not Real?'" opens the collection by focusing on the trilogy's Epilogue as a problem section of the text. It is problematic because it raises more questions than it answers with its abrupt "years later" updates on Katniss's adult status and with its signal that authenticity is an issue in representations of adolescents' voices and experiences. These questions stem from author-narrator tension, structural and chronological inconsistencies across the trilogy, and the frequent multiplicity of narrative voices participating in the challenges of story-telling. This essay is placed in the context of recent scholarship on children's and YA literature, which questions the authenticity of such texts in general since childhood may be unknowable to the adult authors who co-opt it for their own agendas. It is also placed in the context of other works of fiction for or about adolescents that feature difficult epilogues. This essay explores the possibility that epilogues, while indeed problematic, present the current best way to authenticate representations of the voices and experiences of adolescents, because they invite collaborative story-telling and because they provide more creative and interpretive possibilities than do more straightforward and easier-to-manage narratives.

In "Tipping the Odds Ever in Her Favor: An Exploration of Narrative Control and Agency in the Novel and Film," Anne M. Canavan and Sarah N. Petrovic analyze Katniss's varying levels of agency in the novels and the first film adaptation. Like many fans, they find Katniss a powerful female character who has impacted popular culture. They emphasize that their comparison of the two genres does not suggest that one medium—the written word or film—is better or "more correct" than the other; instead, they engage in this comparison to understand the changes to the story's narrative meanings that occur when the story is rendered in different media. Drawing terminology and narrative theory from critic James Phelan's *Living to Tell About It*, Canavan and Petrovic argue that the change in narrative alters Katniss's agency, and that this change occurs, partly, because the two genres alter the way the audience accesses Katniss.

Canavan and Petrovic observe a distinct alternation in Katniss's agency between the novels and the first film adaptation, released in theaters in 2012. They contend, "In the novels, Katniss is fully aware of the multiple narratives in which she is participating, and, moreover, knows the power of employing those narratives to her own benefit. Because the novel's audience accesses Katniss through her interior, first-person narrative, readers discern that she negotiates at least four narratives and that in action she is performing at all times, hiding her true weakness and fear. The audience's access to Katniss's interiority allows them to see her discerning narratives, making decisions, and struggling with her own feelings." Canavan and Petrovic argue that this Katniss has greater agency than the film's Katniss, whose interiority is excised when the cinematic choices in narrative shift from the novel's first-person point of view to third-person. They conclude by arguing that the two different stories about Katniss in the 74th annual Hunger Games forward two different messages and give power to two different figures. While Canavan and Petrovic do not allude directly to "space," they emphasize that the media through which the audience accesses Katniss creates different spaces, resulting in different identities for Katniss and different power structures from one media to the next.

The essays in Parts II and III of this collection, Provoking Change and Creating Radical Spaces and Experiencing Trauma in Safe Spaces, explore how the figures of the child and the adolescent are presented and transformed through Collins's series, as well as how the textual transformation of the child encourages transformations in its child readers. As Tyler argues in her contribution to this collection, the child or adolescent possesses "authentic transformative energy." Because we agree with Tyler, and because *The Hunger Games* literally places the child at the center of political upheaval, we knew that one of our goals for this collection was to explore how Collins's trilogy not only uses the figure of the child within literature to disrupt the social, political, and cultural boundaries of Panem, but also to suggest that her adolescent audience can make similar defiant gestures.

Provoking Change and Creating Radical Spaces provides discussions of the ways in which *The Hunger Games* overtly disrupts traditional understandings of concepts such as gender, as explored in Whitney Elaine Jones's essay "Katniss and Her Boys: Male Readers, the Love Triangle and Identity Formation," and the scapegoat, as explored in Susan Shau Ming Tan's essay "The Making of the Citizen and the Politics of Maturation." Both authors use close textual readings to characterize Collins's trilogy as a space that deconstructs, redefines, and reorders those things that seem to have become commonplace. They suggest that, through the startling reconstruction of literary conventions like *scapegoat* and the love triangle, *The Hunger Games* energizes and enables readers to reconstruct their everyday lives.

In "Katniss and Her Boys," Jones investigates the purpose of the love triangle in Collins's trilogy, asserting that, even though a female protagonist must choose between two romantic love interests, young male readers may benefit most from reading about her choice. Jones ultimately concludes that, at least in *The Hunger Games* trilogy, the love triangle provides a space for male teens to reconsider gendered behavior and expectations. She presents this argument by deconstructing the severed and isolating space of the love triangle into a sliding scale of gendered masculine behavior, on which Katniss is the ever-sliding point with which young male readers identify. "Katniss and Her Boys" continues to disrupt our understanding of *The Hunger Games*, arguing that it is only by transforming the trilogy from a dystopia to a feminist utopia that Collins can offer young boys a comprehensive understanding of gender that balances the best traits of traditionally male and female behaviors. Jones argues that as Katniss finds a balance between the extremes of femininity and masculinity, she promotes the same balancing of identity within a young male audience.

While Jones focuses specifically on a young male audience, the following essay looks at a generalized "child" audience. In "The Making of the Citizen and the Politics of Maturation," Tan uses the concept of the *scapegoat* to suggest that adolescence is a radical space in which the individual gains power, even while excised from the community by the ruling and oppressive system of the Hunger Games. This power enables the scapegoated adolescent to change the community for the better, to transform trauma into opportunity, and silence into storytelling. Tan's essay posits the possibility of a "politics of maturation," in which the real figure of political and social agency is the liminal teenager, a figure in the community but somehow outside of it, on the border between vulnerable child and powerful adult. Her essay shows how this politics of maturation allows Katniss to transcend and transform her oppressive government. It also suggests that for readers of Collins's trilogy, a similar radical adolescence exists, and that a reading of *The Hunger Games* can become an impetus for change, a catalyst to similar radical political transformation in our own world.

Although Jones and Tan insist that *The Hunger Games* is a radical space in which gender, politics, and adolescence collide to transgress boundaries and transform outdated and threatening systems, the authors in Part III, Experiencing Trauma in Safe Spaces, suggest just the opposite. Ann M. M. Childs and Adam Levin explore how Collins's trilogy creates a textual "safe space" that allows readers to investigate dangerous topics and relate to Othered individuals without putting themselves in danger of actually experiencing the trauma depicted in these novels. They argue that readers gain an understanding of trauma that has the ability to change, for the better, the way readers view their actual worlds, socio-economic classes, and religious groups. Childs's essay, "The Privileged Reader as Capitol and Learning Sympathy through Narrative," moves a discussion of Collins's texts from radical transgressions to "safe spaces." Childs is interested in how socioeconomically privileged readers might benefit from a reading of *The Hunger Games*, because its narrator is a member of a culturally and economically oppressed group. She argues that the disparity between the Othered Katniss and her privileged readers should complicate the reader's identification with Katniss, but does not because *The Hunger Games* is, she argues, a "safe space." The safety of textual space made of paper and ink or plastic and computer chips encourages the reader's acceptance of those less privileged than themselves depicted within the text, a move that we hope finds expression in the "real" world through which readers of *The Hunger Games* daily move toward greater respect for real life oppressed and minority groups.

While Childs considers *The Hunger Games* a safe space for YA readers to encounter the Other, Levin argues that it can help strengthen bonds within the Jewish community by creating safe spaces to interpret the Holocaust differently. In "Recreating the Holocaust: YA Dystopia and the Young Jewish Reader," he asserts that educators and parents can use *The Hunger Games* to create a safe, secular place in which to discuss the trauma of Holocaust with Jewish youths. Levin suggests that traditional sites of learning about the Holocaust—reading both fiction and non-fiction genres within Holocaust literature—are hindered by an overwhelming sensitivity toward the subject matter. The students are restricted by framing the Holocaust in faith-based terms. He posits that it is difficult for twenty-first century Jewish youths to understand Holocaust survivors' experiences as well as their emotional and psychological recovery from the trauma; this, he argues, is because parents and educators fear misrepresenting the survivors' experiences.

Levin argues that Collins's trilogy offers a Holocaust-like experience for them to read because it "is not shaped and outlined by an overt Holocaust narrative." While acknowledging that Collins did not write the novel as part of the genre of Holocaust literature, Levin asserts that it can be read this way if the readers are directed toward and choose to read it through this lens. He draws from a vast body of Holocaust narratives, including Anne Frank's *The Diary of a Young Girl*, to alert readers to the parallel images and sensory experiences in *The Hunger Games* and Holocaust literature. By separating the Holocaust from narratives of faith, Levin argues that *The Hunger Games* is a safer space in which to study Holocaust survivors, and is a freer space, where Jewish youths can raise questions about faith, memory, and authenticity.

Although Childs and Levin propose that *The Hunger Games* trilogy provides "safe spaces" for readers to experience dangerous or alien situations, it strikes us that the text's safety encourages radical thought and action in the lives of its readers. Thus, we divided this collection into parts exploring "radical" and "safe" spaces only for the sake of organization, since these spaces are mutually reinforcing, and combined, accomplish change; whether safe or radical, *The Hunger Games* and this book challenge readers to question the order of things, to redefine their worlds.

Launching Part IV, Popular Responses in Actual Spaces, Katie Arosteguy analyzes Katniss's role as mother and "othermother" in "'I have a kind of power I never knew I possessed': Transformative Motherhood and Maternal Influence." Arosteguy turned her attention to the trilogy after reading it in a book club. In both her reading group and online "mommy blogs," she observed several mothers declaiming the novels for depicting children in violent situations. They tied their reactions to their roles as mothers, whose jobs are to nurture and protect their children. Arosteguy argues that these women take issue with the trilogy's exclusion of powerful mothers. Arosteguy argues that through the trilogy, Collins challenges traditional interpretations of mothers and creates a space for a "multi-faceted maternal identity." In other words, the novel provides a new space in which to complicate the ideas of motherhood as a status and mothering as an act.

Arosteguy draws from the emerging and growing body of scholarship on mothers called "motherhood studies." She frames her argument using Elizabeth Podniek and Andrea O'Reilly's theory of "othermothering," in which a character who may not be a mother biologically can perform the role of mother. Expanding the reader's concept of "mother" beyond the biological allows readers to see Katniss's nurturing and transformative potential through the series, working toward her eventual biological and traditional status as mother as depicted in the Epilogue. Arosteguy argues that the trilogy challenges the ways most YA texts include the mother, often making her a combative character or absent from the text. Arosteguy suggests that the space of *The Hunger Games* provides a new way to conceive of mothers, better ways than are offered in other YA texts, because Katniss is challenged to question her rejection of her unnamed mother. This rejection, Arosteguy notes, is typical of YA novels, but she argues that Collins re-assimilates the mother into the narrative as Katniss realizes that she benefits from her mother's knowledge. By understanding Katniss's "othermothering," Arosteguy asserts that we can challenge the narrow roles we ascribe to mothers both in literature and in the world outside the trilogy.

Like Arosteguy, Deidre Anne Evans Garriott drew inspiration for her analysis from the ways in which readers were appropriating and responding to the novels. Garriott's essay "Performing the Capitol in Digital Spaces: The Punitive Gaze of the Panopticon Among Fans and Critics" extends her analysis into the digital spaces that have emerged as a result of *The Hunger Games* through fan culture and how those fans have (mis)appropriated the text to enter civic discourses. Garriott argues that Collins's trilogy is not a warning about a potential future, but is rather social commentary about the present. Most importantly, she argues that this is a text about how surveillance in a space can divide community and contravene identification. Thus, Garriott argues these novels are *rhetorical*—texts about civic performances and responsibilities with consequences outside of the in-text world. She observed the trilogy's consequences through her observation of online publications, specifically articles on the feminist blog *Jezebel*, Tweets, and a film review in *The New York Times* online.

Through this analysis of online media and social networking, Garriott observes that while critics and fans disclose personal investment in the trilogy and how it is adapted to the film, they misappropriate the text. She notes that critics and fans have not seemed to internalize Collins's warning about the ways surveillance is used to divide communities, because these writers have enacted their own panoptic, punitive gaze. Most significantly, she argues, film critics and fans have turned their punitive gazes onto the bodies of the actors depicting characters of the novel. A vocal minority of fans on Twitter espoused racist criticism about casting African-American or multi-racial actors in the roles of Rue and Cinna. Moreover, film critic Mahola Dargis levies attacks on Jennifer Lawrence's body in her portrayal of Katniss for Gary Ross's film adaptation. Garriott argues that these criticisms are instances of the panoptic gaze, which look for social transgressions, disclose them, and seek to punish the transgressors. Additionally, feminist activists, while well-meaning and clearly on-point in their criticism, have also enacted the panoptic gaze by searching for, disclosing, and writing about these instances of body criticism and racism. She suggests that fans seem to have intuited the relevance of the text to their own present context by using it as a way to enter civic discourse on the Internet, mostly through social media such as Twitter and traditional blogs. However, she argues that they have misappropriated the text when they use it to monitor and discipline themselves and other "netizens." Through her rhetorical analysis of these online publications, she argues that the Capitol is not a fictional city in the trilogy, but rather it is us—citizens of the world, right now.

Concluding the part on Popular Responses in Actual Spaces, Linda J. Rice and Katie Wrabel's "Creating a New Ethics: Student Responses, Reality Television and Audience Awareness" connects the importance of Capitol and district audiences depicted within Collins's work to the "real" audiences of the *The Hunger Games*'s readers who are familiar with the trilogy's resonance with current reality TV shows. What is useful about this essay is that it combines academic scholarship on reality TV with the responses of teacher education students who comprise a very unique audience. This audience is unique in that these students are transitioning from adolescents to fully-fledged professionals deemed qualified to teach children and adolescents and to comment as critics on cultural content such as reality TV shows and *The Hunger Games*.

Rice and Wrabel argue that because college students often do not have the same political and professional clout as their older and more seasoned counterparts, scholarly communities would do well to consider students' responses to texts such as *The Hunger Games*, because of these students' liminal and transitional status.

Part V, Envisioning Future Spaces, closes our collection with essays that are the most explicit in exploring how *The Hunger Games* represents what may happen in the world external to the text, and how the external, non-textual world has shaped the ways in which the trilogy might be understood and enjoyed. Carissa Ann Baker's "Outside the Seam: The Construction of and Relationship to Panem's Nature" engages in an ecocritical reading of Panem's environments—both natural and simulated. Baker argues that nature is the primary rather than secondary theme of Collins's work, such that Panem's relationship to nature provides the basis for its politics, culture, and economy.

Most importantly, Baker argues that the trilogy's "frightening images of what can happen when humans disconnect from nature" means that young adults and scholars need to "scrutinize [*The Hunger Games*] from an ecocritical standpoint, in order that we all might understand the trilogy's profound (and prophetic) commentary on humanity's current and future place in the natural world." Placing detailed close readings of the trilogy within the context of the emerging field of ecocriticism and within recent ecocritical conversations about the trilogy, Baker's essay suggests that readers, particularly "young people" with more of a stake in future natural spaces, need to cultivate healthy yet nuanced relationships with nature, "fight[ing] for the earth with the same degree of fervor with which Katniss fought."

Bruce Martin's "Political Muttations, 'Real or Not Real?'" is the final essay of this collection, and using the Frankfurt School critical theory's work with *mimesis* and ritual sacrifice, argues that *The Hunger Games* is a "muttation" from the genre DNA of prior dystopian novels. Because it upgrades its literary genetic legacy, the trilogy "subverts the logic of domination," showing readers "a politics that might help in avoiding a 'real world' future that resembles that of Panem," creating a future "sufficient to honor past sacrifices, built on a foundation other than the continued use of power for dominating others."

Given *The Hunger Games*'s warnings about future "real world" spaces and its specific descriptions of Panem as fictional space, it makes sense that several essays of our collection are interested in open rather than closed possibilities of the spaces that America and the world will occupy years down the road. The text and its surrounding critical space constitute, still, a blank space for readers to formulate their "green"-conscious, political, or literary selves. Dennis Butts argues, "Literature is not a passive construction which simply reflects society. It can react against, protest, subvert or seek to change what appears to be dominant" (xii). It is with these words in mind that we offer you a well-known image:

> ... a stone thrown into a pond, an expected yet random wave of ripples breaking across the previously still surface of the water. The ripples widen out, their circumference growing, reaching depths and lengths unseen.

Ultimately, the purpose of this collection is to promote and investigate the notion that fiction is a stone thrown into the pond of reality, and that it, too, produces ripples, changing the surface of life, the way we (readers, moviegoers, cultural witnesses) view and approach the world. We suggest that Suzanne Collins's *The Hunger Games* trilogy creates ripples beyond the surface level of Katniss braids, Mockingjay tattoos and pins, or increased female enrollment in archery classes. Although those superficial ripples certainly exist, and are important signals of the profound effect a text can have on how we think, feel, and behave, this collection may disturb the proverbial waters below the surface. Gender, race, power, politics: these are the ideologies or sectors of life we insist are disrupted by meaningful readings of fictional texts. In an online interview, Suzanne Collins expressed her desire for readers to look for "how elements of the book might be relevant in their own lives." She asks: "Was there anything in the book that disturbed you because it reflected aspects of your own life—and if there was—what can you do about it?" Collins asks readers about "disturbances" and suggests that being "disturbed" might help each reader to disturb the status quo, to change their own lives and others for the better. "Disturbance," then, and "disruption" are the messages she hopes her young adult audience receive from reading her trilogy. Disruption is also the aim of our own collection of essays, which seeks in every essay to disrupt traditional readings of the child, dystopia, gender, space, narrative, etc. In fact, the essays in this collection often "disrupt" each other, offering contradictory readings on a single topic, identifying *The Hunger Games* as radical, then as safe, the epilogue as authentic, then as false, Katniss's maternal instincts as redeeming or as problematic. The internal disruption within this collection, however, reveals the importance of disruption itself in refreshing stagnant waters, whether they be political, cultural, or critical. As authors, we are not satisfied with retaining the status quo. Inspired by the spirit of the Girl on Fire, we engage in fanning the flames of critical discussion, disrupting the world just a little, so that rebuilding can begin.

Abbreviations

For the sake of brevity, the authors of this collection used the following abbreviations consistently throughout the text:

YA: young adult

In our in-text citations, we refer to the three novels in the trilogy in the following ways:

THG: *The Hunger Games*
CF: *Catching Fire*
MJ: *Mockingjay*

Works Cited

Blair, Carole, Greg Dickinson, and Brian L. Ott. "Introduction: Rhetoric/Memory/Place." *Places of Public Memory: The Rhetoric of Museums and Memorials*. Eds. Greg Dickinson, Carole Blair, and Brian L. Ott. Tuscaloosa: University of Alabama Press, 2010. 1–56. Print.

Butts, Dennis. "Introduction." *Children's Literature and Social Change: Some Case Studies from Barbara Hofland to Philip Pullman*. Cambridge: Lutterworth Press, 2010. vii-xiii. Print.

Collins, Suzanne. *The Hunger Games*. New York: Scholastic, 2008. Print.

———. "Interview by Scholastic Teens: Suzanne Collins Answers Questions about *The Hunger Games* Trilogy." Scholastic Books. Youtubewww. 2 Sept 2010. Web. 16 June 2013.

PART I
Identifying and Challenging Narrative Spaces

Transgressing the Text and Playing Narrative Games
Katniss's Narrative, "Real or Not Real?"

Julie Elizabeth Tyler

In the Epilogue to Suzanne Collins's *Mockingjay*, the finale to *The Hunger Games* trilogy, the narrator-protagonist Katniss Everdeen reports the status of her adult life, more than "five, ten, fifteen years" after surviving the 74th Hunger Games, the Quarter Quell Games, and the brutal rebellion against Panem's oppressive Capitol regime (*MJ* 494). In narrative tones that barely register twenty years' worth of ostensible maturation and transformation, Katniss reveals that she and her fellow Hunger Games victor Peeta have had two children, that there is hope in a positive future for Panem, and that she employs several effective mechanisms for coping with the horrors of her adolescent experiences. Yet, the subtext to Katniss's updates—the duplicitous disclosure of the existence, but not the names, of "girl" and "boy" offspring, and her anxiety about telling her children the horrific story that she tells and retells in her youth—reveal that Katniss's psychological and emotional traumas are extensive (*MJ* 494). Indeed, *Mockingjay*'s final chapters preceding the Epilogue present vivid images of the immediacy of these traumas from the Games, the rebellion, Katniss's act of assassinating President Coin, and the death of her sister Prim whose place she volunteered to take in the 74th Hunger Games. Katniss's actions and traumas render her publically declared a "hopeless, shell-shocked lunatic," unfit for appearing at her own criminal trial and thus exonerated from conviction (*MJ* 480). She returns to District 12, indeed scarred by the flames she herself was instrumental in starting as the "girl who was on fire," as well as reclusive and inactive (*THG* 67).

Katniss's defiance, resistance, and transgression of the Capitol capture the attention of every citizen in Panem throughout the entire trilogy, but by the end of *Mockingjay*, her final challenges are to transgress her post-traumatic psychological limitations and emerge from her reclusiveness. In the portion of Katniss's narrative that depicts her adolescent experiences—or structurally speaking, the *narrative proper*—the last chapter of *Mockingjay* provides some cautious optimism and evidence that Katniss is joining the world again. It concludes the narrative proper with the knowledge that Katniss and her fellow Games victor Peeta "grow back together" and establish a committed romance, that Katniss, Peeta and their mentor Haymitch are recording in a book "those things you cannot trust to memory," from family anecdotes to the experiences of the Games (*MJ* 491). Yet the Epilogue, after all of Katniss's efforts to tell her own story on her own terms, at first seems to undermine Katniss's effort. As chronological and structural "post-narrative," the Epilogue transgresses the narrative boundaries of the trilogy's text in order to supplement and extend a narrative that the audience assumes to be over. And its mere two pages of accounting for years' worth of Katniss's ostensible recovery, tying up loose narrative ends, and answering readers' questions about her future seems abrupt and suspicious, thus raising additional questions about what is "Real, or not real" in Katniss's narrative.

Given Katniss's duplicitous system of disclosing information, the Epilogue as a supplement to the plot raises questions about the real extent of her pain, and about her motivations for returning to a narrative "... fifteen years" later to provide updates. The Epilogue raises related questions about the authenticity of Katniss's adult commentary on her adolescent experiences. For instance, I explore in later sections of this essay the possibility that the Epilogue may *really* represent Katniss's thoughts only weeks between the final chapter and Epilogue, rather than twenty years, and may thus be the product of the adolescent Katniss, transgressing boundaries of age and perspective, in order to "try on" an adult voice and speculate about her future. Readers know that throughout the trilogy, Katniss resists telling the Capitol's story of scripted actions and public statements, and strives to make authentic choices—from hunting on forbidden grounds to assassinating President Coin—that are instrumental in eradicating the Games as well as the Capitol's power and transforming the nation of Panem. But despite these self-authenticating and politically transformative actions, this Epilogue—encouraging, yet sad and reticent—could be Katniss's script, or lie, that she has devised for herself to cover up a much more horrific truth about life twenty years after the Games. Yet another possibility could be that the Epilogue is the current best way to tell the truth, a final anti–Capitol gesture showing that she will tell her own story in the manner that she deems useful, rejecting others' scripts and stories about her, and transgressing the limits that the Capitol worked so hard to keep in place.

With the Epilogue's raising of questions and possibilities, with its problems created and problems solved, and with its evidence of and struggle against the narrative's artificiality, readers' processes of deciphering *what*, if anything, is the final, authoritative, and authentic version of Katniss's story will be extensive. Engaging in these processes, readers may gain some insight into the trilogy's place in a literary tradition specific to young adult fiction. Just as the Epilogue transgresses narrative limits, the trilogy can transgress the limits of current literary forms that are the product of a disparity between adult authorship and adolescent narrators, and that because of this disparity, may be artificial or outmoded, not reflecting the true experiences of the adolescents they purport to represent. The Capitol's engineered "muttations" warn readers about the consequences of appropriating and altering the functions of real nature; likewise, readers might consider the ways in which adult authors appropriate and alter "real" adolescents' voices, creating narrative muttations (such as Katniss's narrative) to fulfill their own agendas. Indeed, readers, scholars, and even authors may be inclined to fuse a hegemonic fascination with the "other" with their critical approaches to texts, either appropriating that which is authentic, or being hyper-protective of the authenticity of the "other." In either case, readers and scholars err on the side of speaking for or silencing those who might identify as ethnic, cultural, or language minorities, or as women, or in the case of *The Hunger Games* and other YA texts, children. Such silencing in texts is not an innocuous issue. Scholars and readers of the trilogy might do well to consider whether children or adolescents can or will tell their own stories through the texts that purport to be about them, as Spivak calls us to ask with other texts in question, regarding whether the "Subaltern" can, should, or will "Speak."[1] I assert that muttations of this sort are particularly dangerous in texts that dramatize adolescents rising to political prominence, if the adult agendas touted therein, no matter how well-intentioned, occur at the expense of, or through the silencing of, adolescent voices, real or fictional. From its depiction of avoxes as the Capitol's servants whose voices have been physically and politically silenced, to the self-authenticating challenge in which Katniss's narrative engages, *The Hunger Games* is keenly aware of these dangers of representation, even though from an authorial standpoint it may be delivering what it critiques.

But unlike the Capitol's muttations which are created for the express purpose of oppressing the districts in one way or another, Katniss's narrative, with all its formal and structural difficulties, may reflect an emancipatory impulse—freeing adolescent narratives from formulaic, straight-forward narratives that restrain creativity and interpretive possibility. Gilles Deleuze and Félix Guattari's "Kafka: Toward a Minor Literature: The Components of Expression" explores "minor" or "revolutionary" literature as that which prioritizes social commentary over aesthetic pursuits, and that reflects a causal, rather than simultaneous, relationship between literature's "minor" or "revolutionary" possibilities and its aesthetic notability. Revolutionary literature, Deleuze and Guattari assert, "begins by speaking and only sees and conceives afterward," such that the "expression must shatter the forms," after which the "contents ... must be reconstructed" (591). *The Hunger Games* trilogy evidences Deleuze and Guattari's theory of revolutionary literature's causal process. Katniss's narrative gives readers immediate access to the trilogy's "expression" of protesting the world's injustices. Then the narrative tensions between the adolescent's experiences and an adult's retrospection "shatter" (or transgress) conventional forms. From these shattered, transgressed forms emerges a "reconstructed" form, culminating in the structurally and chronologically troublesome Epilogue, a form that amplifies rather than reconciles the tensions among plot, narrative, and authorship, and that is politically *and* aesthetically notable. Thus, instead of undermining the work of the whole narrative, as I ponder in paragraphs above, the Epilogue provides models for creativity and interpretive possibility—all toward authenticating adolescent voices and experiences represented in fiction, as well as adults' methods of "writing back," retrospectively and analytically, to their own adolescent experiences.

Readers, scholars, and authors certainly can gain valuable insight about storytelling from their encounters with *The Hunger Games*, from adolescents telling their own stories and from adults looking back on their own experiences about adolescents, to the tradition of young adult literature telling its own story of transformation and prompting transformations external to itself.

* * *

In the preceding paragraphs, I have highlighted a very large and proliferating set of questions and challenges that require more extensive investigations than a single essay can accommodate. Nonetheless, "Transgressing the Text and Playing Narrative Games" seizes the opportunity to suggest ways in which fruitful investigations might begin. This essay's first section, "Transgressing a Transgressive Genre," will place *The Hunger Games* trilogy's adolescent-adult narrative and authorial disparities in the context of recent scholarship on children's and YA Literature. In addition, this section will consider *The Hunger Games* alongside other works of fiction that represent adolescent voices and experiences, that explore graphic content, and that highlight the tensions between plot, narrative, and authorship.

The next sections, "Telling the Story and Re-Scripting the Capitol in *The Hunger Games*," "Telling the Story Again in *Catching Fire*," and "Negotiating Political and Narrative Voice in *Mockingjay*," will investigate how Katniss's narrative is transgressing its own limitations, transgressing the text's form in order to register some external meaning about the nature of storytelling and what it means for authors and readers. These sections will include close readings of several passages and features of the trilogy in order to locate occurrences of textual transgressions.

This essay's penultimate section, "Narrative *Games*," will focus strictly on the Epilogue, as the portion of the narrative that is itself a transgression of the whole text, by virtue of its two most conspicuous features: its structural position external to and chronological position posterior to the narrative proper. This section will also examine Katniss's modes of storytelling in the Epilogue, combining a complex system of disclosing and concealing information, and engaging in dangerous yet therapeutic "Narrative *Games*."

Finally, this essay will conclude with a number of implications and applications for readers and authors, adolescents and adults, who struggle to craft the right voice to tell their own stories, and who may look to *The Hunger Games* and other texts as inspiration.

Transgressing a Transgressive Genre: The Status of Young Adult Literature

The Hunger Games trilogy's plot depicts political rebellion and the districts' grassroots process of transforming the unjust world created by the Capitol. The fact that children are at the center of the rebellion renders this trilogy quite difficult to categorize. Certainly, it does not resemble its "safer" counterparts within a tradition of children's and young adult literature, and adults may deem the trilogy unfit for young adult audiences. Nonetheless, I posit that *The Hunger Games*, despite its graphic content, and because of its transformative energy and unwillingness to be content with safe topics and easy-to-manage narratives, can rightfully be labeled a YA text. Labels aside, though, it seems to constitute its own tradition, one that is invested not only in depicting transformation within plot but also in enacting transformation of the tradition and of the real world. This section looks to recent scholarship on children's literature and compares the trilogy to other works of fiction in order to investigate the trilogy's place within and transformation of the YA literature tradition. Doing so, this essay may provide more insight into the narrative difficulties in texts for or about young adults and how these difficulties may detract from or enhance the experiences of the readers of these texts.

Two critics offer opposing viewpoints on whether children's literature reinforces the traditional and accepted values of a society or whether children's literature can challenge or transgress these values. Jacqueline Rose's groundbreaking work, *The Case of Peter Pan: Or the Impossibility of Children's Fiction*, suggests that the literature for and about children reflects adults' desires to reinforce society's traditions by "preserv[ing] an ideal of innocent children"— images that are comfortable and non-threatening to adults (5). Thus, children's literature has "less to do with children's tastes and development than with adult needs," Rose claims. Specifically, it depicts children's "arrested relationship with language," resulting in "children's literature being arrested as a literary genre" (4). Drawing upon Rose's work in order to offer an alternative assessment of children's literature, Kimberly Reynolds's *Radical Children's Literature: Future Visions of Aesthetic Transformation in Juvenile Fiction* claims that the graphic content and complex forms of children's literature render it radical in ways that adult texts are not and cannot be. Reynolds argues that the "ultimate response" of children when they encounter the world's injustices is "Why? ... Why can't things be different?" Likewise, literature for and about children asks these same questions, and infuses them into textual forms and narratives, to offer "quirky or critical or alternative visions of the world designed to provoke" readers to seek answers to these questions by transforming the world (3). Thus, while many texts traditionally labeled children's literature *do* reinforce norms, Reynolds points out that fiction for and about children that touts an explicit change-the-world message can comprise its own genre.

Whether children's fiction reinforces, transgresses, or creates its own tradition, it is problematic in two significant ways. One problem is adults' appropriation of the literary idea of the child, filling this space with their own agendas, while another problem is children's possession of authentic transformative energy that children's literature is incapable of accessing or reproducing because it is authored by adults. For this essay, "authentic transformative energy" describes the energy that children possess before they grow up, before they compete within Capitol-style political and economic structures, before they become complacent with the status quo and resistant to their own and others' transformation. At best, adults can recall and invoke the transformative energy that they may have once possessed. The same rule applies for children's literature. Although texts and their well-intentioned adult authors cannot access or reproduce the authentic transformative energy that exists in the hearts and minds of children, it is possible that literature for and about children could recall and invoke this transformative energy, as the current best textual model for how to transform the present and future. In other words, we look back to look forward.

From *The Hunger Games* to *Catching Fire* to *Mockingjay*, the trilogy shows that Reynolds's claims can quite possibly be fulfilled within a text's plot. Readers can accept that the *character* Katniss authenticates her own actions in spite of the rules of the Hunger Games—which mold and manipulate Katniss and other tributes into TV personalities that will entertain a

Capitol audience. Although we can accept Katniss as authenticator of her own actions, the questions about adult authorship and complications of the Epilogue that my Introduction section sets up serve as reasons why readers may question the *narrator* Katniss as authenticator of her own story. Yet readers may be willing to consider that *The Hunger Games* represents the effort that children's and young adult literature is making toward authenticating adolescents' voices, and those of adults who want to write back to their youthful experiences in order to write forward.

In this process of recalling and invoking authentic transformative energy, children's and adolescent's literature must be aware of its own limitations. But at the same time, the genre must transgress these limitations to transform itself into something that serves the creative, social, or political needs of adolescents. This awareness of limitations and the efforts to transgress them mean *the genre* is growing up alongside the characters and narrators it depicts. These imperatives—of writing back to write forward, growing up to serve needs of those still growing—are paradoxical, in that a certain literary maturity is required to properly depict adolescent characters and connect to reading audiences who are still maturing themselves. Following *The Hunger Games*'s Epilogue's imperatives of writing back to our experiences, adults might successfully authenticate the processes of writing back to their own adolescent experiences, thereby underscoring these stories and advocating for them. In addition, works of literature for and about adolescents must engage in these imperatives, by writing back to prior texts and forms, by growing up within this literary tradition, and by arriving at a new form that accommodates these challenges.[2]

The Hunger Games trilogy constitutes a logical and obvious comparison to dystopian texts about adolescents, such as William Golding's *Lord of the Flies* or Koushun Takami's novel *Battle Royale*, adapted into a film in 2000, since these graphic plots speculate on the devolution of societies and the horrific "games" they play, in which adults kill other adults, and youths kill other youths. In *Lord of the Flies*, it is an adult, a naval officer, who rescues a pack of boys who are marooned on an island and who have devolved into brutal behavior. The officer arrives just in time to "re-civilize" the errant youths with his comment to protagonist Ralph: "I should have thought that a pack of British boys—you're all British, aren't you?—would have been able to put up a better show than that" (242). In *Battle Royale,* the youths rebel against the adult-designed game in which youths must fight to the death. While several youths manage to escape, the narrative's somewhat open-ended conclusion suggests that the horrors will continue beyond the boundaries of plot. *The Hunger Games* invokes these important plots, but advances them by showing Katniss, as an adolescent, successfully dismantling the Capitol—with her statements, actions, and finally her own narrative, as a way to reconcile, amplify, and complicate the adolescent-adult tensions within herself. And so, the importance of dystopian plots considered, I will examine, in the paragraphs below, *The Hunger Games* trilogy alongside other YA texts in which tension exists among plot, narrative, and authorship—particularly in striking and troublesome post-narratives presented through an ostensible older or adult perspective—as sites for gauging the status and maturation of this genre of fiction. In *The Hunger Games* and other YA texts, post-narrative content exposes storytelling for its insufficiencies and lack of authenticity. More specifically in these texts, narrative is exposed for its questionable representation of time, which makes it impossible to discern whether the "real" present tense of the text is the narrative proper or the Epilogue. And as though this challenge weren't enough, these texts make it impossible to discern the source of narrative tension between adolescent and adult perspectives. This tension may stem merely from the narrative's juxtaposition of two stages in life, or it may stem from the dramatized adult narrator's processes of looking back on adolescent experiences, struggling to reconcile with some trauma, guilt, or other intense experiences from youth. While all of these texts can elucidate our understandings of *The Hunger Games* and other YA fiction, it may be that Collins's trilogy marks one of the YA genre's closest (or furthest) approaches to authentic representations of adolescent voices and experiences.

J. D. Salinger's *Catcher in the Rye* employs a first-person narrator, Holden Caulfield, a self-aware prep school teen who experiences misfit status in every environment, but who is intelligent, well-intentioned, and emotionally sensitive. Holden tells the story of the few days between leaving the prep school from which he has been expelled for bad grades and mustering the resolve to return home to alert his parents of his expulsion. During these few days, he wanders the streets of New York City, "lonesome and depressed," reflecting on his choices, the social behaviors of others, reaching out for companionship, and finding little comfort (81). *Catcher in the Rye* is not a politically transformative text in the way that *The Hunger Games* trilogy set out to be. However, Holden's story provides unique literary insight into adolescent experiences and modes of storytelling, or at the very least, an adult author's attempt to access and depict what it means to be an adolescent. In so doing, Holden's story perhaps succeeds in transforming readers' attitudes about, or inspiring their empathy toward, misfit youth.[3]

More striking than Holden's sad story, his wanderings through New York City, and his sensitivity are Holden's youthful discourse and his identification of and fixation on "phonies." Holden's distaste for social fakery and his admiration for individuals who behave and speak in ways that Holden deems authentic draw attention to the degree to which his discourse and storytelling can reveal the depths of his pain. In addition, as with Katniss's self-authenticating actions, which draw attention to her modes of storytelling and the tensions between narrative and authorship, Holden's critique of all things "phony" raises questions about *Catcher in the Rye*'s tensions between narrative and authorship. Does Holden's narrative authentically capture the experience and voice of youth—with all its sensitivity, struggle, pain, and love? Even Holden narrows the scope of his narrative, and focuses solely on what he calls "this madman stuff that happened to [him] last Christmas" (1). Interestingly, this narrowed scope enables Holden to quantify the magnitude of his breakdown through oblique insinuations of the details: "what I did after I went home, and how I got sick and all, and what school I'm supposed to go to next fall, after I get out of here" (213). And just as he narrows the scope of his narrative at its beginning, he limits, in post-narrative commentary, what he "could probably tell," and what he does not "feel like" telling, thus quantifying the magnitude of his story's impact (213). Furthermore, the possibility that Holden is telling his story to a therapist, an adult in the position to evaluate Holden's psychological (and narrative) stability, makes his system of concealment and disclosure all the more poignant, and demonstrates perhaps how an adolescent might keep his or her story "safe," so to speak, from invasive and appropriating adult insights. Through these choices in storytelling, Holden highlights the (im)possibility of telling one's own story in authentic ways and the pain that would inevitably result from such authentic and full disclosure.

The conclusion to Holden's narrative offers no definitive statements about adolescents telling their own stories, as Holden's breakdown is triggered by an interaction that might otherwise, in another narrative, be a purely positive experience. In the penultimate chapter, the sight of his kid sister Phoebe, innocent and laughing on a park carousel, contributes to Holden's emotional and narrative breakdown that can only be commented upon in retrospective content—which, in this novel is not quite a formal and structurally separate Epilogue, but is a "post-narrative" of sorts. Holden's affection for Phoebe, the person with whom he can be truly honest, highlights his desire to protect and preserve her innocence, as though he were the "catcher in the rye," holding back all the children from danger. Here, I use Jacqueline Rose's claims about adults preserving an innocent ideal of children in the literature about them to observe a parallel in Holden's role as the "catcher," protecting the innocence of smaller children, thereby protecting to some degree his own innocence. This parallel should be yet another alert to readers, alongside Holden's distaste for "phonies," of the questionable authenticity of young adult narratives—specifically because telling one's own story, like telling the story of someone younger, is inherently an act of self-preservation. Like *The Hunger Games*'s Epilogue—which captures either adult Katniss's retrospection on her past, or perhaps more provocatively, capturing adolescent Katniss's experimentation with a future adult voice, Holden's final words operate according to a system of duplicity, as they withhold details of Holden's pain, but convey through his distinctive discourse the magnitude of it. But consistent with his lingo, or even amplifying it, the last sentences, mere indefinite pronouns and vague references to "what [he] did after," deconstruct syntax and meaning into what *cannot* be said about Holden's experiences and thoughts. One question that arises is whether Holden is incapable of finding his voice, or whether the limitations of narrative are incapable of accommodating his voice. Another question is whether some narrative device exists that can transgress the limitations of narrat*or* and narrat*ive* in order to promote healing and restoration of the characters and of literature. Both Katniss and Holden contain the horrors of their experiences within this system, but indicate that writing back is necessary to write forward. Both Holden and Katniss show that telling one's own story to others is painful, but that telling one's own story to oneself involves much more intense pain.

Three other texts depicting adolescents' voices and experiences—J. K. Rowling's *Harry Potter and the Deathly Hallows*, Toni Morrison's *The Bluest Eye*, and Ian McEwan's *Atonement*—might all be appropriately described as transgressive. For one thing, narratively and structurally, these texts make conspicuous and extensive use of "post-narrative" content, even more so than does *Catcher in the Rye*. Like *The Hunger Games*, these three texts provide updates on the adult status of characters whose adolescent experiences are the primary focus of what I call the texts' *narrative proper*. In relation to the post-narrative content, two features of these texts are important: their exploration of weighty issues and the responsibility of the adolescent characters for the fates of the worlds they inhabit. I suggest that these features—weighty issues and adolescents' responsibilities within a larger social framework—indicate that such intense adolescent fiction *requires* Epilogues and post-narratives to negotiate, reconcile, or amplify tensions between adult authorship, adolescent narratives, and adult retrospection, as well as the tensions between artificiality and authenticity of the voices and experiences represented. For the purposes of allowing creativity and interpretive possibility within the text, rather than limiting the text to only closed or fixed meanings, these kinds of Epilogues may be the current best solution for these problems, and may provide more insight into the future of young adult literature which *The Hunger Games* seems to foretell.

Arguably *not* a story written for adolescents to read, Morrison's *The Bluest Eye* concerns itself with the weighty issue of the effects of ubiquitous racism on the black community in Lorain, Ohio, even on the youngest members of this community. The narrative focuses on adolescent Claudia's observations of her peer Pecola, whose shy but desperate hunger for love devolves into insanity, as a result of hatred for her own blackness, a hatred nurtured by the very community and family that should have nurtured her sense of self-worth. In addition to the social and racial complexities, the narrative accommodates several characters' perspectives, including Pecola's interiority, rather than merely depicting the perspective of a single character. And unlike Katniss's narrative in *The Hunger Games* trilogy, Claudia's adult perspective pervades the text as a whole, as she depicts her adolescent self in third-person, thus distancing from and dis-identifying with her former self, and in first-person, thus taking on personal and narrative responsibility. As a painful component of *The Bluest Eye*'s variety in narrative perspective, Claudia's first-person adult commentary in the Epilogue writes back to adolescent experiences and is able to assign the blame for the damage done to Pecola's psyche and self-image. In this post-narrative, Claudia indicts even herself for her own "acquiesc[ence]" to such damage, and for the fact that any attempt, narrative or social, to stop or reverse the damage is "too late ... much, much too late" (Morrison 206).

While Pecola never heals from traumas she experiences, Claudia experiences only partial healing, since her actions on Pecola's behalf, or lack thereof, are implicated in the guilt that is mostly shouldered by the community. Even still, *The Bluest Eye*'s narrative does suggest that it is our adolescent experiences, and those processes of writing back as adults, that provide the most useful insight into adults' (and communities') successes, failures, and futures. More specifically, *The Bluest Eye*'s narrative content, combination of narrative voices, juxtaposition of adolescent and adult perspectives, and its non-linear structure enable repeated and conscientious investigations into the failures of a community that is run by adults and mimicked by adolescents, and that privileges whiteness. Perhaps the most interesting feature of this text is Morrison's own Afterword that functions as a follow up to adult Claudia's retrospection and that presents the author's perspective *on* the narrative, from a postion outside of and after the narrative. The Afterword, as a "*post*-post-narrative," contains Morrison's explanation that the novel expands her own memories of adult conversation and of a child who "wanted blue eyes" and thus implied "in her desire [her] racial self-loathing" (210). In explaining her authorial motivations from a position outside of both the narrative proper and post-narrative, Morrison's Afterword underscores and validates not only her own memory from adolescence, but also the attempt to write back to them, even though the communal (and perhaps personal) atonement for the guilt is partially successful at best. The complications that remain, however, concern Morrison's co-opting of the narrative and experiential space of an adolescent—whether her own memory or otherwise—for the purposes of making a political statement. Another complication concerns how Morrison's self-positioning at the end of *The Bluest*

Eye informs *The Hunger Games*. For *The Bluest Eye*, Morrison's self-positioning serves explicitly to sever any dramatized or co-opted connections between author and narrator beyond Morrison's statement that her own memories inspired the plot. For *The Hunger Games*, the absence of any such explicit posturing from Collins means that Katniss's adolescent-to-adult voice alone is the text's only stated source of insight into the trilogy's depicted horrors and juxtaposed chronologies. Other insights exist and signify external to the text.

Rather than co-opting the narrative and experiential space of an adolescent for political purposes, McEwan's *Atonement* co-opts these spaces to depict the personal and familial consequences of an adolescent's mistakes. *Atonement* tells the story of Briony, an adolescent who "witnesses" and wrongly accuses a family friend, Robbie, of raping her cousin. This lie—motivated perhaps by a desire to seem more adult-like, protective, and in-the-know—results in irreversible consequences. First, Robbie and Briony's older sister Cecilia are in love, but cannot pursue a life together after Briony's testimony to the police results in Robbie's conviction. Second, Briony must live with her guilt. *Atonement*'s plot and narrative are non-linear and comprised of three distinct, third-person forays into Cecilia's, Robbie's, and Briony's experiences. These forays thus pose some problems in representation, yet the fact that they present three sides to the same story in equal proportions indicates at least some narrative attempt at honest and fair representation. By the last chapter of the narrative proper, Briony has reached eighteen years of age and is fully cognizant of her errors, attempting to atone for them in serviceable and difficult employment as a nurse during World War II. The narrative here presents her feeble attempt at confession and to put right her wrongs, during a final meeting with Cecilia and Robbie. Yet readers encounter the Epilogue as an abrupt fast-forward to Briony in her old age delivering a first-person, diary-like account of her experiences writing the story of her youth, and they discover what they may have suspected. Briony is the author; her narrative is an attempt to atone; the final meeting with Cecilia and Robbie is an invention. Even more so than in *The Bluest Eye*, though, the Epilogue in *Atonement* meditates not only on failed actions of atonement, but also failed writings of atonement—both personal and public. Both Claudia and Briony as adults acknowledge their personal failings during their adolescent years. In *Atonement*'s post-narrative, Briony as narrator and as McEwan's dramatized author acknowledges her authorial failings and the narrative proper's failure to atone for her mistake. After all, the triptych narrative perspective, although fair and in a way honest, still contains the fabricated confession scene in the midst of all the layers of truth-telling, and any "real" confession is delayed until the Epilogue. Concerning *The Hunger Games*, Katniss's Epilogue is equally honest if not more explicit, so to speak, about the limits of narrative and authorship. The post-narrative attitude of both Briony and Claudia is that their respective adult selves are the authoritative sources of what their stories signify. Alternatively, Katniss's post-narrative attitude seems to underscore the authority (and "author-ity") as well as the revisable nature of her adolescent narrative, since the act of story-telling throughout all of her experiences and across the gulfs of time, space, and age always poses a challenge in consolidating details and in reconciling experience with memory. Narrative truth is still questionable and multi-versioned, and Katniss's narrative seems aware of the irony that narratives contain the most truth when they *are* questionable and multi-versioned. By being so, narratives necessarily avoid claiming a singular authorial, authoritative reality, and thus can transgress the limits of outmoded, inflexible, and artificial forms, ultimately providing creative and interpretive possibilities.

While *Catcher in the Rye*, *The Bluest Eye*, and *Atonement* each present the first-person "I" of the ostensible adolescent voice in question, the widely read and admired *Harry Potter* series avoids presenting the title character through a first-person narrative. Thus, *Harry Potter* seems to eliminate the ethical problem of the adult author posing as the "I" of a character who matures from adolescence at Hogwarts, inspires a movement of resistance against Voldemort's regime, and enjoys a peaceful adulthood decades after defeating Voldemort. Yet as a consequence of the un-represented "I" of Harry, certain challenges and interpretive possibilities of storytelling are left unexplored. *Harry Potter* eliminates not only a multi-versioned (and thus illuminative and insightful) telling and re-telling of the story, but also a narrator's challenge of writing or speaking back to his or her own experiences. Nonetheless, *Harry Potter* still raises the question of what to do with post-narrative content, depicting the status of Harry and his Hogwarts compatriots "Nineteen Years Later" following Voldemort's defeat, as I explore in paragraphs below (Rowling 753).

The *Harry Potter* series as a whole dramatizes the weighty issues, of course, of the title character's conflict with Voldemort, the dark lord who rises to power and builds an oppressive regime, and of the high-casualty war in the Wizarding world between Voldemort's supporters and those who would stand against him. Alongside these horrors, Harry and his compatriots, Ron and Hermione, must drudge through the usual challenges associated with maturation from adolescence to adulthood, such as teen romance, studying for coursework, and various identity crises, both comical and serious. Most of the action occurs in and around Hogwarts, the educational institution that houses adolescent wizards and witches and that is inextricable from the occasionally corrupt politics of the Ministry of Magic. For Harry in particular, the narrative is rife with depictions of his various identity crises, resulting from his fame as "The Boy Who Lived"—crises that resemble those that Katniss faces as "The

Girl Who Was on Fire." And as with Katniss, many of Harry's actions are defiant and transgressive; even though the narrative voice avoids the challenge of representing the "I," its Epilogue still transgresses narrative boundaries to provide some degree of closure for characters who fought against the evil that oppressed their world.

The Epilogue as closure for *Harry Potter and the Deathly Hallows*, the seventh and final installation to the widely-read series, is problematic in the sense that it constitutes either *Harry Potter*'s most glaring literary weakness or its greatest strength. Some readers may feel that the Epilogue all-too-quickly tidies the untidy by accounting for nineteen years of reconstruction of and peace within the wizarding world, uniting the major characters in marriages with children, and restoring integrity to Hogwarts as the authoritative yet nurturing educational institution. Such readers may be put off by tidy conclusions and deem *Harry Potter*'s Epilogue too good to be true or as leaving too little to the imagination. Other readers may entertain the possibility that the Epilogue works toward satisfying their sense of justice and that, in fact, the Epilogue would do well to provide even more "Where are they now?" details about the characters. After all, readers and the author have written and read about, identified with, and thus shared Harry's battles, grief, and triumphs, and may want to witness a fictional world restored, since complete restoration after political turmoil in the "real" world may not be feasible. Another possibility is that the Epilogue's presentation of happy circumstances can and should be taken at face value, as recognition that adolescents are capable of restoring a broken world, whether that world is fictional or "real," and that characters will receive the happiness in adulthood for which the traumas of adolescence were the price. In *The Bluest Eye*, narrator Claudia experiences only partial healing from racial and communal traumas and her own mistakes, while Pecola is robbed of her sanity. In *Atonement*, Briony, too, experiences only partial healing from her mistakes and from familial discord, while Cecelia and Robbie are robbed of their life together. In comparison, *Harry Potter* may show that post-narrative content can model a system of congruent effort-and-reward, brokenness-and-restoration—a system to strive for in fiction and the "real" world—even though such a system does not always reflect the reality of our lives.

All these possibilities considered, readers may agree that the image of happiness, success, peace, and closure in *Harry Potter*'s Epilogue, whether accepted at narrative face value or regarded as just a model for what to strive for in the real world, is, aesthetically speaking, somewhat heavy-handed. As readers hoped and expected, Ron has married Hermione, and Harry has married Ginny, his adolescent sweetheart. In addition, Harry and Ginny have a son, Albus Severus, named after influential wizards and representing the next generation of adolescent wizards. And if Ginny's confidence that Albus Severus will "be alright" at Hogwarts isn't heavy-handed enough, the third-person narrator closes the series by quantifying the restoration of the wizarding world. This narrator insists that "[a]ll is well," not that some aspects are well, but *all*. Nonetheless, as with Katniss's Epilogue, a mature and somber tone laces the cautious optimism of *Harry Potter*'s Epilogue, as its third-person narrator describes Harry's intuitive reaction to his frightening past, "touch[ing] the lightening scar on his forehead" (759). This last detail to the epic seven-part series suggests that the lingering memories of traumatic adolescent experiences both authenticate and exist in tension with the insisted-upon restoration.

In terms of the interpretive possibilities that the Epilogue enables, readers and scholars would do well to consider Rowling's own claims that she had "long known" how she would conclude *Harry Potter*, having written the Epilogue "in something like 1990," prior to authoring the rest of the series ("Rowling to Kill Two in Final Book"). The fact that she conceived of Harry and his friends as adults means that this post-narrative content inspired the shape and direction of the narrative proper that depicts the wizards' adolescence. In other words, from an authorial standpoint, this YA series and others like it function in service of their Epilogues, representing adolescents all grown up. For the third-person narrative in *Harry Potter*, though, Harry himself does not write back to his experiences, since an external consciousness controls both the adolescent portion and the adult post-narrative. But given what Rose suggests about adolescent texts functioning as conduits of adult agendas, *Harry Potter*'s Epilogue still reflects tensions in plot, narration, and authorship. Accordingly, I am reticent to make a definitive statement about this Epilogue's impact on *Harry Potter*'s plot, narrative, its status within a literary tradition, and even on its readers—as to whether it creates more problems in artificiality than it solves toward delivering closure for characters, deserved or otherwise, and for readers.

These ontologically and epistemologically upsetting texts do not represent the whole of fiction for and about adolescents. However, their consistent ways of transgressing the genre of young adult fiction—including explorations of trauma and memory, personal or political conflict, and the conspicuous use of post-narrative content—facilitate investigations into the ways in which *The Hunger Games* transgresses genres and its own text. For this essay, "transgression" denotes the trilogy's hyper-active, hyper-deliberate, and hyper-assertive revision of outmoded and artificial narrative forms, and by extension, revision of the *world*. Transgression is more than just an implied goal of children's literature as a genre. It is an upgraded, crystallized, and explicit principle for it. The songs of the mockingjays provide symbolic hints toward these transgressions, as their melodically-imitative warblings enable Katniss and Rue to relay messages to one another in the Arena. As several essays in this collection note, the genetic codes of these creatures, as hybrids between the Capitol muttation jabberjays and naturally-occurring mockingbirds, inspire the fashioning of Katniss into Panem's symbol of political transgression during the rebellion against the Capitol. Genetically, they represent nature triumphing over the Capitol's muttations of nature. Aesthetically, their abilities to repeat and alter a given musical melody function like Katniss's modes of storytelling. Both narratively signify new meaning by transgressing prior, hegemonic forms.

The tensions between adolescent and adult voicing, crystallized in post-narrative content, are one *site* of textual transgression, as well as an *agent* of it—sites located in time and space, and agents identifiable as character, narrator, or author—theoretically speaking. To clarify further what I mean by *sites*, I distinguish between textual transgressions that occur within the narrative proper, whereby the narrative proper sets up its baseline form and then conspicuously introduces new forms of itself, and those that occur in the gulf between the narrative proper and post-narrative, whereby a narrative seeks to exit its traditional textual confines, as though creating an out-of-body experience, in order to comment on itself from an external or *post* vantage point. In addition to its chronological and structural post-narrative status,[4] the Epilogue may have some function or significance prior to the narrative proper, thus informing how the narrative proper's beginnings ought to be read. In this regard, the narrative proper constitutes Katniss's attempt to tell the most authentic versions of her stories of 74th Hunger Games, the Quarter Quell, and the rebellion.

The narrative proper constitutes, also, Katniss's attempt to tell the most immediate version, combining present tense and past tense to indicate that she narrates action either in scene as it happens or in the moments that directly follow. These immediacies occur mostly in high-stakes situations across the whole trilogy, from moments in the Arena to one-on-one interactions with President Snow and other political adversaries, suggesting that readers encounter the text in scene and in the present with Katniss as she narrates in "real" time. Yet, once readers encounter the content, form, tone, and "years later" standpoint of the trilogy's Epilogue, they may consider varied possibilities for the timing of these components of the narrative. Perhaps the narrative proper, too, is written from a post-narrative standpoint, even though it manages to convey the immediacy of Katniss's adolescent experiences. *Or*, perhaps the Epilogue is still as immediate as the narrative proper, only days or weeks after Katniss's last chapter, representing adolescent Katniss's effort to "try out" an adult voice.

Simply put, the Epilogue presents three possibilities for Katniss's future: (1) the straightforward possibility, that Katniss does grow up and writes back to experiences from twenty years prior, while updating her audience on her current status, or (2) that Katniss has not yet grown up and the Epilogue enables her experiment of "trying out" the adult voice, or (3) that the entire narrative is written from adult Katniss's perspective—with the narrative proper as a distant memory rather than immediate reality, and the Epilogue representing her current status and state of mind, thus pervading the narrative at large. The plausibility of three possibilities means that time—its reality and its representation—further complicates what readers can know and say about the narrative's accommodations of Katniss's various age-perspectives across the whole trilogy.

Here, I offer possible entry points for readers and scholars for conceptualizing the trilogy's post-, pre-, or intra- and extra-textual processes of transgressing narrative space, structure, and time. Below are two models I have fashioned as (revisable) prototypes for representing or describing *The Hunger Games*'s (and similar texts') narrative time and space, as *sites* where textual transgressions occur as functions larger than actions and events within plot. In this essay, I have experimented with Model 1 to indicate where the Epilogue performs its transgressive work within a structure of plot, narrative, and text. According to this Model, the text contains narrative, and narrative contains plot. The Epilogue, inserted between narrative proper and text proper, signifies meaning (emotional, circumstantial) that exceeds the meanings in the plot and narrative that readers associate with Katniss's adolescence. In addition, Model 1 indicates that although the Epilogue is structurally and materially contained within the text, it offers interpretative possibility outside the confines of this text to signify meaning in other texts and in the real world. Applied more concretely to *The Hunger Games*, Model 1 might usefully describe Katniss's attitude toward childbearing as she presents it across the narrative. While as an adolescent (narrative proper) she cannot conceive of having children in a world such as Panem, the Epilogue reveals a narrative inconsistency in attitude that can only be interpreted as an adult's ability to heal (enough, at least) from past traumas to finally agree to childbearing. Although difficult to reconcile, these narrative inconsistencies within the text might resemble individuals' inconsistencies in attitude based on experience and perspective.

Experimentations with Model 2 suggest possible explorations of the Epilogue's chronological awareness of narrative time, and thus its indication of Katniss's modes of telling and of the times when she tells her story. More largely, it suggests various ways in which the adolescent-adult tension in such texts can be interpreted and transgressed. An important consideration for time

[text proper [narrative proper [plot proper] narrative proper] ▲ text proper]
                                                              Epilogue

Model 1

is whether the Epilogue's *stating* of a particular chronology of plot events is parallel to the *actual* chronology of the telling about these events. For example, *The Hunger Games*'s Epilogue states that Katniss has grown up and speaks back to adolescence from a mature perspective, in which case the chronology of events and of the telling are parallel, such that Katniss tells the story as she matures and the Epilogue is indeed post-narrative. But as the paragraphs above explore, it is possible that the entire narrative is spoken from Katniss's adult perspective, with the adolescent portions representing distant memory; in this case, the trilogy's stated chronology of plot events (Katniss survived two Games as an adolescent, and was instrumental in the Rebellion, and later has children) is acceptable, while the actual chronology of the times when the story is told does not parallel the plot's chronology. This schism would mean that Katniss as adult narrator conceives of the Epilogue's content (life updates and associated emotions) prior to or during the telling of the narrative proper, which details her experiences as an adolescent. To use the terms from Model 2, the Epilogue possibly constitutes a pre-narrative, or could signify meaning throughout the text (as inter-narrative) and surrounding the trilogy (as extra-narrative), such that adult Katniss's experiences of partial healing precede and pervade the telling of the adolescent experiences, with the telling perhaps enabling more complete healing.

And if the entire narrative is spoken from Katniss's adolescent perspective, then this Katniss could be conceiving of the Epilogue *as* she narrates the experiences of the Games and of the Rebellion, in which case the Epilogue pervades the text as pre-narrative, inter-narrative, or extra-narrative. This possibility can be more concretely described as adolescent Katniss imagining, prior to and during the Games and Rebellion, a hopeful future in which healing is possible, meaning that this imagined vision partly inspires her survival of the Arena and facilitates the challenges of telling its stories.

Such schisms between the trilogy's stated chronology (Katniss begins the narrative as an adolescent, then grows up and speaks back through the Epilogue) and what may be the *actual* chronology (the entire narrative is either

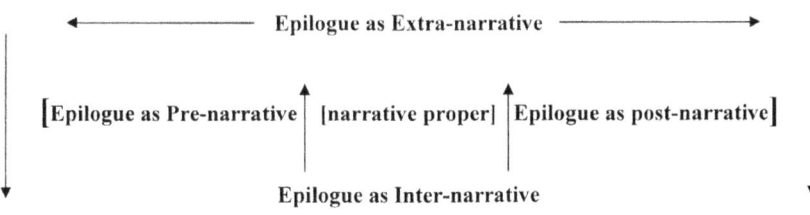

Model 2

Katniss's adolescent experience or it is her adult experience) signify a range of possible meanings. In all possibilities described above and represented in Model 2 that explore *when* Katniss actually tells the narrative proper and Epilogue (as adolescent or adult), the degrees of and relationships among such factors as maturation, looking back, writing forward, hope, and despair are all at stake and matter in terms of their emotional impact on readers.

According to either of these models, the textual transgressions function toward casting off straightforward and (possibly) artificial forms, satisfying and evading readers' expectations, to produce forms that are authentic and up-to-date.

These models for time and space help to clarify what I mean by *agents* of the text, which can refer to characters, narrators, and authors who are at work at the aforedescribed sites—processing, becoming aware of, dealing with, and thus transgressing the conspicuous boundaries between adolescence and adulthood, narrator and author, and between the text and the "real" world.[5] *Agents* also include readers, who are prompted by these boundaries to actively respond to, become aware of their positions within, and participate in the creative and interpretive possibilities which Epilogues or other post-narrative structures enable for YA fiction.

Telling the Story and Re-Scripting the Capitol in The Hunger Games

In *The Hunger Games*, Katniss as character authenticates herself through her actions against the Capitol's control over the districts, their citizens, and even media reports of the goings on in Panem. Some of these actions are motivated strictly by Katniss's desire to survive and to ensure her family's survival, while others are more politically motivated. It is this combination of motives, rather than a single motive, that makes Katniss transgressive, since such internal complexity eludes the Capitol's attempt to categorize her and thereby oppress, silence, and limit her power. In the first installment of the trilogy, *The Hunger Games*, Katniss begins telling her own story of transgressive action well before the real action of the plot begins. Readers find that she is a seasoned trespasser and hunter on District 12's forbidden woods beyond the boundary of the electric fence, selling the game she kills on the District's black market. Katniss's transgressive nature and authenticity catalyze the action of the plot, when she volunteers during the District's annual reaping ceremony to replace her sister Primrose as tribute in the 74th Hunger Games—thenceforth establishing her place in Panem's gaze.

Katniss's narrative in *The Hunger Games*, as the first book in the trilogy, is even more elusive and transgressive, as I claim in this essay's introduction, and alerts us to a unique form of storytelling, characterized by sparse yet varied syntax, embedded with environmental detail—a form that is apparent from her very first paragraph: "...the other side of the bed is cold.... This is the day of the reaping" (3).[6] While throughout *The Hunger Games* she discloses all dialogue and action and even her immediate thoughts about them, Katniss as narrator explicitly delays the process of deep reflection from the immediacy of her actions and experiences as character. This delay is especially apparent at the Ceremony concluding the 74th Games, which Katniss calls "the most dangerous part of the Hunger Games." At the Ceremony, Katniss must "pull off the girl-driven-crazy-by-love scenario" that Haymitch co-scripted with her for her survival in the Arena and which the Capitol scripts after the Arena to minimize Panem's attribution of Katniss's "trick with the berries" to rebellion (358). Carefully managing the rate of disclosure in this moment of performing the Capitol's script and telling its false story, Katniss authenticates her internal story by delaying the process of reflection, or "separat[ing] out [her] feelings about Peeta," until she can figure out what's real and what's not, what she "did as part of the Games," and what she "did out of anger at the Capitol" (358). In her internal honesty, Katniss insists on three "luxur[ies]" of time, space, and privacy for authentic reflection, stating that her "questions [are] to be unraveled back home, in the peace and quiet of the woods, when no one is watching" (359). These luxuries of time after the Games and space outside of the Arena where she is not required to perform scripted actions and statements foreground the Epilogue's textual imperatives of proper timing and spacing. Initially, Katniss may appear to be eluding her own need for answers or closure, as well as the readers' needs for these things—by dis-allowing readers and herself access to certain narrative and emotional undertones. In addition, Katniss's system of disclosure and delay may seem duplicitous, or a negotiation of two disparate agendas in the telling of her own story. Yet, just as the Epilogue is placed chronologically and structurally after the narrative proper in order to do its best authenticating work, Katniss's narrative delay at the end of the first book in the trilogy begins to teach its audience some things about storytelling. There are advantages to narrative processing the adolescent's experiences, delaying in order to confirm the accuracy of memory, and thus transgressing its own elusive mechanisms. This happens well before the Epilogue raises its troublesome post-narrative questions.

Telling the Story Again in Catching Fire

As the trilogy progresses, Katniss's narrative evolves from its initial attempts to relay events in real time to its revisions, retellings, and delays in reflection. These evolutions work toward producing an authentic version of the story that represents the teller's nuanced emotions, motivations, actions, and reactions. In order to be authentic, this version cannot resemble what another character would tell—certainly not an adult, or someone from the Capitol, or any oppressive consciousness and its modes of storytelling. At the level of plot, the Quarter Quell Games in *Catching Fire* raise the stakes of the horrors that the Capitol can create. Each District's veteran victors, rather than inexperienced tributes, are entered into the reaping, meaning that Katniss and Peeta must represent District 12 again in the Arena merely a year after surviving the 74th Games. Gamemakers' rules for the Quarter Quell force Victors to repeat the Arena experience, while dis-allowing a repeat of the 74th Games' exception—offered, revoked, then reinstated—that victor-tributes from the same District could mutually survive the Arena. At the level of narrative, the Quarter Quell Games mean that *Catching Fire* is essentially about Katniss facing the circumstantial and narrative horrors of telling the Arena story a second time.

As with the 74th Games and thereafter, the Quarter Quell necessitates Katniss's surface-level complacency with performing the victor and star-crossed lover roles that the Capitol, and even the Rebels, have scripted for her. Katniss's actions in the Quarter Quell's clock Arena conversely demonstrate that her transgressive sensibilities deepen and become more subtle and complex in *Catching Fire*. For starters, she must upgrade her "trick with the berries" by plotting to save Peeta in the Quarter Quell, knowing that he will plot to save her. Secondly, as with her alliance with Rue in the 74th Games, Katniss's alliances with misfit victor-tributes rather than "career" tributes show her willingness to value unexpected or overlooked potential—potential even in tributes she initially dislikes and distrusts. However, whereas her alliance with Rue reflected almost immediate affection and trust between these two tributes, Katniss's alliances with outspoken Johanna, heartthrob Finnick, engineer Beetee, and elderly tribute Mags reflect that Katniss gradually cultivates trust and affection. In addition, she gradually goes along with these tributes' plans—of which Katniss is initially unaware—to begin a rebellion from within the confines of the Quarter Quell Arena. Katniss's act of shooting an arrow into the flaws in the Arena's force field, its "chink in the armor," shows her condensing of the "*Enemy*" down to a singular entity, the Capitol, rather than myriad bloodthirsty tributes (*CF* 378). Despite all these upgrades to Katniss's transgressive actions, the form of the narrative depicting an adolescent's voice and experiences still reflects YA literature's hesitancies, anxieties, and tensions between adolescent narrators and adult authors. Katniss's actions exceed others' scripts, but *Catching Fire*'s narrative still has work to do toward exceeding the script of the YA tradition.

Catching Fire's concluding narrative complication is that it is the voice of Gale, a childhood friend and fellow rebel, who dialogically and narratively tells the story of District 12's fate, as the final words of this novel. Gale tells Katniss that "there is no District Twelve" after the Capitol obliterates it (391). And while Katniss processes that her family has escaped ruin, in asking, "They're not in District Twelve?" she does not process the destruction of her home, and thus dialogically (and psychologically) resists the responsibility of telling this circumstantial part of the story (391). But even though Katniss psychologically resists the truth and the dialogic telling of it, it is this resistance that tells another story—one of turmoil, pain, and self-preservation. While *The Hunger Games* emphasizes Katniss's actions and statements in conflict with the Capitol's scripts, *Catching Fire* emphasizes conflicts among storytellers—or, the question of who among characters is qualified to tell various aspects of the story—and thus emphasizes the challenge of authenticating versions of the story and the manner in which they are told. It may be the case that this dialogic and psychological resistance to processing and disclosure, along with the conflicts between storytellers and story versions, show the possibilities for more authentic narration—by virtue of the choices available, as readers might consider with *The Bluest Eye*, *Atonement*, and *Catcher in the Rye*.

Given Katniss's mental and physical state at the end of *Catching Fire*, and in keeping with Katniss's own patterns of delayed reflection, *Catching Fire's* abrupt conclusion emphasizes the narrative's act of delaying its reflective and authenticating work until the third novel of the trilogy.

Negotiating Political and Narrative Voices in Mockingjay

In *Mockingjay*, Katniss's actions of invading the Capitol and assassinating District 13's President Coin are certainly her most transgressive and authentic actions, and are fused with her own first-hand accounts of the rebellion, recorded by District 13's media and broadcast crew. Indeed, District 13's media crew realizes that scripting and costuming Katniss as the Mockingjay are not useful "in winning the war" (*MJ* 100). Rather, Katniss as Mockingjay must express "something real" about herself, her experiences, and her voice, and must even engage in real combat, "out in the field" while the crew "just keep[s] the camera rolling" (102). These and other circumstantial and narrative conflicts between storytellers and story versions amplify the conflicts, in the trilogy, between adolescent and adult voices.

In *Mockingjay*, Katniss functions in three capacities—(1) as self-authenticating character, (2) as the embodied symbol and actor for the scripted "Mockingay" for District 13's media-driven rebellion, and (3) as narrator. In all these capacities, Katniss engages in a series of narrative exercises—enabling her as character some degree of control over plot and narrative. At the level of plot, Katniss can control the outcomes of her negotiations with political figures. For example, she dictates the terms of a Mockingjay deal with District 13's President Coin, promising to act as the Mockingjay in exchange for other tributes' protection, including the rescue of Peeta whose memories the Capitol has hijacked and replaced with horrific lies. At the level of narrative, Katniss begins to manage with more alacrity the rising conflict within herself between two life perspectives—that of the adolescent she was before the Hunger Games and that of the adult whom trauma and circumstances are forcing her to become. This narrative management shows the importance of recovering the true stories of her past and present, no matter how gruesome they are. To achieve this recovery, Katniss periodically engages in material storytelling, gathering personal and family artifacts from District 12, thus exercising control over the parts of her life that signify meaning and memory for her.

Yet even with these successes, Katniss's challenges of storytelling become more complex; questions arise about the authenticity of stories' versions and about the legitimacy of authorship in relation to voices and experiences represented. In this regard, Katniss's narrative in *Mockingjay* upgrades *Catching Fire*'s concluding complication of having Gale deliver circumstantial truth and thus function as temporary co-storyteller, supplementing the plot details that readers and Katniss must process. In *Mockingjay*, Peeta is absorbed as long-standing co-storyteller, as his process of reconstructing accurate memories of his experiences prompts him to play a "Real or not real?" game with other characters, with Katniss, and even with readers who notice all the challenges to narrative authenticity.

Katniss's narrative also absorbs the alcoholic and cynical Haymitch as co-storyteller, thus demonstrating the imperative of sharing storytelling responsibilities between adolescents and an adult who mutually understand and experience traumas. In creating this micro-community of storytellers, across age difference but within the realm of shared experience, Katniss, Peeta, and Haymitch engage in one of the most important acts of recuperative storytelling. These victors of the Games co-author a scrapbook of sorts, documenting their common and individual memories of the Games and other experiences, or as Katniss describes it, "those things you cannot trust to memory, ... all the details it would be a crime to forget" (*MJ* 491). The scrapbook, recording anything from "twenty-three years of tributes [Haymitch] was forced to mentor" to "[s]trange bits of happiness," enables Katniss, Peeta, and Haymitch to decondition themselves from the Capitol's damage and its lies, and to reconcile the plot events of their mutual past with their mutual memory of it, in the spirit of confirmation and truth (491).

Most importantly, Katniss concludes the narrative proper by connecting the hope and love she feels with Peeta—who can provide "the dandelion in the spring ... the promise that life can go on, no matter how bad our losses"—with the shared process of storytelling and confirming emotional truth. Peeta asks her, "You love me. Real or not real?" and Katniss answers, "Real" (493).

Narrative Games

Between the trilogy's narrative proper and the Epilogue, the narrative transgresses its forms in *The Hunger Games* and *Catching Fire*, and indeed transgresses boundaries of time and space, and possibly the boundaries of the text itself to comment on YA literature and on storytelling in the "real" world. As I argue from the outset of "Transgressing the Text," the most important textual transgressions occur in "post-narrative" content, in the Epilogue, Katniss's final and retrospective narrative commentary, which Katniss's narrative has deferred from (or even conceived of prior to) what she tells in *The Hunger Games*, *Catching Fire*, and most of *Mockingjay* until this Epilogue. Regardless of Collins's purposes in writing the troublesome Epilogue, readers can play a number of doubting and believing *Games* with it in order to continue grappling with the problems associated with representing adolescent voices and experiences—problems that this trilogy alone is insufficient in solving. In the Epilogue, Katniss plays a game with herself and with readers—a game of narratives, stories, of silence and disclosure—to deal with horrific memories, when "bad mornings" make it "impossible to take pleasure in anything," because she fears them being "taken away." Katniss's game is the final aspect of her mode of storytelling that she chooses to explore. It reveals that Katniss will always struggle to believe that life is worth living:

> ... on bad mornings... That's when I make a list in my head of every act of goodness I've seen someone do. It's like a game. Repetitive. Even a little tedious after more than twenty years.
> But there are much worse games to play [*MJ* 495–96].

One *Game* that readers might play is to accept the Epilogue at face value—believing that this portion of the story can and does represent the authentic voice of a grown-up Katniss, whose adolescent voice in the narrative-proper is authentic too, believing that this "five, ten, fifteen" years later version of Katniss speaks back to earlier experiences. This Katniss, if she is to be believed, faces two primary post–Games, post-rebellion challenges: (1) producing children willingly, and (2) deciding how to tell them her version of her story, knowing that school lessons and peers will offer competing versions. Katniss has been playing this *Game* throughout the entire trilogy, asking and answering "Why?"—which Reynolds calls the "ultimate response of the child." In *The Hunger Games*, Katniss must tell her own story of survival against the "lovers" story that Haymitch and the Capitol have scripted for her to perform in public. In *Catching Fire*, Katniss must tell the story again for the Quarter Quell. Even *Mockingjay* involves Katniss telling the story of the rebellion that District 13 has scripted for her. More than "fifteen years" later, there are children, to whom she must tell the story "without frightening them to death." She repeats her anxieties about what the children "know" and "will know," how to "tell them," and how to answer their questions, as she will have to one day "explain" the horrors to her children when they ask, as Reynolds claims all children ultimately will, "why?" when faced with the reality that the world is broken (*MJ* 494).

Yet, readers might question this "face-value" Katniss, and choose to play another game, one with higher stakes, regarding the Epilogue as yet another device of the narrative to call attention to its own artificiality, and to the game it plays with itself. Katniss raises the stakes in figuring out a way to tell her story to herself, the most dangerous game of all, even though she claims that some games are "much worse," referring to the horrors of the Games and the rebellion. Katniss's earliest and most audacious tactics in playing the Games by her own rules are notable in *the Hunger Games* as her "trick with the berries" and shooting the arrow so close to the Gamemakers during the pre–Games training sessions—thus, in both cases disclosing her defiance, temper, and ultimately her authenticity. Yet this Epilogue functions in the opposite way and does not reveal so audaciously Katniss's greatest narrative assets. Or rather, it might be appropriate to say that for this post-narrative version of Katniss, the very act of playing the storytelling Game of guarded disclosure *does* reveal her greatest asset to authors and readers, who are the literary gamemakers in the "real" world, who design discursive Arenas for storytelling. As with Holden's post-narrative in *The Catcher in the Rye*, Katniss's Epilogue potentially reveals more than it conceals. In particular, it reveals the sound logic of saving a more forthcoming narrative for the telling of another story, one that is unencumbered by her nightmares about her past and fear of the "pleasure[s]" of her present being "taken away," one that is unencumbered by narrative Games as psychological mechanisms for telling the stories of the past that shape those of the future (495).

And not to be forgotten are the three interpretive possibilities for how the Epilogue deals with the issue of time: (1) the straightforward one, that Katniss does grow up and writes back to those experiences while updating us on her current status, or (2) that Katniss has not yet grown up and the Epilogue is her experimentation with "trying on" the adult voice, or (3) that the entire narrative is written from adult Katniss's perspective—with the narrative proper as a distant memory rather than immediate reality, and the Epilogue the current status. Possibility (1) seems to suggest that the adult authenticates the adolescent's experience by confirming the plot events that happened and underscoring the adolescent's various modes of telling the story, even "five ... ten ... fifteen years" later. But possibility (2) suggests that the adolescent Katniss "tries on" the adult voice that she hopes will one day be able to do the authenticating, while possibility (3) still suggests that for Katniss's story, an adolescent voice does not and will not register.

In all cases, the question remains as to whether the adolescent's voice is still in need of an adult voice to authenticate it, or whether a collaboration between adolescents and adults is sufficient for doing the authenticating work. Certainly, no matter which *Games* readers choose to play, we detect the narrative's artificiality and its possible failed attempt to authenticate the voice of an adolescent who doesn't want children for the majority of the narrative and to reconcile it with the voice of an adult who agrees to have them years later. Until the narrative disparities between representor and represented can be reconciled in narrative forms, the best that we can do, as authors, readers, adults, and adolescents producing and consuming these books, will be to play narrative games, no matter how "[r]epetitive," or "tedious," considering the possibility that Katniss's claim is correct, that "there are much worse games to play" (*MJ* 496).

Conclusion

In "Transgressing the Text," I have argued that *The Hunger Games* trilogy functions to transgress existing literary traditions and to transgress narrative confines within its own pages, in very specific ways—teaching readers new things about the nature of storytelling, and about the creative and interpretive possibilities in certain features such as "post-narrative" content in Epilogues. Also, I have considered the potential for these transgressions to enact the transformation of the YA fiction tradition. Such a transformation can perhaps begin authorizing and "author-izing" adolescents, who may be readers and aspiring authors, to decide the ways in which their voices and experiences will be represented in fiction. Likewise, works like *The Hunger Games* may inspire adult readers and authors to recall and reproduce our own authentic trangressive and transformative energy, rather than settling for the artificial adult muttations to which we have grown accustomed. How do we learn to tell our own stories—striving for authenticity, but leaving room for creative and interpretive possibility—especially when we express desires to transform the world and establish our place in it?

For the Epilogue in *Harry Potter*, and the questions of storytelling and world-changing, it is less about the telling at the level of narrative and more about the fulfillment of deserved closure on the level of plot. The other novels explored in connection to *The Hunger Games* are useful places to make some assessments in terms of storytelling and world-changing. *The Bluest Eye* reveals the communal and personal consequences of that community's perpetration of a "quiet as it's kept" system of responding to Pecola's tragedy, alongside Claudia's complicity with that system (Morrison 1). On the other hand, *The Catcher in the Rye* reveals the individual consequences of self-disclosure, consequences in the degree and manner of telling. Holden advises, "Don't ever tell anybody anything. If you do, you start missing everybody" (Salinger 214). These opposite ends of the spectrum—the one of silence and the other of telling—show that neither can achieve healing or atonement. This is the case for the narrative proper and the post-narrative content of these novels. *Atonement* depicts a different sort of storytelling—perhaps some achievement of healing in the telling, even though it will never be complete. Briony seems content with her lifetime of writing about her mistake, and says "[a]tonement ... was always an impossible task, and that was precisely the point. The attempt was all" (McEwan 479). Contentment or satisfaction with the "attempt" sounds plausible, but then again, readers may not feel the same contentment or satisfaction that Briony insists upon. It may be that she does not either.

And in returning over and over to *The Hunger Games*'s Epilogue, I remain fixated on Katniss's claim that "there are much worse games to play" than the story-telling game she plays with herself (*MJ* 496). Her claim sounds very pithy, accommodates her emotional state, and seems to convey a good bit of truth. I want to believe that Katniss's process of transgressing the text by playing a narrative game, the same game repeatedly, is in fact less dangerous than the Hunger Games, the Quarter Quell, the rebellion, and her re-scripting of her own actions and statements against the Capitol's design. But I am more inclined to believe that *not* playing this storytelling game is "worse." I wonder if I should be saddened, in this case, that Katniss's narrative and ours can never be 'Real,' and that to do their best work, they must always play with being 'Not Real?'

At some location along the spectrum of silence and disclosure, of Briony-like "attempt(s)" and Katniss-like Games, Harry-like scar-touching, and Holden-like silence and telling, the Epilogue shows us that Katniss's narrative system of disclosure and expression may be the current best solution for storytelling and world-changing, though it still involves some artificiality. We hope that we can be authentic in our expressions and not have to play Games, but we must understand that even though we can tap into our authentic childhood transformative energy, circumstances need not be tidy or fully disclosed.

Rather, the telling of them must be attempted, refined, re-told continuously. In fact, we must understand, also, that closed meanings, authoritative and singular versions, and definitive statements, even for one's own story, constitute the "worse game" to play, because it is the one the Capitol has designed.

Notes

1. Originally published in 1983, Gayatri Chakravorty Spivak's "Can the Subaltern Speak" explores the ethical dangers of representing race, class, and gender of "subaltern" groups in literary or political discourse, as well as the dangers of excluding members of these classes from such discourse, or "insisting" that they participate in it (2207). The results of these impulses on the part of readers, scholars, and authors include "essentializing" groups' difference from dominant or elite classes, as well as relegating certain members of these groups to different roles through harmful narratives, such as "White men are saving brown women from brown men" (2204).

2. *The Hunger Games* is especially important to examine not only as extending prior texts and forms, but also in the context of its representation of and pervasive impact on current social consciousness, as fans and scholars are already exploring, including other essays appearing in this edited collection. For instance, Deidre Anne Evans Garriott's "Performing the Capitol in Digital Spaces" points out that current popular discourse about the trilogy and recent film adaptations reflects a "real world manifestation of what Collins critiques in her trilogy: surveillance and oppression" at the level of racism and disparaging comments about actors' body types. So, if *The Hunger Games* is eliciting these kinds of harmful public comments about adolescents, then its service to adolescents is questionable. Yet, many readers would and have agreed that *The Hunger Games* resists this kind of Capitol-style policing of physical appearance, and as Garriott qualifies in her analysis, fans and scholars have issued statements that counter the Twitter users cited above.

3. Frances FitzGerald's "The Influence of Anxiety: What's the Problem with Young Adult Novels" appeared in a 2004 issue of *Harper's Magazine* and comments that *Catcher in the Rye* was one of several texts that were written before the 1970s and intended for adult readers, but that appeal more often to adolescents. This issue of audience is inextricable from the issue of purpose; scholars might ask why certain texts are written for particular audiences and with what messages. Simple answers for *Catcher in the Rye* and *The Hunger Games* might be that the texts are didactic, teaching readers to sympathize with adolescents' struggles or to value their capabilities. What complicates these answers are considerations of whether the questionably authentic adolescent voices and experiences represented are qualified, so to speak, to deliver such messages. Furthermore, scholars might consider the consequences of these messages, namely whether they reinforce readers' (potentially inaccurate and harmful) assumptions about adolescents or produce new ones.

4. Gerard Genette's structuralist theories on literature offer "paratext," among other terms, for exploring the ways in which a text is affected by other texts that exist externally. For Genette, in *Paratext: Thresholds of Interpretation*, "paratext" might include a text's "other productions," such as "an author's name, a title, a preface, illustrations," that signify meaning by virtue of their position surrounding or extending the text in question (1). Genette notes, too, that paratext signifies "spatial, temporal, substantial, pragmatic, and functional" meaning about a text (4). For this essay on *The Hunger Games*, I focus less on the trilogy's printed paratext, and more on negotiating theoretical, circumstantial, structural, or chronological (even if just implied) meaning in Katniss's narrative.

5. Wayne Booth's *The Rhetoric of Fiction* explores the relationships among the author, narrator, text, and reader, all as agents of fiction. A linear continuum of fictional agents might

arrange agents in the following way to indicate relationships of agents to each other and to a fictional text: actual author—implied author—dramatized narrator—narrated story—imagined/implied/ideal reader—actual reader. However, the relationships among them are more abstract, tenuous, complicated, and multi-dimensional than this model can accommodate. For instance, the actual author may not resemble the author that readers imagine through reading the text. And of course, the narrator cannot be assumed, in every case, to represent the experiences of the author. Still, authors at best can imagine an ideal reader, who may or may not intersect with actual readers. Shared agency in *The Hunger Games* rallies around the character and narrator Katniss. Although this essay does not explore fully Booth's theoretical implications for the text, such an exploration is worth doing in a larger scholarly undertaking than this one. Such a larger study might consider the following theoretical implications: (1) the presence of an *implied author*, as a manifestation of readers' expectations and impressions of *actual* adult author, Suzanne Collins, and (2) the *implied author's* narrative collaboration with Katniss, as self-authenticating character and questionable narrator.

6. See Baker's essay in this collection, "Outside the Seam: The Construction of and Relationship to Panem's Nature," for an extended analysis of "Katniss and Her Language of Earth."

Works Cited

Booth, Wayne. *The Rhetoric of Fiction*. Chicago: University of Chicago Press, 1961. Print.
Collins, Suzanne. *Catching Fire*. New York: Scholastic, 2009. Print.
_____. *The Hunger Games*. New York: Scholastic, 2008. Print.
_____. *Mockingjay*. 2010. Large Print Edition. Detroit: Gale, Cengage Learning, 2012. Print.
Deleuze, Gilles, Felix Guattari and Marie Maclean, "Kafka: Toward a Minor Literature: The Components of Expression." *New Literary History* 16.3 (1985): 591–608. *JSTOR*. Web. 23 Sept. 2011.
FitzGerald, Frances. "The Influence of Anxiety: What's the Problem with Young Adult Novels?" *Harper's Magazine* (Sept 2004): 62–70. *EBSCOHost*. Web. 14 June 2013.
Genette, Gérard. *Paratexts: Thresholds of Interpretation*. Trans. Jane E. Lewin. Cambridge: Cambridge University Press, 1997. Print.
Golding, William. *Lord of the Flies*. New York: Coward-McCann, 1962. Print.
Morrison, Toni. *The Bluest Eye*. 1970. New York: Penguin, 1993. Print.
Reynolds, Kimberley. *Radical Children's Literature: Future Visions and Aesthetic Transformations in Children's Literature*. New York: Palgrave MacMillan, 2007. Print.
Rose, Jacqueline. *The Case of Peter Pan: Or the Impossibility of Children's Fiction*. London: MacMillan, 1984. Print.
Rowling, J. K. *Harry Potter and the Deathly Hallows*. New York: Scholastic, 2007. Print.
"Rowling to Kill Two in Final Book." *BBCNews.co.uk*. BBC News, 27 June 2006. Web. 16 May 2013.
Salinger, J. D. *Catcher in the Rye*. 1951. New York: Little, Brown Books, 1991. Print.
Spivak, Gayatri Chakrovorty. "Can the Subaltern Speak?" From *A Critique of Postcolonial Reason*. 1988. *The Norton Anthology of Theory and Criticism*. Ed. Vincent B. Leitch. New York: Norton, 2001. 2197–2208. Print.

Tipping the Odds Ever in Her Favor
An Exploration of Narrative Control and Agency in the Novel and Film

Anne M. Canavan *and*
Sarah N. Petrovic

In writing about the then-future casting of *The Hunger Games*, Meghan Lewit calls protagonist Katniss Everdeen, "the most important female character in recent pop culture history" ("Casting"). While other heroines in YA fantasy literature, like Hermione Granger or Bella Swan, can certainly contest Katniss for this title, there is no doubt that Katniss has captured the popular imagination with every imaginable product branded with images and spin-offs from the novels and film.[1] One of the reasons for this success may well be how in Suzanne Collins's YA novel, *The Hunger Games*, Katniss Everdeen consciously creates a series of narratives that give her both a feeling of control as well as actual agency in the events that take place around her. In the blockbuster film adaptation of the novel directed by Gary Ross, however, that agency is noticeably decreased, making Katniss a pawn in a larger game rather than a major player in a game of her own choosing, even though the role of narrative creation is increased in the film. The novel's audience likely transfers their understanding of and belief in Katniss's agency to the film, but a close reading of both reveals that her power is quite diminished. The purpose of this essay is not to suggest that either the novel or the film is more correct, but to examine the differences that each version of Katniss presents and what that means for the construction of the narrative.

Narrative Control

When discussing what it means to have agency in a narrative, it is helpful to begin with a definition. James Phelan in *Living to Tell About It* states, "narrative itself can be fruitfully understood as a rhetorical act; somebody telling somebody else on some occasion and for some purpose(s) that something happened" (18). Telling, of course, can occur in a wide range of verbal and non-verbal forms, and the somebody else in question is often the narrator him or herself. Traditionally, when critics write about the narrative of a piece of fiction, they are referring to the heterodiegetic level of the work, which goes on outside of the world that is created by the characters and the subsequent actions. In other words, the heterodiegetic level is the external level of the story, as opposed to the in-world level. The narrative of the heterodiegetic level is controlled solely by the author of the work, and generally characters within the work (those on the homodiegetic, or in-world level) are never made aware of forces of narrative control at work. To use an example, characters in a horror story generally do not know that they are in a horror story until late in the narrative; therefore, walking alone up the dark staircase to investigate the strange sounds from the attic seems like a reasonable action. The reader is, of course, aware of the norms of this type of narrative (nothing good is at the top of those stairs), but because the character does not have access to that same knowledge, he or she makes choices that seem ill-informed or foolish. However, Katniss is no fool.

The creation of identity through narrative is one that is important not only to Katniss but also to her readers. In his article "The Changing Face of Young Adult Literature: What Teachers and Researchers Need to Know to Enhance Their Practice and Inquiry," Jeffrey S. Kaplan notes, "Questions about self-identity and self-discovery continue to underlie narratives for teens, and no matter the literary style or genre, young people often find comfort and solace in engaging reads that attempt to define their journey toward self-understanding" (20). Katniss's ability to control her own identity and thus her own destiny may be one of the reasons behind *The Hunger Games*'s incredible success in connecting with teen readers. Thus the construction of the narratives within the novel and film is important not just for the advancement of the story but for the model it provides for its readers.

The Novel

In the trilogy, Katniss is fully aware of the multiple narratives in which she is participating and, moreover, knows the power of employing those narratives to her own benefit. While we typically think of agency as resulting from actions, as Michel Foucault observed in "The Order of Discourse," speech, and the control of the speech of others, is a fundamental source of power in a society. It is primarily through her words, which shape her actions, that Katniss is able to manipulate the narratives in which she is involved. In the novel, Katniss manages four, at times conflicting, narratives—the role of the strong daughter and sister, the star-crossed lover, the tribute, and finally the Girl on Fire. At various times in the novel, Katniss consciously makes choices to further these narratives, using them to leverage the audience of the Hunger Games into supporting her. These narratives, particularly that of the star-crossed lover, while powerful tools that help Katniss survive the Hunger Games, also severely limit her agency in terms of her ability to end her participation in a given role. Because Katniss has chosen the narrative of the strong and mysterious tribute, she cannot allow herself to show weakness when she is in front of the camera.

Similarly, agreeing to engage in the role of the star-crossed lover means that she *must* act in this way until the Games are over and she believes she will no longer be under scrutiny. No matter how she feels about Peeta or Gale, she must always appear to be in love with Peeta. Being the girl who breaks Peeta's heart or, worse yet, the girl who deceived a Capitol audience threatens her survival. Within the confines of the roles she has chosen to embody, the ways in which Katniss manages the narratives in the film and in the novel are markedly different, ultimately presenting two different levels of control and complicity in the creation of the various narratives. While the management of the homodiegetic narratives continues throughout Collins's trilogy, because of the interest in the interplay between word and film, this essay is limited to a discussion of the first novel and its film adaptation.

Within the novel, Katniss is perpetually aware of the way others perceive her, even before Haymitch drives the point home during training by explaining the importance of other people liking her in order for her to get sponsors. In the first chapter, she discusses how she has learned to control both what she says and her expressions to keep her family safe, and how she puts on a bright face for Prim to make her less afraid during her first Reaping. Even before the Reaping takes place and Katniss is thrust into the public eye, she tells the reader of her experience holding her tongue and turning her "features into an indifferent mask" (*THG* 6), all designed to keep her family safe. While the Hunger Games are the foremost threat in the events of the novel, Katniss reminds readers that simply living in District 12 is a constant balancing act, where a stray word could lead to harsh punishment. This foundation of control paves the way for Katniss's narrative agency in the novel, as she is already practiced at maintaining a public image in a way that Peeta is not. Peeta, who comes from a more privileged background, is less practiced at presenting a public face against the constant dangers of starvation and subjugation, and this difference in world views explains some of the tension between Katniss and Peeta in the first novel. Katniss, naturally cynical, regards Peeta's expression of love as a ploy, and Peeta, naturally trusting, believes that Katniss's kisses have more to do with him than simply surviving the Arena.

The difference between the narrative in which Katniss participates and her own emotions is that participating in the narrative of the strong provider for the family makes Katniss act in ways that hide her true emotions or thoughts. However, her inner thoughts reveal that the "true" Katniss is weaker and more afraid than the persona she has adopted for the public and her family; it is only through acting out her role of strength that she is able to exercise control over her situation. Perhaps the clearest example of this division between the outer and inner self is when Katniss is preparing for the reaping and thinks, "The anguish I always feel when she's in pain wells up in my chest and threatens to register on my face. I notice her blouse has pulled out of her skirt in the back again and force myself to stay calm" (15). Because the reader knows what Katniss is thinking, it becomes clear when she is furthering a particular narrative and when her reactions are genuine.

When Katniss volunteers for her sister at the Reaping, she instantly begins to create a new narrative for herself, that of tribute. Protecting her sister moves her embodiment of a narrative from a private, domestic event to a constant public performance. From the moment she volunteers, Katniss begins to control her identity as tribute: "'Prim, let go,' I say harshly, because this is upsetting me and I don't want to cry. When they televise the replay of the reapings tonight, everyone will make note of my tears, and I'll be marked as an easy target. A weakling. I will give no one that satisfaction" (23). In the split second after her almost involuntary decision to volunteer in Prim's place, Katniss is already in control of her narrative as a tribute, masking her feelings in order to perpetuate a public image.

This control continues on her way to the Capitol, as Katniss repeatedly demonstrates an awareness of the cameras that are recording her every move, and she responds by hiding her emotions from everyone else. By being aware of the public persona she is presenting, she is able to take control of that image and create an appealing story out of it, a story that might make her more likely to survive the Hunger Games. Katniss knows that the Hunger Games are not simply a gladiatorial battle between twenty-four children; rather, the Games are designed to favor those with the most interesting or appealing stories and those most likely to survive through the mechanism of the sponsors and the interventions of the Gamemakers. Even before Haymitch begins crafting the star-crossed lover narrative, Katniss has begun to create a story for herself as the strong mysterious tribute, who has the added interest factor of having volunteered for her sister.

While the narrative of Katniss as the provider for her family and the protector of her sister receives little development in the first novel of the series, it is important because it marks the first instance when Katniss deliberately assumes a persona that fits into a particular narrative for a certain reason, in this case, to protect her sister. When Katniss is taken to the Justice Building, she refuses to let herself cry and, instead, orders her mother to stay with Prim and not to retreat into herself as she did after the death of Katniss's father. Katniss's instructions to her mother are clear and detailed, explaining that the family can survive without tesserae if they sell Prim's goat's milk and cheese and her mother's remedies. There is no discussion of Katniss's feeling about being a tribute, just a plan for the family's survival. Katniss realizes that because her life is suddenly a part of the show of the Hunger Games, she must choose a narrative that she can embody in order to survive the Games, and she chooses a path of outward strength, both for her family and for the viewers and participants in the Hunger Games: "I cannot afford to get upset, to leave this room with puffy eyes and a red nose. Crying is not an option. There will be more cameras at the train station" (34). While the narratives that she participates in do restrict her actions, they also allow her to exercise her agency by placing her in positions of power—the strong sister, the smart and competent tribute, the object of Peeta's desire.

However adept Katniss is at creating her own narrative and manipulating public perception, her narrative is also shaped by those around her, including Haymitch, Cinna, Peeta, as well as by the Capitol via Caesar Flickerman and Effie Trinket. By coaching her behavior in the Capitol on everything from how she should react to her stylists and the four-hour long content session, Haymitch attempts to help Katniss craft her narrative into a more successful version:

> "I'm trying to figure out what to do with you," he says. "How we're going to present you.... People are intrigued, but no one knows who you are. The impression you make tomorrow will decide exactly what I can get you in terms of sponsors" [116].

His assistance, however, has little effect before Katniss goes into the Arena, as it is Cinna who helps Katniss in her interview, telling her, "'Remember, they already love you… Just be yourself'" (123). This advice flies in the face of the deliberate crafting of Katniss's narrative as tribute that Haymitch had undertaken and underscores that for Katniss to be able to construct and use a narrative to her advantage, it must be in some way organic to her personality. Just as she was naturally protective of Prim and her mother, Katniss has to find a part of herself that furthers her persona as a tribute—dedicated to her family, strong, and somewhat mysterious. For Katniss, constructing the narrative of herself as tribute is less about manufacturing feelings and actions that do not exist, and more about hiding those aspects of herself that are antithetical to the narrative, such as her hatred of the Capitol and her own fears. Even though Cinna has crafted her public persona as the Girl on Fire, it is clear that his costuming of her was meant to bring out part of her personality that already existed, rather than to create something from nothing.

Even before the Games begin, Katniss is adept at hiding the parts of herself that do not lend themselves to her survival, as she recounts that she used to frighten her mother with the things she "would blurt out about District 12, about the people who rule our country" (6), but that she learned to conceal those thoughts from others. Katniss also hides her distrust of Peeta's motives, as well as her feelings for those in the Capitol because those sentiments are at odds with the narrative she is creating. Because the novel allows the reader to see what Katniss is hiding as well as what she is embracing, her agency becomes clear. Almost all of Katniss's actions are the result of a conscious decision, a decision that the reader sees her making.

These decisions are often at odds with her true feelings, making it clear that her actions further a particular end, which in this case is her participation in a series of narratives designed to keep her alive. Her narratives, which are created by her conscious choices that often run counter to her true feelings, allow her greater latitude in her actions. The case in point, of course, is when the Capitol is forced to (re-re)modify the rules to allow two victors in the Hunger Games. If Katniss and Peeta had not become so wildly popular in the Games, it is at least possible that the Capitol would have allowed them both to die. Moreover, if Katniss, who was still profoundly conflicted about her feelings towards Peeta, had not played her role of the star-crossed lover so well, it is likely that Peeta would never have agreed to the plan. Her subjugation of her personal feelings is the only source of her agency; the fearful, angry girl that the reader sees in Katniss's private thoughts would never have survived the Games, let alone have made the Capitol reverse itself in such a public way.

Katniss is not the only one with a vested interest in her participation in these narratives; she also recognizes that Haymitch is the co-author of her story as a tribute and interprets his actions through the lens of how they further the narrative that they have created. When Katniss is seeking water in the Arena, she realizes that Haymitch can see how her struggle has made her a prime target for the ever-present cameras (169). It is Katniss's awareness of how she appears to the audience that leads her to interpret correctly Haymitch's lack of action as an indicator that she has almost found water herself, and she uses the camera's mediation to further her own narrative as a tribute. Haymitch's coaching is most effective when it is least present, as with the gifts from sponsors while Katniss is in the Arena. Katniss knows that as a victor, Haymitch has a clear view of the sort of narrative that audiences will respond to for a tribute, and when he sends gifts to her, he is helping her present that narrative to the cameras. Nowhere is that clearer than when Peeta is sick in the cave and Katniss realizes that "one kiss equals one pot of broth" (261);

there is no note from Haymitch telling Katniss that she is furthering the narrative that is most likely to keep herself and Peeta alive. Katniss simply understands the ramifications.

Of the three fully-developed narratives in which Katniss participates throughout the novel, the role of Peeta's lover is the one that is most disparate from her natural inclinations and the one over which she has the least control. When Peeta drops the bombshell of his love for her during his interview with Caesar Flickerman, Katniss is thrust into this story, whether she wants to participate or not. Before Katniss has time to understand fully her role in this new narrative, the tributes are thrown into the Arena, and she has to balance her uncertain position in this new narrative with her already-established individual identity as tribute. The lover narrative is more complex for Katniss because she did not initiate the storyline, because she is dependent on Peeta to preserve the appearance of the relationship, and because she is personally unsure whether Peeta is creating a narrative designed solely to further his own survival. Because of Katniss's experiences with presenting herself in ways that are designed to further her own survival, she finds Peeta's sudden declaration of love as more likely to be a manipulative play on the audience's emotions rather than a genuine outpouring of sentiment.

Katniss does not, however, reject the narrative that Peeta has created, even while she is unsure of his motivations. When Katniss finds out that Peeta is working with the Careers, she realizes that seeming uncertain about Peeta's loyalty will give away any advantage that is to be gained from that narrative, so she gives the cameras a knowing smile, leaving the audience to figure out what it means (164), and as she hikes along, she decides that there is still the potential to "get some mileage out of" the narrative (165). Clearly Katniss is her most cynical about this narrative, and it functions as a secondary concern to her primary Arena narrative of being a tribute for the first half of the Games. Immediately after the near run-in with the Careers, Katniss goes to check her traps, finding a rabbit: "I want sponsors to see I can hunt, that I'm a good bet because I won't be lured into traps as easily as the others will by hunger" (164). While not rejecting Peeta's star-crossed lover dynamic, Katniss is still most interested in perpetuating her own individual narrative for the cameras, and this will continue until the rule change that allows for two victors.

This preference for the tribute narrative over the lover story is strongly tied to the level of agency that each narrative affords Katniss. As a tribute, Katniss has been establishing a solo identity in the woods, relying on her own prowess as a hunter to further her reputation for competence and survivability. The way she is seen as a tribute is entirely in her own hands, whereas her identity as Peeta's lover is, by its nature, dependent on Peeta's actions as much her own. Complicating this narrative is the lack of communication between Peeta and Katniss during the initial stages of the Hunger Games. When Katniss sees Peeta with the Careers, she is not sure where she stands in this shared narrative, because her actions are necessarily dependent upon whether Peeta is furthering the narrative. While the narrative of the lover has given Katniss some additional avenues for agency by making her seem more desirable, not to mention more personable, they have also made her dependent.

The star-crossed lovers is also the only narrative that Katniss ever lets drop in the course of the first novel. When Katniss teams up with Rue, she mentions that she thinks that Peeta might have saved her from the Careers but dismisses his actions as "just part of his act" (206). When Katniss speaks with Rue, whom she trusts, she is able to treat the star-crossed lovers as a tool for survival rather than the truth she is presenting it as for the Capitol audience, clearly demonstrating that for Katniss, there is a clear divide between reality and the fictions she must adopt to stay alive. This scene highlights Katniss's discomfort with the narrative that is the least organic to her personality and the one requiring her dependence on Peeta to make the narrative successful, and at that moment, Katniss is not sure if Peeta is still participating in the story or what his strategy might be. Given the information that she has, Katniss feels that Peeta is likely abandoning the narrative and here begins to distance herself from it as well so that she still appears to be in control of the situation.

Her ability to engage and disengage with various narratives indicates that Katniss ultimately has control over the stories she has created. While she will eventually become trapped by the star-crossed lovers narrative that President Snow uses to force her into an engagement to Peeta, and later by her role as a symbol for the revolution, within the first novel Katniss is still able to use the narratives that she creates to triumph in the Games and to protect those that she loves. At the end of the novel, though, Katniss begins to get an idea that the power she wielded in furthering these narratives may have a terrible price, as she is confronted by Peeta about her true feelings for him. Fittingly, the novel closes with anther performance for the cameras for which Katniss must participate in a narrative that has become painful for her and that has begun to blur the lines between a convenient fiction and reality: "I take his [Peeta's] hand, holding on tightly, preparing for the cameras, and dreading the moment when I will finally have to let go" (374).

The Film

While the trilogy's Katniss finds significant power in the creation of her various narratives that lead to her victory, the film's Katniss is less obviously in charge of her own story. In looking at the novel and film *The Hunger Games*, the authors of this essay do not seek to create a hierarchy between the two media forms or evaluate the film based on its adherence to the novel; instead, the film will be analyzed according to how it differs from the novel and, more importantly, what effect those differences create in the film's story. We hope to respond to Thomas Leitch's call to adaptation studies to "loo[k] more closely at the ways adaptations play with their source texts instead of merely aping or analyzing them" (76). Though we are looking at the success, so to speak, of Katniss as a composer of narratives, we do not equate this success with the success of the particular text, rather we hope to provide an analysis of how the film changes the control of the narrative. Ultimately, the film trades Katniss's role in the narrative of the Games for the Gamemaker's, highlighting the constructedness of the Arena situation itself rather than Katniss's ability to control it.

The grim and gritty world of District 12 closely reembles Dorothea Lange's Depression Era photography of the homeless and unemployed. That photography, like the opening to the film, highlights the helplessness of the people and their need for someone to tell their story to the larger world. Here, Katniss lives with her family, and she is introduced as comforting and encouraging her younger sister Prim, while moodily ignoring her mother. Without the explicit backstory of Katniss's father's death and her mother's depression that the novel provides, Katniss's treatment of her mother appears as evidence of a sullen teenage disposition at best or worse, a spiteful personality. Here she is not obviously and consciously fulfilling a role of family leader so much as emotionally responding to her mother and sister. Instead of showing her as family protector through her backstory of providing for them over the years, the film depicts this role through the gift of the Mockingjay pin. No longer representative of the district and given by Katniss's friend Madge, Katniss discovers it in the market and brings it home as a gift for Prim. Katniss tells Prim it will protect her: "And as long as you have it, nothing bad will happen to you. Okay? I promise." The pin originally a symbol of Katniss's protection of her sister, and while it does not mystically keep Prim's name from being drawn, it means that in order to keep her promise, Katniss must volunteer as tribute to protect her sister. Later, it is returned to Katniss, now representing her promise to Prim to try and win, and functioning as a reminder to her of the responsibility she has to fulfill her role as the family's provider. More pressure is placed on Katniss in this role in the film because the pin is not a reminder of home and how her district is rooting for her as in the novel when it comes from the community, but is rather a symbol of Katniss's individual need to succeed for her family. This burden isolates her from them all the more rather than connecting them to her, forcing her to now more fully and consciously take on the role of family leader, which she had previously occupied in more of a de facto sense.

As Katniss transitions from her role as family provider to tribute, the Games as entertainment is emphasized to her by others around her though not by her, suggesting that she needs to be taught an awareness that she does not already possess. Her hunting partner Gale reminds her, "They just want a good show. That's all they want," and Haymitch and Cinna impress upon her the need to make people notice and like her. The film also highlights the role of the Gamemakers, particularly Seneca Crane, in ways the novel's limited narration cannot. There are commentaries by Claudius Templesmith and Caesar Flickerman, interviews with Seneca and President Snow about the narrative of control, hope, and fear being crafted by the Games in general and the 74th Games in particular, and several scenes depict the production studio that controls both the Arena and all of the televised events surrounding the Games. This expansion impresses upon the film viewer the constructedness of the Games and how what happens in the Arena is a result of careful planning rather than "natural" progression. Resultantly, the role of tribute that Katniss must occupy is not just one that can survive in the wilderness and is willing to kill others, but one that is entertaining to watch. And in order to win, her persona must be as deliberately crafted as the Games themselves. This critique of the barbarism of the Capitol audience and the horrifying schadenfreude that fuels reality television is present in the novel though not as explicitly as in the film. Because it now exists as a part of that media machine, the film's heightened implications of the manipulation of story and audience create a separation between itself and that which it critiques.

It is within Katniss's role as tribute, particularly leading up to and immediately following the Games, that the film's Katniss varies most from Collins's writing of her. Starting with the tribute training, Katniss seems slower to pick up on the political implications of her actions during the opening ceremonies, interviews, and judging than Peeta, particularly in regards to seeking to curry favor with potential sponsors. However, with the other tributes, Katniss shows a greater sophistication. Whereas in the novel, Katniss and Peeta readily listen to Haymitch's instructions not to show any strengths prior to the individual judging, Katniss urges Peeta to show his physical power by throwing a heavy piece of equipment to impress the Career tributes. Katniss goes against Haymitch's orders so that Peeta does not appear too easy of a mark for the Careers once the Games begin. In doing so, she arguably helps lay the groundwork for Peeta's ability to join the Careers at the beginning of the Games instead of that team being purely formed from Peeta's desire to keep the Careers away from Katniss. However, here she shapes a narrative for Peeta, not herself, and it is not clear that she is acting out of a desire to control her narrative rather than a reaction to immediate personal cues. This ultimately suggests that Katniss and Peeta together share some of the creation of their narrative, rather than Peeta solely creating one for Katniss before the Games begin.

Katniss's insight as to how she (and Peeta) are appearing to the other tributes does not transfer into the Games themselves. While the novel's Katniss is sensitive to the fact that everything she does is on and for the camera, the film's Katniss is not explicitly so. At one point, Katniss finds a camera in a tree she's sleeping in, but this explains the mechanisms of the Games more than her knowledge of how she's being perceived by the watching world of the Capitol and the rest of Panem. Actress Jennifer Lawrence's blank expression at the camera may merely be indicative of the inner control of Katniss, but it fails to register recognition of the camera and its significance. Furthermore, the filmmakers choose not to use a voiceover to make explicit Katniss's inner thoughts that are revealed through the novel's first-person narration, and thus Katniss's keen awareness of how her actions will be perceived by those in the Capitol is lost.

One instance in which the film's Katniss does seem to use the cameras to her advantage is when Rue dies. In the novel, Katniss adorns Rue with flowers to "shame them, to make them accountable, to show the Capitol that whatever they do or force us to do there is a part of every tribute they can't own. That Rue was more than a piece in their Games. And so am I" (237). Because the movie audience does not have access to Katniss's internal monologue, her intentional subversion of the Capitol here is not as clear in the film. Picking flowers and placing them around Rue could as easily come from Katniss's own grief and feelings of now being alone in this cruel world. Once she finishes this funeral though, Katniss begins to walk away, but then stops and looks around, halting when she is looking directly in the camera; she then kisses her middle three fingers and holds them up to the screen. The film cuts to the same image of Katniss being projected on the screens in a public square in District 11. In response, the citizens hold their fingers up to Katniss and then begin to riot against the Peacekeepers on the edges of the crowd. The film does not show the subversive intentions of Katniss in her hatred of the government, but it does preview, more so than the novel, the power she has in leading others, in symbolizing the revolution that is to come in the next two novels, and her role as the Mockingjay.

However, in the film *The Hunger Games* in general, Katniss's political machinations and game strategy are inscrutable. Like the viewers of the Games themselves, the film audience is left to puzzle out Katniss's emotions and decisions based on her actions, rather than her thoughts, and the audience is unaware of the vast disparity between Katniss's external and internal self. To overcome this loss of motivation, the film substitutes others' savvy for Katniss's, like Rue's, who in the film is responsible for the idea that Katniss drop the tracker jacket hive on the Careers, but most particularly Haymitch's. The film's

Haymitch is certainly a drunk (though sadly a svelt one), but not the angry-fall-off-the-stage-oblivious-to-how-his-actions-affect-his-tributes drunk that he starts off as in the novel. He is not even at the Reaping. But, by the time the Games are underway, the Haymitch in the film is wining and dining sponsors, advising the Gamemaker Seneca on how to put on the best show, while keeping Katniss and Peeta alive, and most importantly instructing Katniss on how to act, not just as a tribute, but as a "star-crossed lover from District 12." Rather than Katniss and Haymitch being co-conspirators as in the novel, the film's Haymitch has more power over Katniss's strategy and control directing, rather than merely aiding, her role as tribute. Rather than Katniss aptly discerning and evaluating the minimal communication from Haymitch and the Gamemakers into the Arena as she does in the novel, the film's Katniss is given more overt directions. We do not see Katniss struggling to find water and successfully interpreting a lack of help from Haymitch as a sign she's nearby and should keep going.

Nowhere is Haymitch's leading more obvious than in his schooling of Katniss. He seeks to show Katniss that to be successful as a tribute, she must play at being a lover. Immediately after the interview with Peeta's declaration of a long term crush on Katniss, Katniss is angry, but Haymitch tells her, "Now I can sell the star-crossed lovers from District 12," and "It's a television show. And being in love with that boy might just get you sponsors, which could save your damn life." These are much more overt instructions than the novel's, and they do not end there. When Katniss's leg is burned, the parachute containing medicine from Haymitch also contains the obvious note, "Apply generously and stay alive.—H." Once the rules have been changed so that two victors from a single district are allowed, and Peeta and Katniss team up, their roles as lovers and tributes become one and the same. Peeta is desperately ill, and Katniss's affection for him seems to be out of pity when she kisses his cheek comfortingly. In response, a parachute arrives to a surprised Katniss. Haymitch only sends a pot of broth along with the note, "You call that a kiss?" He is reminding her of the rules of performance, of the audience, and of the role she must play rather than waiting for her to come to that knowledge on her own. Instead of Katniss being the brilliant chessmaster, manipulating the various pieces of the Games to her own advantage, she appears more passive as she follows Haymitch's lead.

At the film's conclusion, as in the novel, Katniss is clever enough to discern that the Capitol must have a winner to fulfill the purpose of the Games, which is to give enough hope to the districts that they do not try to revolt once again. The film's subtle alteration of Katniss's funeral for Rue, which activates the malcontent in District 11, foreshadows the film's Games' conclusion. By threatening her and Peeta's double suicide, Katniss unlocks the ultimate power narrative and openly defies the Capitol. This is a portent to the role she will later play in the series as the symbol of the rebellion. However for now, she must subsume this identity within hers as lover. When President Snow crowns her the victor and remarks on her pin that Katniss notes is from her district, the film alludes to the coming conflict between the districts and the Capitol that Katniss has enabled through her participation as a Hunger Games victor, participation through unity not isolation.

Conclusion

As its publisher Scholastic categorizes, *The Hunger Games* novel originally was intended for a sixth to eighth-grade audience, though the novel's readership has grown well beyond that. By the time the film was produced, the audience included many fans of the trilogy who were not from that narrow YA segment. This more diverse audience combined with a $78 million dollar budget—comparatively small for a franchise blockbuster, though still a significant amount—created a film less concerned with capturing the inner experience of its teen girl protagonist than with depicting the world in which she lives.

We argue that while the high-profile media attention the first film garnered has multiplied the impact of Collins's work, the film's depiction of Katniss provides less insight into her success being on her own terms. The trilogy's Katniss is savvy about her presentation of herself and creates her own narratives rather than living out the ones assigned to her by the Capitol—a message with significant appeal for its target audience. While later in the series, Katniss becomes increasingly trapped by the roles she has created for herself as being in love with Peeta and as the symbol of rebellion against the Capitol, the first novel allows Katniss to successfully control how she is perceived by others. Rather than showing Katniss's ability to transcend the system of the Capitol's control and how she manipulates it to her advantage, the film shows the inverse—why the system is in place and how its power works. The film's audience does not see Katniss figure out how to break the system, but rather sees how the system is constructed, a move that expands the critique of exploitative media that the novel employs, though at the expense of empowering the teen girl protagonist. The emphasis on narrative creation and control as a source of agency remains the same in the film as in the novel, but the power has shifted from Katniss to the Gamemakers, President Snow, and even Haymitch. As it currently stands in the filmic world—though with a projected *three* sequels this may change—Katniss cannot break out of the system in the film by her own initiative. Therefore the ultimate messages of the two narratives are quite different. While Collins's novel indicates that there is hope for individual action triumphing over a government-police state through the creation of a personal narrative, the film puts forth a world where the power resides with more obvious figures than a poor, teen girl, and Katniss's agency is largely illusory.

Note

1. Beyond the predictable t-shirts, bags, and jewelry—the most popular being a mockingjay pin—there are journals, cookbooks, and Barbie dolls.

Works Cited

Foucault, Michel. "The Order of Discourse." Untying the Text: A Post-Structuralist Reader. ed. Robert Young. Boston: Routledge & Kegan Paul, 1981. 48–78. Print.

Kaplan, Jeffrey S. "The Changing Face of Young Adult Literature: What Teachers and Researchers Need to Know to Enhance Their Practice and Inquiry." In Teaching Young Adult Literature Today: Insights, Considerations, and Perspectives for the Classroom Teacher, eds. Judith A. Hayn and Jeffrey S. Kaplan. Plymouth, UK: Rowman & Littlefield, 2012. 19–40. Print.

Leitch, Thomas. "Adaptation Studies at the Crossroads." Adaptation (2008) 1 (1): 63–77. Print. doi: 10.1093/adaptation/apm005.

Lewit, Meghan. "Casting 'The Hunger Games': In Praise of Katniss Everdeen." The Atlantic. 9 March 2011. Web.

Phelan, James. Living to Tell About It. Ithaca: Cornell University Press, 2005. Print.

Part II
Provoking Change and Creating Radical Spaces

Katniss and Her Boys
Male Readers, the Love Triangle and Identity Formation

WHITNEY ELAINE JONES

Since the publication of *The Hunger Games* in 2008, critics and readers have highlighted Katniss's status as a rough and tumble feminist icon. A 2011 article in *The Atlantic Online* even proclaimed Katniss "the most important female character in recent pop culture history" (Lewit). However, in the same year, marketing for the film adaptation of Collins's trilogy shifted the emphasis of the novels from Katniss to "the men of *The Hunger Games*." This shift was most apparent on the May and August covers of *Entertainment Weekly*, the first of which featured Katniss, alone and armed with bow and arrow, and the latter of which featured only Gale and Peeta. The shift from the central feminist heroine to her male sidekicks is initially, and undeniably, disturbing because it sidelines the central female character in favor of her male romantic interests; however, it is my object in this essay to show how this particular marketing interpretation of the trilogy, that centers not on a single individual, but on the love triangle she is a part of, identifies a key, yet overlooked, component of the text itself: masculinity.

Beginning with the *Entertainment Weekly* covers—which highlight the love triangle and isolate its components by placing Katniss alone and separate from the combined men in the later issue—I trace the issue of masculinity back to the text and investigate its relationship to the love triangle, and to Katniss. Katniss, the most important corner of Collins's love triangle, is torn not only in her romantic options, but also in her gendered identity. Many have identified Katniss as a character who easily manipulates the boundaries of gendered identity.[1] These discussions of Katniss's ambiguous gender are valuable in understanding how Collins's trilogy expresses an undeniably radical formation of gender that positions both male and female characteristics in one highly masculinized female form. Ultimately, I will argue that, while Katniss may be "the most important *female* character in recent pop culture history," *male* readers have most to gain from her fictional experiences.[2] Although love triangles are often considered appeals to female readers in search of romance, I suggest that the triangle presents the complicated double bind of masculine identity that expects men to be protective, but not aggressive, strong, but not violent, and never emotional. I argue that the resolution of the love triangle offers male readers a new definition of gender that is comprehensive and utopian rather than divisive and dystopian.

This comprehensive gender embraces both femininity and masculinity to create a single, utopian site within the trilogy in which the traits that define masculine and feminine unite rather than separate the sexes. The seemingly incompatible masculine and feminine aspects of Katniss's character identify her as a girl with a divided self, a broken girl downtrodden and defeated by the divided and broken world around her. I suggest that even though Katniss may begin with a divided, broken self, by the end of the trilogy, her identity is healed, the rift in her sense of self mended through a new understanding of gender, making Katniss a model of selfhood for a future utopian community inside and outside of the trilogy. By exploring how the male corners of the love triangle work as projections of Katniss's torn self, I will show that Collins creates the possibility of a future utopia through the balancing of gender traits, offering young male readers an example for healthier behaviors and attitudes to mend their own torn worlds and conflicted identities.

My essay joins a body of scholarship concerned with the "invisibility" of masculinity for contemporary readers. As John Stephens notes in the preface to his collection of essays entitled *Ways of Being Male*, until recently, "[u]nder the influence of various feminisms, the application of gender studies to children's texts has focused predominantly on issues of female representation" (x). The essays in Stephens's collection seek to illuminate and remedy the seeming disregard for the masculine child in criticism. Although work on fictional male children and animals in children's literature, literacy, and historical masculinities, and on masculinity in other cultures, have appeared in the last several years, discussions of contemporary depictions of masculinity in children's and young adult literature is still playing catch-up to the copious studies on femininity.[3] The contributors to *Ways of Being Male* agree that, through children's literature, "masculine subjectivities may be reconfigured, resignified, and rewritten" (xiv). However, as Beverly Pennel concedes, "the realization of such a possibility seems utopian" (61).

By "utopian," Pennell means ideal, out of reach, a lovely, but highly improbably if not impossible, dream or fantasy of a perfect world. My essay hinges on that very word—"utopian"—but in a much more hopeful sense. I define utopia as a state of unity, balance, and synthesis free from the divisions, contradictions, and oppositional, competitive binaries of a broken—and thus dystopian—world; utopia and dystopia are oppositions whose central features I identify as, respectively, unity and division.[4] Rather than despair at the possibility of ever achieving a massive cultural revision of masculinity, in particular, and gender in general, I suggest that, through a text like *The Hunger Games*, which I argue has a hidden utopian impulse despite its obvious dystopian appeal, the process has already begun.

In pursuit of this thesis, I have divided my essay into three sections. In the first section, I explore Gale and Peeta as representative of opposing gender traits—masculine and feminine—and as projections of Katniss's torn identity. In the second section, I destroy, then reconstruct, the love triangle to reveal Katniss's position on a sliding scale of masculinity that identifies her as a relatable character for young male readers. Finally, in the third section, I argue that the resolution of the love triangle solves the issue of conflicting masculine identities and offers an alternative model of self-construction for Katniss and her male readers, mapping for both the way to a utopian future. Katniss's choice does not define her as a feminine character, but is symbolic of the possibilities for the evolution of masculine identity.

The Boys in the Corners: Masculinity and Severed Selves

The love triangle is, at its very core, divisive; it tears the chooser in two and pits the two romantic choices against one another. The love triangle causes conflict and, often, as is the case in *The Hunger Games*, offers the chooser two romantic choices who are complete opposites of one another.[5] For Katniss, this choice is between Gale and Peeta, the hardened warrior and the sensitive baker. Gale represents extreme Western notions of active and destructive masculinity while Peeta represents Western ideas of passive and nurturing femininity. Even their physical descriptions evoke different genders: Gale—tall, dark, and handsome—is the picture of the swoon-worthy hero of romance, while Peeta—with golden hair, pale skin, and blue eyes—bears the physical markers of the pure and innocent romantic heroine. While neither character is one-dimensionally representative of a single gender—like Peeta, Gale is capable of the softer emotions and like Gale, Peeta is brawny and tough—the main driving force behind each boy's personality can be associated with either masculine or feminine gender traits. The choice between these basic oppositions is located within Katniss herself and corresponds to the dueling gendered poles of her own personality. The choice between Gale and Peeta is a choice between two warring factions of Katniss's self, each of which has its own particular worth for her survival and happiness.[6]

Collins's description of Gale is hyper-masculine; he is the emotionally-hardened warrior, hunter, provider, and overall alpha male. He fits a traditional model of masculinity associated with power, aggression, and sexuality. Although Gale is usually interpreted as appealing because of these very qualities, the trajectory of the narrative across all three novels reveal him as a character limited by the strict masculine stereotypes he represents.[7] Susan Lehr's description of how boys are depicted "in popular culture as active, loud, aggressive, unemotional, independent... strong, handsome, bold, curious, adventurous, tough, and naturally smart" maps easily onto Gale (1). In District 12, Gale is the sole financial supporter of his family, and this associates him with traditionally masculine characteristics such as strength, security, power, and cunning. These are all good qualities, but they become magnified to an unpalatable and violent extreme in District 13 when Gale transforms from hunter to soldier and Katniss transforms from tribute to Mockingjay. Gale's need to "protect" those around him turns lethal in District 2 when he suggests "one of his death traps" that would simultaneously take out a major Capitol military base, a fortified mountain nicknamed the Nut. Katniss realizes that Gale "has no interest in preserving the lives of those in the Nut" and is willing to sacrifice lives in exchange for military victory (*MJ* 203). Gale's willingness to participate in the violent competition of battle associates him with strict notions of masculinity that privilege dominance and strength over empathy and life. However, his adherence to normative masculinity comes with a price. Perry Nodelman observes, "we often tell boys that their wildness is inevitable, even desirable, while also telling them that to enact it is wrong" (5).

This claim rings true in Katniss's changing perception of Gale from the beginning of *The Hunger Games* to the end of *Mockingjay*. His aggressive masculinity makes him, ultimately, destructive and careless of innocent life, a sin for which, eventually, Katniss cannot forgive him. The possibility that he may have had a hand in killing Prim and other innocents profoundly alters her, and perhaps the reader's, understanding and appreciation of Gale's attractively masculine qualities. Taken to the extreme, Gale's masculinity becomes destructive, and his worth for Katniss—previously found in his mental and physical strength, his aggression, and his ability to protect her family—becomes a liability for her.

Whereas Gale's job as first hunter and then warrior associates him with the worldly, masculine sphere of nation-building and commerce outside of the home, Peeta, the second male corner of the love triangle, enacts those traits that Lehr notes as associated with popular cultural representations of girls: "passive, quiet, sweet, nice, emotional, more mature ... dependent, hardworking" (1). Peeta spends years in love with Katniss, yet, passively, makes no attempt to express his feelings. He is both sweet and nice (though also brave and tough) when he rescues Katniss from starvation by throwing her burnt bread, and his various strategies during the Games—plotting with Haymitch, joining a (fake) alliance with the Careers—mark him as more dependent upon others, if resiliently and intelligently so, than Katniss.

Peeta also participates in a traditionally feminine occupation: baking. He has been born and bred for work that associates him with the domestic sphere. He is also an "artist"—he paints both baked goods and canvases—a role that links him with the more feminine act of creation, and that places him immediately opposite Gale's role as "destroyer." Peeta Malark is a sensitive baker with an imagination capable of envisioning beautiful works of edible art as well as of taming nightmares by bringing the Games "back to life" on canvas (*CF* 53). His gentle, deft finger work makes his artistic visions a reality. Through his art, and through his occupation, Collins situates Peeta firmly within the home and the kitchen, and constructs a character as emotionally sensitive as Gale is seemingly callous. Although Peeta is capable of destructive acts of violence, especially after he is mentally "hijacked" by the Capitol, his defining traits, his worth for Katniss, lies in his empathy, his sensitivity, and his artistry, which he explores and expands through the domestic art of baking, associating him with traditionally female qualities.

Why offer Katniss romantic options who are completely opposite from one another in physical description as well as in personality, values, and behavior? Gale and Peeta are more than character foils, and they offer more than romantic tension. They are physical and male manifestations of Katniss's competing values and personality traits, which shift uncertainly between feminine and masculine expectations. I seek to show how Collins's radical use of gender in *The Hunger Games* trilogy—the projection of a female's inner identity conflict onto two male characters—works with the love triangle to transform the familiar romance convention into something completely new. I argue that Katniss's ambiguous and thus radical gender identity is manifested through the love triangle itself, creating for Katniss not a triangle of romantic choices, but a triangle of identity and gender choices. Katniss is the apex of the love triangle, the point halfway between the extremes of Peeta and Gale. Her choice is not necessarily love or government, rebellion or conformity, but a set of character traits associated with femininity and masculinity, Peeta or Gale. Her journey to selfhood is not in determining which boy she loves, but which set of values and behaviors, masculine or feminine, she accepts as her own.

Katniss experiences a unique bond with each boy that amplifies the aspect of character that she shares with each. Like Gale, Katniss is angry and violent; like Peeta, she is a sympathetic artist. The synchronicity of purpose and action between Gale and Katniss ultimately threatens to overwhelm her, to override the compassion and empathy, represented by Peeta, that balances out the more aggressive and masculine aspects of her personality. When Gale suggests blowing up the Nut, killing all those inside—even the innocent—Katniss admits that the notion is temporarily tempting, thinking, "I want everyone in that mountain dead" (*MJ* 204). Throughout the trilogy, Katniss is tempted to slide increasingly toward the extreme, violently masculine part of herself manifested as Gale; however, the opposing part of herself that finds expression in the other male corner of the triangle, in Peeta, counters this temptation, keeps it in check. Though she "want[s] everyone in the mountain dead," and is "about to say so," there is a pause, a moment of internal indecision that characterizes the pendulum swing of her personality: "But then...I'm also a girl from District 12. I can't help it. I can't condemn someone to the death he's suggesting" (204–5). The death Gale suggests is that of underground explosions, suffocation, being buried alive; it is a death similar to the one experienced by their fathers, and by so many other coalmining men of District 12. What stands out here is the ellipsis, which signals hesitation, doubt, shifting values, motivations, decisions. It is in the textual blank space of the ellipsis that we most clearly see Katniss's divided sense of self. Is she the vengeful girl who, like Gale, can sentence a mountain of innocents to death; or is she the girl from District 12, who values all life because she has experienced the loss of so much of it?

The "But then," the ellipsis, signals Katniss's shift from those traits that align her with Gale, to those that align her with Peeta, whose bond with Katniss is perhaps even stronger than that between her and Gale. Ultimately, Peeta's pain and death are pain and death for Katniss, a fact of which President Snow is well aware. When the Capitol holds Peeta hostage and Katniss asks Prim what she thinks they will do to him, her astute little sister's answer is "whatever it takes to break you" (151). The breaking of Peeta means the breaking of Katniss's more vulnerable self, the destruction of the intuitive, artistic, lover embodied by Peeta and hidden within the girl he loves. Katniss may see herself as "Violent. Distrustful. Manipulative. Deadly," but she is a more complex character than she gives herself credit for (232). She can be as "coldhearted" and calculating as Gale, but she also "contains multitudes." Katniss may be, to her own weary eyes, a violent and distrustful killer, but if she is a hunter and destroyer, she is also a singer and creator, sharing the artistic, sensitive qualities embodied by Peeta.

To talk about the "Peeta part" of Katniss is to talk about Katniss's "feminine" traits, her compassion, her sensitivity, and her creative capabilities.[8] Peeta's other pursuits, namely baking and painting, dangerously feminize his own particular brand of toughness. While Peeta's baking even earns him a nickname—"the boy with the bread"—I am most interested in exploring Katniss's artistic commonalities to Peeta. Art, in *The Hunger Games* trilogy, is feminine, an act of creation that directly opposes Gale's violent, destructive tendencies.[9] Katniss—a singer and, most importantly, an actress—has the qualities of an artist. She creates just as surely as Peeta does, though instead of baked paintings, she creates symphonies of melody in the trees and multiple, believable personas for the capital and viewing audience.

However, Katniss views art, and more generally acts of creation, skeptically, assigning them both dubious value within her dystopian world. Because of its seeming uselessness when compared to a bow and arrow, art ranks "somewhere between hair ribbons and rainbows" (*THG* 211). Music, painting, and creativity understandably appear pointless in a world ruled by fear, death, and destruction, and she associates creation not with beauty, but with pain suffered after creation. When, in *Mockingjay*, she sings to a forest of the titular birds, she creates a symphony within nature that is "quite beautiful" and has the power to arrest the attentions and stir the emotions of those watching her: "Everyone is watching me intently. And Pollux has tears running down his cheeks" (126). However, Katniss fails to see these reactions as positive or sincere, guessing that "my freaky song has dredged up some terrible incident in his life" (126). Katniss's inability to understand the beauty of creation underscores her initial refusal to have children. She rejects her creative abilities at all levels. Katniss's resentment of her role as an artist or creator indicates the unbalanced state of her own identity. She is both artist and warrior, feminine and masculine, but cannot reconcile these two opposing parts of her character; instead, she reads herself as torn and fragmented, a broken reflection of the broken world she lives in, violently volleyed between the two boys who represent her internal fragmentation.

A Third Masculine Corner; or, Who Will Katniss Choose?

Just as it is possible to read the triangle as constructed around two males and one female, all of whom exhibit differing levels of masculinity and femininity, it is also possible to read the triangle as one constructed around varying levels of masculinity alone. To clarify a masculine reading of the love triangle, I want to break the construction apart, destroy it, and reconstruct it from a shape of sharp corners and bisecting lines to one of fluid continuity: a line, a spectrum, a scale.[10] The purpose of this reconstruction is to clarify how a text like *The Hunger Games* with a female narrator can successfully address issues of masculine identity. Lem and Hassel observe that "One of the ways that *The Hunger Games* bridges the divide between boys' and girls' culture is Collins's portrayal of a heroine who embodies traditionally masculine characteristics—

in her role within her family, in her behavior, and in her adherence to patriarchal expectations regarding masculinity" (121). This is true, and in order to see the masculine construction of Katniss more clearly, I suggest we slide the bottom corners of the love triangle (Gale and Peeta) outward, letting the top point (Katniss) descend, until all three points occupy a position on a line, a scale of masculinity that slides from the extremity of Gale's hyper-masculinity, through Katniss's conflicting sense of self, to Peeta's more sensitive and feminized representation of manhood. Once we transform the triangle into a scale of masculine behavior, we can more clearly see how the triangle is actually a reflection of contemporary masculine identities, and how Collins's trilogy, and her heroine, become tools through which young male readers can reflect on their own selfhoods.

And Katniss, occupying a sliding position on the love-triangle-turned-masculinity-scale, is a girl torn in identity as well as in love. Within Katniss are the defining traits of both Gale and Peeta, and her first-person narrative expresses the confusion and frustration of her fragmented and warring sense of self. According to the co-authors of *New World Orders in Contemporary Children's Literature,* "[Adolescent fictions] construct narratives of personal growth or maturation, stories about relationships between the self and others and between individuals and society" (12).[11] It is this very trait of adolescent fiction that lies at the heart of the love triangle between Katniss, Gale, and Peeta. Katniss, in search of selfhood, is susceptible to what Susan Bordo identifies as a masculine "double bind," or "any situation in which a person is subject to mutually incompatible instructions, in which they are directed to fulfill two contradictory requirements at the same time" (242).[12] Bordo illuminates the dual yet paradoxical role expected of men in the twentieth century: beast and gentleman. She explains the impossibility of this duality that requires men to be "warrior males" but to also contain their aggression within certain suitable spheres, particularly the bedroom, and to act with the sensitive manners of a gentleman at all other times (236). She notes:

> What a quandary all this places boys in! On the one hand, the official and unofficial wisdom is declaring that to be a 'real male' ... requires that one be fiercely competitive and aggressive in 'manly arenas' like athletics and have a predatory, promiscuous, get-all-you-can attitude toward girls, and woe to the boy who doesn't [240].

The boy's dismissal of this double bind has obvious social ramifications, despite the, also obvious, limitations it puts on their lives and choices. Huck agrees that boys

> are caught in this web of gender stereotyping. They can be and do anything except be a ballet dancer, an artist, or a homemaker. Yet most of us know men today who do all of the cooking in the household, home school their children, and change

the diapers of their babies. And increasingly there are more single fathers. Our books need to reflect this changing culture [viii].

The Hunger Games signals "this changing culture" through a love triangle that breaks the traditional placement of a beautiful woman between two terribly different, but equally masculine suitors.[13] Instead, the corners of Collins's love triangle are occupied by male figures who are characterized by varying levels of masculinity, and so have as much to say about male identity formation, the struggle with the double bind, as they have to say about female identity.

It is safe to assume that a biologically female character may appeal to a young male reader, but can he identify with her as an individual who shares his life experiences? I suggest that, yes, he can, and that, in many ways, Katniss, as a biological female, can shed light on constructs of masculinity better than male characters of young adult texts.

Recent sociological and literary criticism on masculinity suggests that, while masculine character traits may retain hierarchical power in American culture, masculinity itself remains "invisible" (Nodelman 2). Nodelman's use of children's literatures with his students has challenged the way we read and interpret gender. Not only does he argue that the masculine is invisible, but when he and his students changed a protagonist's sex from male to female— Max in *Where the Wild Things Are* becomes Maxine—they noticed admirable traits in the character that they had not identified before and discovered their limiting assumptions about masculinity (10–11). Discussing the formation of American masculinity, sociologist Michael Kimmel argues, "the quest for manhood... has been one of the formative and persistent experiences in men's lives. That we remain unaware of the centrality of gender in our lives only helps to perpetuate gender inequality" (3). In other words, if we remain unaware of the formative importance of "the quest for manhood" in the lives of young men, we can never attain gender equality. Masculinity, and boys, as Nodelman notes, will remain invisible.

I want to expand Nodelman's observations on the invisibility of masculine identity through a reading of *The Hunger Games* trilogy that emphasizes Katniss's gender ambiguity, which makes it possible for her to be an identifiable figure of masculinity. I suggest that it is because of her female sex that Katniss is an ideal figure for highlighting to young boys what it means to be masculine. By locating competing male identities within the love triangle and, more importantly, in Katniss's female body, Collins puts sufficient distance between the young male reader and the presentation of the double bind to which his identity formation is subjected, to allow him a safe distance from which to witness the negotiation of masculinized and feminized personality traits and make the invisible masculine bind visible. As Katniss navigates the sliding scale of masculinity through her interactions with Gale and Peeta, so too can young male readers engage in questioning the gendered behaviors their own social structures expect of them.

Though biologically female, Katniss is essentially masculine; even her motivation and relationships derive from masculine sources.[14] According to Michael Kimmel, "[m]anhood is less about the drive for domination and more about the fear of others dominating us, having power or control over us" (5). Kimmel's assertion relates to both Katniss and Gale, and their desire to perish by their own hands rather than by the hands of others. Gale, Katniss, and the other District 13 soldiers go into battle with nightlock tablets—self destruction in case of capture—and even discuss other ways to end their own lives or each others' quickly if they are caught by the enemy. Gale has several tricks up his sleeve: "'Beetee showed me how to detonate my explosive arrows by hand. If that fails, I've got my knife. And I'll have Katniss,' says Gale with a smile. 'She won't give them the satisfaction of taking me alive'" (*MJ* 336). Not only is Katniss a part of the pact to ensure she and the other soldiers remain in control of their own lives or deaths, she is the vehicle of that death, the arrow that is supposed to pierce Gale's heart and stop his life.

I realize that I use, here, an extreme example of power struggle, one that, hopefully, a young male reader will never find himself in. However, the pact Katniss and the others make with one another excellently shows the importance of power and control with regard to the masculine dynamic. While young male readers most likely do not occupy positions comparable to Katniss's in their everyday lives, the battlegrounds of school and home, where they vie for power with teachers and parents and siblings, offer related if distanced means of understanding Katniss's power struggles with Gale, with Coin, with Snow, and with an entire system that works to suppress and control her.

Katniss's central and lethal position within this group of soldiers reveals yet another masculine characteristic; her most important relationships, outside of her relationship with her sister Prim, are with other men. Kimmel notes that, for "masculine" men, relationships with other men are more important than relationships with other women (5). Haymitch, Katniss's dead father, Gale, Peeta, and Cinna are closer to Katniss than are her mother or Effie, and these relationships certainly garner more attention within the narrative than even Katniss's relationship with Prim, who is mostly "off camera."

The most important masculine relationship for Katniss is the one she shares with Gale. An analysis of their relationship reveals a kinship between herself and Gale that goes beyond friendship and partnership to definitions of selfhood.[15] Collins establishes Katniss's unity with Gale almost immediately in the series. Not only do Gale and Katniss physically resemble each other, with "straight black hair, olive skin... the same gray eyes," but, as Katniss recognizes, they are "a team" (*THG* 111), keeping each other alive and offering a safe space for each other in which to voice those thoughts too dangerous for "inside the fence" of the Capitol-controlled District 12 (112). "[C]onfidants," Gale and Katniss represent for each other freedom, trust, and "mutual need" (112). Collins continually emphasizes their symbiotic relationship throughout the trilogy until it surpasses the status of a relationship between two close individuals. Gale and Katniss seem to become a single soul inhabiting two different bodies. *Mockingjay* particularly emphasizes the similarities between Gale and Katniss, possibly because, in the final installment of the trilogy, Katniss is most worn, most cynical, and most determined to survive at all costs. When Katniss demands that District 13 allow her to go above ground to hunt, she thinks not only of herself, but also of the pleasure it will bring to Gale: "We hunt, like in the old days. Silent, needing no words to communicate, because here in the woods we move as two parts of one being" (*MJ* 53). Her thoughts identify their pleasure as synonymous and as intuited by Gale, who has the ability, even, to finish Katniss's sentences.

In *Catching Fire*, Katniss's relationship with Gale takes a more forceful move toward the romantic, creating a closer connection between Katniss's "choice" and her torn identity. Katniss expresses complete sympathy with Gale, kissing him and imagining her life exchanged with his: "I imagine watching Gale volunteering to save Rory [his brother] in the reaping, having him torn from my life, becoming some strange girl's lover to stay alive, and then coming home with her" (*CF* 117). At this moment, Katniss's love for Gale overwhelms her—"Gale is mine. I am his. Anything else is unthinkable"— and her identity as rebel and warrior overtakes the other aspects of her personality (117). She knows, in that moment, that "[t]he answer to who I am lies in that handful of poisonous fruit," lies in the berries of rebellion she uses to save Peeta's life, to win the Hunger Games and to defy the Capitol (118). Katniss's inner monologue reveals that her sense of self intimately intertwines with the identity of the boy she loves. Let me make a clarifying distinction: Katniss does not become a rebel and warrior to be like Gale, who in that moment she loves. Rather, Gale is a projection of that inner part of herself, which, in that moment, she identifies with more than she does with compassion and creation.

Katniss's warrior viciousness is not her only "masculine" trait. Unlike either of her suitors, Katniss does not do well with emotion, an interesting reversal since, as Kimmel points out: "the pressures to live up to the 'boy code' leave many boys suppressing emasculating emotions like vulnerability, dependency, and compassion and affecting, instead, a hypermasculine unemotional pose" (269). In March of 2011, Meghan Lewit, of *The Atlantic* online, discusses Collins's reversal of gender. In her article, "Casting 'The Hunger Games': In

Praise of Katniss Everdeen," Lewit admires Katniss through a comparison to Peeta: "Peeta Mellark—is carefully crafted to serve as the yin to Katniss's occasionally abrasive yang. She hunts; he bakes. She's churlish and closed-off; he's unfailingly open and sunny. She's not looking to commit; he's eternally devoted. To put it simply, she's totally the guy in the relationship." As Lewis's commentary suggests, Katniss's emotional distance from everything and everyone makes her "the guy in the relationship" to Peeta's "girl." Jennifer Mitchell takes Lewis's comment further, observing:

> Peeta is an equally complicated match for Katniss. Just as Katniss's masculinity is expressed in her status as hunter, so Peeta's femininity is expressed in his role as baker. Even Peeta's shrew of a mother undercuts his masculinity by suggesting that Katniss might actually win this year, a sharp testament to his perceived feminized weakness. Prior to the Games, both tributes spend their day-to-day lives doing things that undercut conventional gender delineations [132–33].

Mitchell emphasizes how Katniss and Peeta similarly undercut gender conventions in opposing ways. While Mitchell investigates the superficial markers of gender—occupation, for example—the important ways in which Katniss and Peeta transgress gendered boundaries are internal and emotional, rather than external or physical.

While Peeta exhibits the emotional characteristics we have come to expect from a girl, Katniss exhibits a lack of, or suppression of, emotion we feel necessary for acceptable boyhood. Collins reverses the association of emotional suppression with young boys, placing this trait within a young female instead. It is Katniss, not Gale, who does not want to talk about "feelings," and it is Katniss, not Peeta, who finds their intimate pillow talk and emotional candor awkward and uncomfortable:

> Ugh. Peeta makes comments like this in such an offhand way, and it's like being hit in the gut. He's only answering my question honestly. He's not pressing me to reply in kind, to make any declaration of love. But I still feel awful, as if I've been using him in some terrible way. Have I? I don't know. I only know that for the first time, I feel immoral about him being here in my bed [*CF* 86].

Katniss's clear discomfort with, and even ambivalence toward, Peeta's heart-on-the-sleeve brand of emotion not only associates her with Western traditions of stoic masculinity, but causes her to question her sense of self, tugs on the seams of her torn identity. Peeta's emotions, and her discomfort with her own emotions, cause Katniss to question her own values, morals, and actions. Has she been using Peeta? If she has, does this make her immoral? Katniss does not know what she wants or why she might want it. She does not know why she acts the way she does. Because she does not know what she wants, who she is, or what matters to her most, she cannot choose a romantic partner, let alone a path in life. Katniss's emotional ignorance creates internal confusion on every level. Critics like Bordo and Kimmel are concerned with young male confusion—of identity, of emotion, and otherwise. Bordo suggests that "our culture has a small problem knowing what it wants from men" (234) and Kimmel asserts that "[p]roving masculinity remains vitally important to young men, even as the opportunities to do so seem to be shrinking" (Kimmel 269). Katniss's confusion over what appears to be her harsh or immoral and unemotional treatment of Peeta offers young male readers an opportunity to see the results of adhering to a strict, unemotional "boy code" and offers them a model of dealing with those emotions through a highly powerful, masculine figure—Katniss—who must herself confront the confusion and pain of surviving and feeling.

Katniss—powerful, resourceful, and active—is the perfect female character to benefit a young male audience as her problems with self-definition mirror their own. She is a figure of masculinity, uncomfortable with the feminine roles occupied by her mother and sister, a figure who eventually allows emotion and vulnerability into her life and embraces those parts of herself that are creative rather than destructive. The trilogy's bittersweet ending reveals a traumatized Katniss no longer at war, who seeks redemption and healing through the creation of a scrapbook, an artistic outlet that embraces her ability to create and neutralizes, though it can never completely erase, her violent and destructive past. Through Katniss's scrapbook, creation and destruction collide and coexist, as do the masculine and feminine within Katniss herself. While Collins could have completely abolished our own divisive concept of gender, rather than merely synthesizing established and restrictive terms, she does not, creating, instead, recognizable and perhaps related, rather than unisex characters, a textual choice Charlotte Huck identifies as necessary for endearing, rather than alienating, young contemporary, and particularly male, readers (viii). I applaud this move, despite its lack of revolutionary flavor. If a male audience, or any readership for that matter, is to move toward a utopian future, then they must work with what they have, what they know, synthesizing the positive traits of each gender to revise their divided dystopian present and reveal their unified utopian futures.

Toward Utopia: Healing Rifts and Breaching Divides

Collins's love triangle, because it can function as both a representation of division between masculinity and femininity, and an expression of the double bind of masculinity, reveals multiple gender identity conflicts. But how does Collins's trilogy attempt to resolve these conflicts? Collins resolves the love triangle through Katniss's choice of Peeta over Gale. However, does romantic resolution solve the issue of Katniss's fragmented sense of self? Does choosing Peeta make her whole? And, if the resolution of the love triangle does unify a torn girl's understanding of herself, can it also help young male readers reach a similarly coherent sense of self? I insist that, yes, Collins's resolution to the love triangle offers not only a solution to Katniss's fragmented interiority, but also a model of self construction for those reading the trilogy that emphasizes a comprehensive, and utopian, redefinition of gender generally and masculinity more specifically. In this final section, I claim that the trilogy's position as a dystopian text requires a swing toward a feminist utopia that, through a radical and transgressive female figure—Katniss—radically transgresses the binary divisions of the dystopian world.

Though I ultimately argue that the trilogy's ending suggests utopia, its position as a dystopia is essential to understanding why utopia is the necessary means of resolution. Collins immerses Katniss so fully within a fragmented dystopian nightmare that the "girl on fire" is worse than burned by the end of the novel; she is a charred shell. Fragile, a single touch could crumble her frame to ash. The only possible relief from the nightmare of dystopia is a swing towards its opposite, a gradual approach toward utopianism. Though opposites, utopia and dystopia are, like Gale and Peeta with masculinity, extreme examples of the same state. Krishan Kumar notes the horror of the symbiotic nature of the utopia/dystopia dichotomy:

> As nightmare to its dream, like a malevolent and grimacing *doppelganger*, anti-utopia has stalked utopia from the very beginning. They have been locked together in a contrapuntal embrace, a circling dance, that has checked the escape of either for very long. ...utopia and anti-utopia are antithetical yet interdependent. They are "contrast concepts," getting their meaning and significance from their mutual differences [99–100].

The very definition of dystopia relies on its opposite, the utopia, suggesting even in the oppositional nature of the words, a reliance, a co-existence that hints at balance and perhaps even synthesis. Where there is division, there will also be unity; where there is nightmare, horror, and torn identity, there is a possibility of healing and wholeness. The conflict and resolution of Collins's love triangle underscores the "contrapuntal embrace" and "circling dance" of the two opposing genres; Collins eventually resolves the divisive dystopian triangle by purging extremes from the text and creating a comprehensive, and thus utopian, gender category (Kumar 99). I suggest that Katniss's utopian resolution to her divided dystopian crisis of identity offers a model for achieving "utopia" on a communal level inside the trilogy, and on a personal level outside of the trilogy with young male readers who are susceptible to the same "double bind" that marks Katniss's identity confusion and creates the romantic tension of the love triangle.

The division of dystopia in *The Hunger Games* exists in Katniss's very nature; she is a girl torn, as I have already shown, down to the very core—a "wasteland," fractured not only by her nation and its war, but by her romantic possibilities as well. Katniss, torn between Gale and Peeta, painfully suppresses her instinct as sensitive artist and a confrontation with her conflicting emotions, for the more masculine role of hardened warrior, a role her torn and brutal world requires of her. Robert S. Baker notes that the central character of the dystopia is an analogue to the broken and divided society that shapes her: "The characterization of the hero... [is] informed and shaped by this central tension between the oppressive organization of the state and the revitalizing anarchy of the individual" (45). I suggest that this is true of Katniss who, as Collins's representative fighter against the dystopian social structure, is not "informed and shaped" by the conflict between her own powerful individuality and Panem's insistence on conformity and obedience, as she is bent and broken. The conflict between Katniss and Panem creates for her a conflict of self characterized by rifts, divides, and breaks—the nightmare of division over the dream of unity.

While political and personal divisions equally shatter Katniss and her dystopian world, Collins's trilogy achieves the mended, healed ending of a feminist utopia. Tom Moylan identifies the feminist dystopia and utopia relationship as a "continuum," in which there are sliding degrees of meaning and unlimited levels of adherence to either genre or both, banishing the notion of oppositions all together (qtd in Mohr 51). In expanding Moylan's idea of the continuum, Dunja M. Mohr emphasizes the centrality of "transgressing binary thought" to both the continuum that synthesizes two contrary genres and to the plots of the texts themselves (51). She identifies the feminist utopia as a genre that works to transgress gender boundaries and to synthesize contraries like masculine and feminine:

> there are stories, drawn from the abyss of polarizations, that have begun to move beyond the either/or dichotomy and that tell not of a void but of futures in the plural sense. The pandemonium from whence such unheard tales arise is a literature of subversion that speculates about the future, while desiring the transformation of the present, and that demands the (im)possible: the transgression of dualism [1].

Mohr argues that contemporary female dystopias are, in fact, utopian, and work to "imagin[e] and creat[e] from a world riven by binary logic an alternative world of transgressions" (3). *The Hunger Games* only masquerades as a dystopia in order to transgress gender and other boundaries and to create a better future, characterized by creation rather than destruction, union rather than division. Since Katniss's identity is split, since Panem itself is a country divided, the notion of transgressing binary thought is imperative to healing the dystopian rift on personal and political levels.

Collins's trilogy, which abounds in political, economic, and gendered divisions, seems to share nothing with contemporary feminist utopian works, which transgress divisions and create unity between opposing forces. However, a closer inspection of Katniss and her love triangle suggests alternate readings of the trilogy that more closely align it with feminist utopian texts. According to Joanna Russ, "Feminist utopias offer an alternative model of female puberty, one which allows the girl to move into a full and free adulthood" (143). Tom Moylan observes that the "young women at puberty" who are central to feminist utopias act as "leading models for the radical new subjectivity explored in these novels" (81). Katniss is certainly a "leading model" of "radical new subjectivity" within Panem, so much so that she sparks a nation-wide rebellion, and even influences rebellion (at least symbolically, if perhaps, also, unconsciously) outside of her trilogy as evidenced by the mockingjay pins attached to the jackets and backpacks of teenage girls across the nation.[16] I suggest that Katniss represents the "full and free adulthood" of the feminist utopia and is, through her personality, actions, emotions, and choice, also a physical manifestation of the feminist utopian dystopian continuum, a notion revealed, ironically, through an inspection of the divisive love triangle and the various modes of gendered identity represented in its corners. When Katniss chooses Peeta, she moves herself to a more balanced position on the scale of masculinity, thus resolving the triangle as well as gaining peace and a greater sense of self.

The Epilogue to *Mockingjay*, in particular, reveals a transformative understanding of gender within the text. Whereas before the resolution of the love triangle, the frustrating conflict of Katniss's romantic choice expresses her own frustrated conflict over who she is and what she values, after she chooses Peeta, Katniss realizes that identity does not have to be an "either/or" sort of thing; rather, it can be inclusive, comprehensive, broadening instead of narrowing. What Katniss learns, in the Epilogue, is that identity can be multifarious, and that rather than two choices—Gale or Peeta, warrior or baker—there is a third choice, one that synthesizes competing gender traits and creates a comprehensive identity suggestive of healed breaches and unified communities, suggestive of utopia.

The feminist utopian attempt to construct a better future world that transgresses boundaries parallels a similar pattern in young adult dystopias, including *The Hunger Games*. According to Kay Sambell, "very often the conclusions to the children's dystopia sentimentally depict an adolescent couple ... striking out to forge a new and better life elsewhere" (253). Is this not what Katniss and Peeta attempt in Collins's Epilogue? Although oppressed by the gloom and weight of experience, and haunted by dark memories of a dark past, Katniss's newly developed position in the Epilogue, as mother and giver of life decidedly moves the narrative from bleak dystopian present, to obscure yet hopeful future. The birth of Katniss's children gives birth also to hope, despite fear, that is anchored in her love for Peeta: "what I need to survive is not Gale's fire, kindled with rage and hatred. *I have plenty of fire myself.*[17] What I need is the dandelion in the spring. The bright yellow that means rebirth instead of destruction. The promise that life can go on, no matter how bad our losses. That it can be good again. And only Peeta can give me that" (*MJ* 388). Katniss realizes that it will never be possible for her to lose her "rage and hatred," but that it can be tempered when united with Peeta's patience, hope, and understanding.

Because Katniss is most like Gale, choosing Peeta moves her not away from a balanced gender position, but toward a middle ground. While she can never forget the pain and violence of her prior life, nor should she, by choosing Peeta over Gale, she embraces that opposing and contradictory part of herself that is "soft-hearted," the part of herself that is creative, not destructive. Her subsequent separation from Gale excises from the text the sole individual in the love triangle unwilling, ultimately, to find middle ground between strategy of the mind and sympathy of the heart, who is willing to sacrifice his heart, those he loves, and himself for his political cause. "Gale would sacrifice his life ... for the cause—no one doubts it," but he potentially sacrifices much more than that, perhaps even Katniss's sister, negating the protective impulse of love—Katniss's protection of Prim from the Games—that propels the trilogy's plot into motion (*MJ* 205).

Gale's refusal to compromise negates love itself. When Katniss asks him if the bomb that killed her sister was his, he claims ignorance, but his disturbing potential for senseless violence severs their connection: "[e]ven now I can see the flash that ignites her, feel the heat of the flames. And I will never be able to separate that moment from Gale" (*MJ* 367). When, after the war and Katniss's return to District 12, Gale accepts "some fancy job" in District 2, Katniss can't even muster enough feeling for him to manage "anger, hatred, longing"; there is "only relief" (384). The "relief" Katniss feels at her separation from Gale is also relief at releasing from her own life the violence and aggression now so closely and dangerously associated with him, and signals her release, and the trilogy's release, from his destructive influence. When Gale is purged from the text, purged also is Katniss's torn and conflicted sense of self. She becomes, if not a whole, then a more evenly balanced individual.

The idea of Katniss as a balanced individual, hard to believe though it may be with her nightmares and terrifying memories, brings me back to the deconstructed love triangle, lying flat now, a scale indicative of sliding possibilities, with no one corner or point higher, more important than the others. The love triangle-turned-gender-spectrum reveals that Collins's representation of gender—masculine and feminine—within her trilogy seeks equality between differences and opportunity for expression no matter an individual's biological sex. Beverly Pennell suggests that, to challenge and perhaps change children's views of gender and gender formation, "masculinity needs to be redeemed" (56). She suggests two ways in which masculinity can be redeemed from negative stereotypes, which we see Gale and Katniss suffer under from *The Hunger Games* to *Mockingjay*. First, "traditional normative masculinity must be made visible" and second, the "concept of the unitary masculine subject ... needs to be replaced by a diverse range of self-reflexive masculine subjectivities whose intersubjective experiences with women and girls are not premised either implicitly or explicitly upon unequal relations of power" (56). In other words, Pennell suggests that, ultimately, to "degender" children's literature, and through the genre, children themselves, we must reconfigure gendered behaviors "so that the positive human attributes formerly cast as binary opposites, as either masculine or feminine, become potentialities for everyone" (61).[18] My deconstruction of the love triangle, with Gale at one end and Peeta at the other, makes apparent Collins's attempts to make "normative masculinity" "visible"; it flashes grotesquely at the far end of the scale, in opposition to Peeta's normative femininity. It is Katniss—who fluctuates between the two, trying out various possibilities between extremes—who suggests that "positive human attributes" should not oppose one another, but should be considered "potentialities for everyone" (Pennell 61). Katniss does not have to be either strong or sensitive; sliding from one end to the other of flattened love triangle, she has the opportunity to be both.

Conclusion: Love, Romance, and Utopian Selfhood

The love triangle Katniss, Gale, and Peeta inhabit is a version of a major aspect of all dystopian texts: the love affair.[19] According to Baker, the dystopian love triangle is usually illicit or forbidden and is not between three individuals, but between two individuals and a dystopian government that wants complete commitment from the lovers through a sacrifice of their love for each other. Love, in the dystopian novel is rebellion, an assertion of self over community, and it alone has the ability to create a utopian microcosm between two people. However, if the love triangle is, as I argue, a manifestation of internal division and conflict of self, then "love" has the ability to unify the fragmented self, to unite, to create wholeness within.

Arnold L. Weinstein notes, "[y]oung love alters all givens, redistributes light and dark, sound and silence, makes a world of its own" (112). The love between Peeta and Katniss is no exception. Their marriage symbolically unites the gendered traits each represents and takes physical expression in their two children, a boy and a girl, each with the combined light and dark coloring of their father and mother: "[t]hey play in the Meadow. The dancing girl with the dark hair and blue eyes. The boy with blond curls and gray eyes" (*MJ* 389). The implication here is that these two children, born into a world free from the terrifying uncertainty of violent death, each carrying the traits of both mother and father, will enter into a world characterized by unity in which the boundaries of contraries, the boundaries of gender, no longer remain.

The synthesis of gender suggested by Katniss and Peeta's marriage is a template for a future utopian world and the key to a better future, particularly for young male readers. Belinda Y. Louie notes that it is essential for authors of children's literature to work towards a gender balance in their texts in order "to create a better world in their books" (143).[20] She also notes that boys "like stories in which the characters are powerful, resourceful, and active. There is little indication that boys will reject the books if the female protagonists are the ones who possess such qualities, provided that the male characters are not portrayed in a negative way" (144). My own experiences have proven this claim true time after time as I have watched my university-level male students support Katniss when their female classmates have attacked her for a lack of "feeling," or when my (considerably "all boy") brother has sat in rapt attention watching Disney Pixar's *Brave*, attempting immediately after the movie to make himself a bow and arrow out of the most available materials.

Because, "[i]t is often the case in the field of children's literature that texts for children lead in new directions while the existing critical paradigms lag considerably," perhaps, by witnessing the balancing out of the double bind through the love triangle, young male readers of this particular "children's" story can begin the work of shifting current, constricting paradigms of masculinity that confuse and harm the development of young boys (Bradford, Mallan, Stephens, McCallum 7). If it is true that "utopian and dystopian tropes carry out important social, cultural, and political work by challenging and reformulating ideas about power and identity, community, the body, spatiotemporal change, and ecology," and that "Children's literature is marked by a pervasive commitment to social practice," then *The Hunger Games* is doing more important work for young male readers than it is for female readers, who have already made strides and enjoy, in many ways, more flexible boundaries when it comes to expression and identity formation (Bradford, Mallan, Stephens, McCallum 2). Boys can find, through reading *The Hunger Games*, a model of a unified utopian self, free from the dystopian double bind of masculinity.

While claiming that Collins's text has the potential to create utopia in the world outside of the one she fictionally created may be unreasonable, claiming that it has the ability to change the lives of young readers for the better is not. I cannot count the number of times a book has made my life brighter, smarter, more hopeful, and I am sure my own readers can name at least one title that positively changed who they are and how they think of themselves. This is the power of fiction, but especially the power of children's and young adult literature; it is a power particular to fiction we read when we are at our most vulnerable, our most confused. We want to know who we are, and books tell us. If a young man, searching for a sense of self, reads Katniss, what will he learn, what will he carry away from the reading? That a strong, masculine warrior can encapsulate love and compassion, that there is no line between masculine and feminine, and that we are all just jumbles of good traits and bad, and that we can *choose* which of those traits best define who we are.

Notes

1. Jennifer Mitchell argues that Katniss's gender is ambiguous, and that her gendered liminality enables her success in the Hunger Games because of its similarity to the Capitol citizens' own gender ambiguity. Lem and Hassel, on the other hand, center their discussion of Katniss's ambiguous gender in Collins's use of traditionally male and female genres—the war novel and the romance—in one text.
 2. Italics are mine.
 3. For various examples of these discussions, see: Troy Potter's "(Re)constructing Masculinity: Representations of Men and Masculinity in Australian Young Adult Literature," Ken Parille's "'What Our Boys Are Reading': Lydia Sigourney, Francis Forrester, and Boyhood Literacy in Nineteenth-Century America," Wynn William Yarbrough's "Masculinity in Children's Animal Stories, 1888–1928: A Critical Study of Anthropomorphic Tales by Wilde, Kipling, Potter, Grahame and Milne," and Shawn Thompson's "Robinson Crusoe and the Shaping of Masculinity in Nineteenth-Century America."
 4. For further reading on the contested, complex, and ever-shifting definitions of "utopia" and "dystopia," see the following authors: Frederic Jameson's *Archaeologies of the Future,* Tom Moylan's *Scraps of the Untainted Sky,* Krishan Kuman's *Utopia and Antiutopia in Modern Times,* as well as Lyman Tower Sargent's "The Three Faces of Utopianism Revisited."
 5. Other examples of love triangles that offer oppositional choices: Darcy, Wickham, and Elizabeth in *Pride and Prejudice,* and more recently, Edward Cullen, Jacob Black, and Bella in *Twilight.* The following novels/series, also feature similar oppositional options for the romantically-confused heroine: George Eliot's *The Mill on the Floss,* Lauren Oliver's *Delirium* trilogy, the *Matched* trilogy, and many more.
 6. Jennifer Lynn Barnes' essay, "Team Katniss" in the fascinating collection entitled *The Girl Who Was on Fire: Your Favorite Authors on Suzanne Collins's The Hunger Games Trilogy,* attempts to move young readers beyond the love triangle, arguing, "Sometimes, it's about the girl" (15). She emphasizes the centrality of identity formation to YA texts and suggests that "When people sit around debating who Katniss would choose, maybe what they're really debating actually *is* her identity—and the romance is just a proxy for that big, hard question about the ever-changing, unaware girl on fire" (19). Barnes rightly identifies that particular attempt to read Katniss as "dangerous" in its identification and definition of a

female character through her male peers. I want to emphasize the difference between that train of thought and my own argument. I do not argue that Katniss is Gale or is Peeta, but that these boys are manifestations, projections, of her own character. Katniss is neither Gale nor Peeta. They are her.

7. To return to the August issue of *Entertainment Weekly*, the cover presents Gale as strong, handsome, and undeniable cocky; it seeks to advertise Gale's "swoon-worthy" qualities, which have attracted female readers who identify themselves as "Team Gale." Various online spoofs have satirized Gale's appealing masculinity, insisting that Gale is "hotter" than Peeta, a point that has actual textual origins. When Peeta and Katniss first begin their public romance, Gale's very existence is threatening, and his appeal must be neutralized by completely shutting out the possibility of any romantic entanglement between himself and Katniss. To eliminate Gale's threatening sex appeal, they must position him as Katniss's cousin.

8. While other discussions of Katniss's femininity—such as Amy L. Montz's "Constuming the Resistance: The Female Spectacle of Rebellion" and Rodney M. DeaVault's "The Masks of Femininity: Perceptions of the Feminine in *The Hunger Games* and *Podkayne of Mars*"— focus on fashion and beauty, I choose to look beyond the superficial and physical markers of gender because, in *The Hunger Games* trilogy, I argue that gender conformity and transgression or rebellion go much further than appearances. Instead, I focus on those "inner" qualities that associate Katniss with more-feminine attitudes and behaviors and on the ways in which Peeta becomes an embodied presentation of Katniss's more sensitive impulses.

9. I am also interested in artistic acts of creation as characteristics of the feminine because of shifting paradigms in this stereotype. While "true" art used to be considered a masculine pursuit—Virginia Woolf's Lily Briscoe is tormented by the echoing claim that "women can't paint, women can't write"—male artists are now commonly made to appear effeminate in popular culture, a change that, according to Andrew Dowling, began in the nineteenth century, as male novelists struggled to succeed in a genre associated with female authors while simultaneously maintaining their status as active and virile males (51).

10. I want to thank Dr. Amy Billone, who allowed me to present this idea during a lecture on *The Hunger Games* to a group of students in her upper-level children's literature course.

11. Co-authors are Clare Bradford, Kerry Mallan, John Stephens and Robyn McCallum.

12. The term is one developed in 1956 by psychologist Gregory Bateson in reference to "double messages that parents send to children" (Bordo 242).

13. A good example is the love triangle from the overwhelmingly popular *Twilight* phenomenon. Bella's suitors are both physically stronger than herself, though Edward is feminized by his incredible beauty. If we go back further, to Jane Austen's *Pride and Prejudice*, we see both Wickham and Darcy as opposing but equal figures of masculinity.

14. Ellyn Lem, Holly Hassel, and Lauren Mitchell all make arguments for Katniss's masculinity. Mitchell in particular argues that Katniss's masculinity is a sign of gender "transness" in *The Hunger Games* trilogy that enables rebellion and survival and, according to Lem and Hassel, explains the cross-gendered appeal of the trilogy (Mitchell 135).

15. Jennifer Mitchell also observes the masculine similarity between Katniss and Gale: "While the insinuation of possible sexual attraction between Katniss and Gale may serve to reinforce notions of our heroine as a heterosexual girl, she is an equal partner to Gale in virtually every way, a deliberate erasure of gender differentiation" (13). However, Mitchell notes this point as proof of Katniss's masculinity and moves on. I want to investigate further how Gale *is* Katniss, or more specifically, the masculine portion of Katniss's personality.

16. Perhaps more telling is the popularity of the mockingjay tattoo, a permanent symbol of affinity for the trilogy and of support for Katniss's rebellious nature.

17. Italics are mine.

18. Perry Nodelman also notes the oppositional nature of gender as constructed by West-

ern, and particularly American culture: "We tend to understand it [masculinity] in terms of how it is not femininity and how it is oppositional to femininity" (12).

19. Patrick Parrinder observes that the love affair of the dystopian text is often complicated by technological advances and governmental control. Parrinder investigates how the eugenic aspect of dystopian texts changes issues of love, romance, courtship, and marriage.

20. Kimberley Reynolds argues that children's literature is the perfect place to rethink not only gender, but masculinity specifically, because "Irrespective of sex or sexuality, gender roles have expressive dimensions which are continually being revised, rehearsed, and represented—especially in adolescence. One forum for trying on and rehearsing different identities is fiction, which is why it is worth looking closely at the range of identities and the ideological stances provided by the literature directed at and/or consumed by (not always the same thing) young people" (99).

Works Cited

Baker, Robert S. *Brave New World: History, Science, and Dystopia.* Boston: Twayne, 1990. Print.
Barnes, Jennifer Lynn. "Team Katniss." *The Girl Who Was on Fire: Your Favorite Authors on Suzanne Collins' Hunger Games Trilogy.* Dallas: Smart Pop, 2010. Print.
Bordo, Susan. *The Male Body: A New Look at Men in Public and in Private.* New York: Farrar, Straus and Giroux, 1999. Print.
Bradford, Clare, Kerry Mallan, John Stephens, and Robyn McCallum. *New World Orders in Contemporary Children's Literature: Utopian Transformations.* Houndmills: Palgrave, 2008. Print.
Carter, Cynthia. "Sex/Gender and the Media From Sex Roles to Social Construction and Beyond." *The Handbook of Gender, Sex, and Media.* Ed. Karen Ross. Malden: Wiley-Blackwell, 2012. 365–82. Print.
Collins, Suzanne. *Catching Fire.* New York: Scholastic, 2009. Print.
_____. *The Hunger Games.* New York: Scholastic, 2008. Print.
_____. *Mockingjay.* New York: Scholastic, 2010. Print.
DeaVault, Rodney M. "The Masks of Femininity: Perceptions of the Feminine in The Hunger Games and Podkayne of Mars." *Of Bread, Blood and* The Hunger Games: *Critical Essays on the Suzanne Collins Trilogy.* Ed. Mary F. Pharr and Leisa A. Clark. Jefferson, NC: McFarland, 2012. 190–99. Print.
Huck, Charlotte. "Introduction." *Beauty, Brains, and Brawn: The Construction of Gender in Children's Literature.* Ed. Susan Lehr. Portsmouth: Heinemann, 2001. vii–xi. Print.
Kumar, Krishan. *Utopia and Antiutopia in Modern Times.* New York: Blackwell, 1987. Print.
Lehr, Susan. "The Hidden Curriculum: Are We Teaching Young Girls to Wait for the Prince?" *Beauty, Brains, and Brawn: The Construction of Gender in Children's Literature.* Ed. Susan Lehr. Portsmouth: Heinemann, 2001. 1–29. Print.
Lem, Ellyn, and Holly Hassel. "'Killer' Katniss and 'Lover Boy' Peeta: Suzanne Collins's Defiance of Gender-Genred Reading." *Of Bread, Blood and* The Hunger Games: *Critical Essays on the Suzanne Collins Trilogy.* Ed. Mary F. Pharr and Leisa A. Clark. Jefferson, NC: McFarland, 2012. 118–27. Print.
Lewit, Meghan. "Casting 'The Hunger Games': In Praise of Katniss Everdeen." *The Atlantic.* 9 March 2011. Web. 20 February 2013.
Louie, Belinda Y. "Why Gender Stereotypes Still Persist in Contemporary Children's Literature." *Beauty, Brains, and Brawn: The Construction of Gender in Children's Literature.* Ed. Susan Lehr. Portsmouth: Heinemann, 2001. 142–61. Print.
Mitchell, Jennifer. "Of Queer Necessity: Panem's Hunger Games as Gender Games." *Of Bread, Blood and* The Hunger Games: *Critical Essays on the Suzanne Collins Trilogy.* Ed. Mary F. Pharr and Leisa A. Clark. Jefferson, NC: McFarland, 2012. 128–38. Print.

Mohr, Dunja M. *Worlds Apart: Dualism and Transgression in Contemporary Female Dystopias.* Jefferson, NC: McFarland, 2005. Print.

Montz, Amy L. "Constuming the Resistance: The Female Spectacle of Rebellion." *Of Bread, Blood and* The Hunger Games*: Critical Essays on the Suzanne Collins Trilogy.* Ed. Mary F. Pharr and Leisa A. Clark. Jefferson, NC: McFarland, 2012. 139–47. Print.

Moylan, Tom. *Scraps of the Untainted Sky: Science Fiction, Utopia, Dystopia.* Boulder: Westview Press, 2000. Print.

Nodelman, Perry. "Making Boys Appear: The Masculinity of Children's Fiction." *Ways of Being Male: Representing Masculinities in Children's Literature and Film.* Ed. John Stephens. New York: Routledge, 2002. 1–14. Print.

Parrinder, Patrick. "Utopia and romance." *The Cambridge Companion to Utopian Literature.* Ed. Gregory Claeys. Cambridge: Cambridge University Press, 2010. 154–73. Print.

Pennell, Beverley. "Redeeming Masculinity at the End of the Second Millennium: Narrative Reconfigurations of Masculinity in Children's Fiction." *Ways of Being Male: Representing Masculinities in Children's Literature and Film.* Ed. John Stephens. New York: Routledge, 2002. 55–77. Print.

Reynolds, Kimberley. "Come Lads and Ladettes: Gendering Bodies and Gendering Behaviors." *Ways of Being Male: Representing Masculinities in Children's Literature and Film.* Ed. John Stephens. New York: Routledge, 2002. 78–95. Print.

Russ, Joanna. *To Write Like a Woman: Essays in Feminism and Science Fiction.* Bloomington: Indiana University Press, 1995. Print.

Sambell, Kay. "Carnivalizing the Future: A New Approach to Theorizing Childhood and Adulthood in Science Fiction for Young Readers." *The Lion and the Unicorn* 28.2 (2004): 247–67. Print.

Stephens, John. "Preface." *Ways of Being Male: Representing Masculinities in Children's Literature and Film.* Ed. John Stephens. New York: Routledge, 2002. ix–xiv. Print.

Weinstein, Arnold L. *Morning, Noon & Night: Finding the Meaning of Life's Stages through Books.* New York: Random House, 2011. Print.

The Making of the Citizen and the Politics of Maturation

SUSAN SHAU MING TAN

The Hunger Games is a story of political violence, set in a world where to come-of-age is to be the target of state aggression. The project of the Hunger Games is clear: they are "the Capitol's way of reminding" its citizens "how totally [they] are at their mercy" (*THG* 19). The rhetoric and pageantry of the Games centers around this one, ineluctable message: "[l]ook how we take your children and sacrifice them and there's nothing you can do'" (*THG* 19).

This message is directed towards the citizens of the districts: adults. Yet, the objects of governmental violence are the district's children and adolescents. Indeed, vulnerability to the Games spans traditional notions of adolescence, beginning at age twelve and ending at age eighteen, with the odds of being selected for the Games increasing each year. While, outwardly, the Games target poverty—with the tesserae system that allows children to make additional entries in the reaping lottery in exchange for food—age, actually, is of greater importance to the reaping system. Indeed, this is driven home as it is not Katniss who is initially selected as tribute, with her name entered twenty times in the lottery, but her younger sister Prim, whose name is entered only once, mortally endangered through the simple act of turning twelve. The Capitol actively targets and effectively punishes children for maturing, for coming of age, within Panem. And, as children are used to buy the obeisance of their parents, another function of the Games emerges: these children, victimized and vulnerable, are being groomed as the next generation of adults—the next generation of passive and scarred citizens of the districts. Thus, to be a mature citizen of the districts is to have lived despite the system of Games. Adults are intrinsically survivors.

In this essay, I will explore the roles of the child, adult, and adolescent citizen within *The Hunger Games*, tracing the various modes of maturation presented by the text. Elucidating what I refer to as an overarching "politics of maturation," I will draw on René Girard's notion of the scapegoat, a union of the sacred and political, to explore how the child's expulsion from their communities through the Games becomes inherent in the formation of adult identity. A political project in maturation emerges as the loss of childhood becomes essential to social definition and Capitol control. As child-violence is linked with adult formation, I will demonstrate that only the adolescent can offer an escape from the binaries of victimized child and silent adult, enabling the development of revolutionary identity—proffered through Katniss—and disrupting the Capitol's model of stunted maturation. *The Hunger Games* trilogy presents the adolescent as central to revolutionary power, a defining figure who makes the cohesive identity of citizenship possible.

As I trace these intersections of violence, community, and the state to map the joint-formation of citizenship and identities of child, adult, and adolescent, I will simultaneously extend these discussions outwards. Exploring the trilogy's staging of competing visions of "maturation" through the institution of the Games, I will interrogate how notions of scapegoat and *pharmakos* situate the child-as-victim in pertinent contemporary discussions of adolescence. Linking adolescence in *The Hunger Games* trilogy with the highly popular genre of YA dystopian literature, I will conclude with a consideration of the ways in which violence and notions of the scapegoat operate in texts for YA audiences.

By extending my discussion of community and identity formation outward, first through the idea of the scapegoat, then through a discussion of YA dystopian literature, I will demonstrate, ultimately, that *The Hunger Games* trilogy emerges as a vehicle of a similar "politics of maturation," and significantly, one caught between radical and reactionary impulses. The trilogy works to empower the "real world" adolescent citizen by encouraging an escape from the mechanisms of scapegoat. Exploring these tensions within *The Hunger Games* trilogy, I will uncover a vision of citizenship and violence that transforms the adolescent, within and without the text, into an object of profound political power: a symbol of cultural hope and fearful potential.

Between Tribute and Citizen: Coming of Age and the Capitol

I begin with a consideration of the model of maturation proffered to the citizens of the districts by the Capitol—a model completely dominated and shaped by the political apparatus of the Hunger Games. Against this backdrop, Girard's notion of the scapegoat illustrates the models of communal displacement and identity-formation at work within this state-sanctioned vision of maturation. Adult community-identity, and the obedient adulthoods that the

Capitol demands, are formed through expulsion of the tribute and the tribute's associated identity of "child." Contradictions emerge, however, as powerfully conflicted notions of fear and vulnerability surrounding the figure of the child are uncovered through the concept of scapegoat, and the boundaries between traditional evocations of the Romantic "innocent" child and the potentially-dangerous child are revealed as unstable. As all children become potential participants within the Games, childhood itself becomes an object of perpetual danger: a notion which I will ultimately show has real-world implications, embedded in contemporary cultural discourse surrounding "evil" and violent children.

Following the model of the scapegoat, the victimized youths of *The Hunger Games* become tools for the definition of adulthood. Girard's conception of scapegoat imagines an object of religious sacrifice who, through expulsion, allows for the formation of communal identity. The scapegoat exists as both a reviled and sacred figure: hated for her "crimes," real or imposed, yet worshipped for the resulting group-cohesion and community that her expulsion enables. The scapegoat, the "apparent cause of disorder becomes the apparent cause of order because she is a victim who rebuilds the terrified unity of a grateful community, at first in opposition to her, and finally around her" (Girard 50). For Girard, the scapegoat allows for the articulation of an innate human propensity for violence, enacting cultural violence, and becoming a symbolic figure of suppressed violence:

> it is a substitute for all the members of the community, offered up by the members themselves. The sacrifice serves to protect the entire community from *its own* violence; it prompts the entire community to choose victims outside itself. The elements of dissension scattered throughout the community are drawn to the person of the sacrificial victim and eliminated, at least temporarily, by its sacrifice [8].

As the Capitol sends child-tributes—affixed with the crimes of their districts' pasts—to their deaths, their status becomes reminiscent of Girard's notion of "displacement." The government imposes the collective "crimes" of the community onto the figure of the tribute, displacing not only *guilt*, but significantly, *punish*. Indeed, substitution emerges as central; the child-tribute becomes a means of focalizing punishment. While all are vulnerable to punishment as potential tributes, the selection of the tribute ensures one more year of safety for the unselected collective. Thus, the reaping and the Games act as a social contract—a promise that the disciplining attention of the government will be focused on the bodies of the tributes, not the community at large.

To survive, then, necessitates a degree of removal from the scapegoat. To be young is to be vulnerable, and to reach adulthood indicates a separation from this vulnerability. For children and adults alike, then, the "otherness" of the tribute must be immediately enforced, even as the scapegoat-tribute was, moments before her name was drawn from the reaping bowl, a member of the community. The tribute's selection in the Hunger Games lottery immediately underscores the individual's alienation, and Katniss reflects that Peeta "has two older brothers, ... but one is too old now to volunteer and the other won't. This is standard. Family devotion only goes so far for most people on reaping day" (*THG* 31). Tribute status denotes an expulsion on all communal levels, including family, and expands to indicate an expulsion on a broader, literal level: "the word *tribute* ... pretty much synonymous with the word *corpse*" (27). Indeed, even as the district itself is not the expelling force—rather, the Capitol selects the tribute—the district becomes an agent in the expulsion, bidding Katniss farewell in "an old and rarely used gesture ... occasionally seen at funerals. It means thanks, it means admiration, it means goodbye to someone you love" (29). While this is a defiant act, honoring Katniss and protesting the Games, its underlying message is inescapable; through the funerary gesture, the district recognizes Katniss's expulsion, that she is no longer one of them, and that, in all likelihood, she will never return. District communities find form through opposition to the scapegoat; they are defined through the scapegoat's enforced "otherness" and absence.

As the mechanisms of the Games victimize children, however, complications emerge within this model of childhood vulnerability, nuancing the adult's status as "survivor" and the resulting affirmation of community identity. The construction of a vulnerable childhood is rooted in British Romanticism, which envisions children as innately innocent and good (Nikolajeva).[1] Prim, the consummate child, is continually described as "sweet" and "tiny" (*THG* 33), and becomes "teary" when anything is in distress (42). Even Rue, who demonstrates an ability to fend for herself in the Arena, never kills, and relies on Katniss for protection. At first glance, the path to adulthood within the narrowly confined and controlled world of Panem seems a clear one: survive the reapings and become an adult, or survive the Games and become a victor and adult. However, as this model of innocent childhood becomes central, a duality emerges: while the child is profoundly vulnerable, in line with Romantic representations of childhood, the child is simultaneously always a potential threat. Children are inherently victims, but part of this victimization—selection for the Games—assumes the potential to engage in a fight-to-the-death. Thus, despite the represented vulnerability of the child, this Romantic link is connected, innately, with the child's potential deadliness—at least if they want to survive into adulthood. The child is characterized by this dichotomy, at once vulnerable and dangerous, simultaneously victims and threats to the adults of their world. As it locates danger in the Romantic innocence of childhood, *The Hunger Games* seems to suggest a new vision of childhood, conflicted in its treatment of children, as the child emerges as vulnerable both to danger and to becoming *dangerous*. The resulting threatening child must be banished through the expulsion of the scapegoat.

Thus, childhood, in all its associations of idealism and inexperience, is actively expunged, and to survive is to join the ranks of the jaded and removed: the older "family members" who can only stand silently "around the perimeter" as their children's fates hang in the balance, or the many adults "who have no one they love at stake, or who no longer care, who slip among the crowd, taking bets" on children's imminent deaths (*THG* 20). The "successful" adult citizen, the adult who has survived the Hunger Games system, is one stripped of both threat and promise: who has successfully left childhood behind, relinquishing innocence, but also relinquishing the element of danger implicit in this model of childhood. Indeed, adults are subsumed into a model of mute, impotent political community. With the tesserae system, the adult world is denied true agency, power stripped from them in a reversal of family nurture and provision. The notion of "circus" implicit in Panem's name based on the Roman model of *"Panem et Circenses"* gains a Bakhtinian valence (*MJ* 260).[2] In a profound inversion, children provide for their parents through their own susceptibility to the Games. A carnivalesque reversal of family hierarchy emerges: children possess an agency which enables them to provide for their families but puts them in danger as a result, while adults are "safe," and yet, because of their safety, unable to provide.

Adult disempowerment emerges as a direct result of the child/adult role reversal. Katniss's mother "can only hear so much," and is not equipped to deal with the realities of the adult world, evidenced by her inability to care for her children after her husband's death, and later, by her inability to care for Katniss after Prim's (*MJ* 40). Katniss's only friend, Madge, has parents characterized by absence as well, with a mother who retreats from the world with "fierce headaches that force her to stay in bed for days" (*CF* 107). Even Haymitch, Katniss's mentor, is represented as ineffectual and incompetent, an alcoholic who we first see "hollering something unintelligible" as he "staggers" onto the reaping stage (*THG* 19). Haymitch is helpless in his drunkenness, and Katniss reflects with disgust having to "take in the scene of [her] mentor trying to rise out of the slippery vile stuff from his stomach" (*THG* 58). Unable to control the functions of his body, Haymitch is effectively infantilized.

As the trilogy progresses, however, adult disempowerment emerges as the consequence of the adult world's own childhood trauma. Katniss learns of Maysilee Donner, a tribute who was her mother's friend, Madge's aunt. This knowledge shakes Katniss, and she reflects: "I think of Madge's mother.... Who spends half her life in bed immobilized with terrible pain, shutting out the world. I think of how I never realized that she and my mother shared this connection," a connection and loss which neither adult has ever spoken of (*CF* 236–237). As Katniss learns more about Haymitch, she realizes that his alcoholism comes from a similar past, and concludes, "maybe he wasn't always a drunk. Maybe, in the beginning, he tried to help the tributes. But then it got unbearable. It must be hell to mentor two kids and then watch them die. Year after year after year" (*THG* 373). The adults of the districts are scarred—broken by their experiences and losses. Their traumas run deep, and can only be "discovered"; they are never directly mentioned, never spoken of. Silence becomes another facet of expulsion: adult identity focalized around the loss of voice, and the expulsion of linguistic agency.

Thus, all child figures are expelled within *The Hunger Games*—either banished through the traumas of adulthood, or literally killed by the violence of Panem (a point I argue elsewhere in an essay entitled "'Burn with Us': Sacrificing Childhood in *The Hunger Games*"). Even the most resourceful or privileged of children are inherently vulnerable. This "war" against childhood itself is best illustrated, perhaps, through the case of the children of the Capitol. In one of the only appearances of Capitol children, toddlers are shepherded into a "protected area" only to be showered in bombs in a rebel maneuver designed to turn Capitol citizens against their government. Here we see Capitol children used for the same symbolic, scapegoating purposes as children in the Arena: to provide a new national rallying point. The governing system in Panem firmly relegates all children—in the capital and in the districts—to the role of sacrificial victim; children are scapegoats, symbols, and tools of the adult world.

To grow up, then, is innately political, a movement from a position of an innocent-yet-dangerous childhood to that of traumatized adult subsumation. The child emerges as a symbol of hope, the "future a rebellion could bring" (*MJ* 176). However, the child who sparks this hope cannot survive. Prim, whose selection for the Games sets off the events of the trilogy, continually motivates Katniss: the promise of her future igniting "[s]omething small and quiet, like a match being struck, light[ing] up the gloom inside" (*MJ* 176). Prim's motivational influence, however, brutally contrasts with her ultimate fate—the child who sparks hope ultimately consumed by the same imagery, becoming "a human torch," killed by the bombs that brutalize the Capitol's children (*MJ* 352).

As the Games reveal that the innocent child is dangerously close to the violent child, necessitating the expulsion of both, this vision of maturation taps into larger, contemporary conversations of the nature of childhood. Terry Eagleton offers his own take on the scapegoat or *pharmakos*, as he terms it. It is perhaps telling that in the same volume, he writes of the "uneasy complicity of good and evil" that "can be observed in the case of children," citing "the ease with which "Victorian Evangelicals found them so sinister, as indeed do some modern horror films" (258). For Eagleton, children's threat lies in their intimacy: they are "uncanny, very like adults but not at all like them" (258). The idea of the unsettling child becomes central in a consideration of representations of child violence and violent children, and Eagleton addresses this explicitly, bringing the horror surrounding that which is at once intimate and "other," to bear on the figure of the *pharmakos*, arguing:

> The victim is thus both themselves and not themselves, both a thing of darkness they acknowledge as their own as well as a convenient object on which to off-load and disown their criminality. Both pity and fear, identity and otherness, are at stake. [...] The *pharmakos* being both poison and cure, symbol of both transgression and redemption, has a homeopathic doubleness rather like *catharsis*, which similarly provokes sickness in order to cure it [279].

Like the *pharmakos,* the child's threat is an intimate one, both of the community and alien to it. The same notions of "pity and fear, identity and otherness" are at risk within Eagleton's conception of the evil or violent child as an innate danger to adult society, as a threat to basic definitions of humanity. Joseph Zornado discusses an adult drive to "make monsters" of evil or violent children (xiv). The alternative to this demonization—to acknowledge that children possess a capacity for evil—is to acknowledge that humanity possesses the same innate potential. Therefore, violent children are made strange in an attempt to deny and expel the insular fears they evoke. The disruption of Romantic childhood innocence, then, emerges with far-reaching implications. All children are potentially violent: the most terrifying of innate threats, who, when positioned as scapegoat, necessitate absolute communal disavowal.

Thus, *The Hunger Games* trilogy taps into larger, contemporary cultural impulses surrounding violent children. The only "comfortable" resolution to violent childhoods lies in complete expulsion, and to survive into adulthood is to leave childhood behind. To be tribute is to be the object of constant surveillance, control, and punishment. Collins's trilogy stages real-world anxieties surrounding the figure of the violent child: first in the space of the Arena, where the action of the Games expels all but one tribute, and then later, in the surviving tribute's life as "victor." Even for the tribute who survives the Games, expulsion is complete. It is not enough that victors have endured unspeakable trauma within the Arena. Victors can never integrate back into their communities, indelibly relegated to status as "other." Those who win remain objects; the Capitol prostitutes them as political pawns, forcing them to continue to act as representatives and embodiments of their district, as well as forcing them to mentor their district's tributes and preside over the next generation of scapegoats. Indeed, segregation in the Victor's Village—the celebratory homes given to victors to live in—is a literal illustration of this isolation. The Victor's Village is a space of unreal wealth and sanitation that forever separates the victor from the starving poverty of his or her district. Within *The Hunger Games*, the violent child can never return to society; the child-scapegoat's expulsion is eternal.

The Mockingjay's Rebellion: Katniss and Radical Adolescence

As noted in my introduction, vulnerability to the Games occurs during a period that spans the range of possible definitions of adolescence, from twelve to eighteen. This reflects a duality within the conception of adolescence itself. A developmental stage which encompasses both adulthood and childhood, adolescence emerges as an inherently transitional state, the adolescent a figure in flux.[3] Within *The Hunger Games*, the adolescent's exposure to the Games denotes a child-like vulnerability and threat. However, the Games also reveal that adolescents possess an agency traditionally associated with adult power, but in Panem, unavailable to the adult world. Thus, inhabiting a subject-position in between the vulnerability of Panem's childhoods and the impotency of Panem's adulthoods, adolescents emerge as the only figures capable of significant political action. As Katniss—a radical adolescent—negotiates the violence of her world, she disrupts the cyclical violence of Panem, locating revolutionary identity in the very act of growing up.

From the moment Katniss volunteers to take Prim's place in the Games, she emerges as the ultimate sacrificial figure and actively claims the identity of scapegoat.[4] Once in the Arena, a profound difference emerges between Katniss and the other tributes. Katniss is focused on the *survival* of the scapegoat, in a sense of survival that extends beyond herself to the larger notion of *pharmakos*. Katniss's power, the nebulous "effect she can have" is traced, continually, back to her desire for others, and specifically other scapegoats, to live (*THG* 111). Katniss becomes a revolutionary symbol the moment she demonstrates that her own individual survival is not as important as that of another tribute's—Peeta. Her power is born of a "handful of berries" and the willingness to either save Peeta or to die alongside him, denying the Capitol its scapegoat (*CF* 26). So subversive and radical are the proffered berries that threaten to negate the scapegoat that they possess the potential to "bring [the nation] down" (*CF* 26). Katniss is the scapegoat who refuses expulsion, who fights to keep the scapegoat *within* the community.

As a result, the Capitol does not succeed in excising Katniss as the scapegoat is meant to be; instead, she is put on increasing display. The very fact that the Capitol sentences Katniss and Peeta once more to the Arena in *Catching Fire* highlights Katniss's role within the system. Katniss draws attention to the entrenchment of the scapegoat, and as a result, the Capitol makes Katness, Peeta, and other past victors into official scapegoats once more, in a second round of Games—the Quarter Quell. Katniss's threat to the community has prompted a mass reiteration of the scapegoat process—necessitating the recapitulation of a whole generation of scapegoated children inscribed into a new round of sacrifice. Emphasizing the inescapability of the identity of scapegoat, this re-entry underscores the profound centrality of the scapegoat and the need for its expulsion. Because Katniss stops the act of sacrifice—because, despite the deaths of twenty-two other children, both Peeta and Katniss remain alive—the Capitol must repeat the sacrifice in order to reestablish community identity. Indeed, Katniss's refusal to be "a piece in [the Capitol's] Games" underlines the scapegoat's threat and also directly correlates to the disintegration of the communal identity that sacrifice is meant to maintain, leading to district-wide rebellion and a collapse of the political system (*THG* 172).

Katniss's ability to elide the scapegoat system emerges as a direct result of her adolescent status. Katniss is a transitory figure even before volunteering for the Games, forced to act as parent to her mother and sister alike after the death of her father, while still firmly occupying the identity of "child" at only eleven years old. Katniss's decision to volunteer in Prim's place is not a disinterested act of self-sacrifice, but rather, a natural extension of the role of adult-parent that Katniss has taken on. Similarly, Katniss's later focus on survival, which morphs into her protection of Rue and determination to save Peeta, is initially centered solely around the desire to return to Prim. While Capitol law restricts district residents from marrying, and presumably, from having children until thirty years of age, Katniss's family position puts her in a role that highlights the adolescent's liminality. Unlike the stunted adults of the districts, Katniss has the responsibility of a parent long before she sheds the identity of youth.

That the teenager is the most powerful and dangerous figure within Panem is unsurprising in the YA dystopian genre—a body of literature characterized by "social and political awakenings" (Hintz and Ostry 9). It follows that the ability to recognize and address the wrongs of society becomes an "awakening" only available to the adolescent, with the adolescent simultaneously empowered and burdened with the "righting" and saving of the world. If Katniss's society punishes children for the act of aging, adolescents emerge as the only figures capable of exacting change. They are not yet the stunted adults of the districts, but at the same time, they are victims of, and remain vulnerable to, the Games. The surviving adolescent transgresses the political boundaries of child and adult, and in her hybridity, locates radical political potential. In a world of victimized children and infantilized adults, Katniss pioneers a subject-identity that emboldens the rest of her world. Adolescent rebellion is made quite literal as Katniss's model of adolescent maturation and identity formation leads to civil war.

Indeed, as Katniss's radical adolescence wreaks political havoc, and Katniss herself becomes a mouthpiece for revolution, an emphasis on voice emerges, disrupting the silent model of adulthood previously presented. This corresponds with an ability that only Katniss seems to possess, to identify the silence and traumas endemic in her society. I have previously written on the role of silence and voice within *The Hunger Games* trilogy through a Lacanian analysis, exploring Katniss's world as one of a "stunted Symbolic," where adulthood remains trapped in a mute Real and Katniss gains power through her entry into the full Symbolic order (Tan). Here, however, while acknowledging these psychoanalytic valences, I want to focus on Katniss's use of voice as a disruption of social reproduction. Katniss continually details her fear and fascination with the transgressors known as "Avoxes." An Avox is a criminal-turned-slave of the Capitol, their tongues cut "so they [can] never talk again" (*CF* 262). An Avox is reduced to a body—his or her voice forever silenced in a literal embodiment of the Capitol's power over the individual and the individual's ability to express themselves. And indeed, in a world where "muttations"—creatures made of human, machine, and animal components—are created mainly to kill, Avoxes remain among the most horrifyingly personal of the Capitol's human-mutilations. They are used repeatedly to torture Katniss, as people she knows are turned into Avoxes, and Avoxes are punished in her stead.

Katniss seems to recognize the horror that Avoxes embody, and one of her greatest fears is the physical silencing they endure. Tongues "feature prominently in [her] nightmares," as she dreams that she must "watch frozen and helpless while gloved hands carry out the bloody dissection" (*CF* 265). With her nightmares of "mutilated-tongues," Katniss envisions the psychological violence of her society made manifest, the political silence bought with and through the sacrifice of the tribute represented through the maiming of voice (*CF* 267). Katniss fears the silence of the adult world, a world in which the "boldest form of dissent" is, in fact, silence as "[t]o the everlasting credit of the people of District 12, not one person claps" after Katniss volunteers to takes Prim's place (*THG* 28). This silence, ironically, the only political commentary available to the citizens of the districts "says we do not agree. We do not condone. All of this is wrong" (*THG* 28–29). Katniss's fear of silence corresponds to her ability to identify the violent structures that govern maturation in her world, an acknowledgment reflected in her initial refusal to have children. To have children is to recognize adult inability to protect and nurture. Such an inability along with the potential death of her own possible children is "the thing [Katniss] dreads the most ... about the future," to the point where she has "spent [her] life building up layers of defences until [she] recoil[s] even at the suggestion of marriage or a family" (*CF* 310). Katniss rightly identifies that to have children is to perpetuate the silence and cycle of the scapegoat, to offer potential tributes to the machine of the Capitol's violence, to accept transformation into the passive citizenship of the adult world.

Katniss, however, forces her world to face its own mechanisms. Her power and the rebellion it inspires returns voice to people and traumas. It is significant that, throughout *Mockingjay*, televised segments named "*We Remember*" pay tribute to past victims of the Games and comprise a significant aspect of rebel outreach (*MJ* 129). Katniss has enabled childhoods hitherto characterized as unspeakable to be articulated and remembered. Ultimately, Katniss as scapegoat not only resists the scapegoating cycle, but also removes what Girard identifies as a veil of "*misunderstanding*" from the scapegoating process (7). For Girard, the cycle of the scapegoat can no longer function when societies recognize overarching communal displacement, when the community becomes aware that the threat of the scapegoat is in fact a projection of their own violence (7). As Katniss urges the community to "remember," the Games are transformed, "misunderstanding" removed, and their mechanisms laid bare as the Arenas become memorials rather than sites of entertainment.

As the radical adolescent disrupts the process of the scapegoat, however, the scapegoat's connection to the nation does not invert. Even as community identity deteriorates—the identity of a united Panem giving way to rebellion—Katniss still emerges as a national, almost sacred figure. Katniss retains the symbolic, defining significance of the scapegoat, even as she refuses communal expulsion. Katniss becomes intimately connected to the national identity, "wedded" to Panem as the plumage of her bridal-dress-turned-mockingjay would suggest. While Katniss refuses to leave the community to which she belongs, refusing the scapegoat's status as outsider, she simultaneously enables the creation of another vision of a group identity, not through opposition, but through inclusion. She becomes the symbolic Mockingjay around which the district rebels rally, uniting them through her status of survivor, victor, and adolescent rebel. It is Katniss's living action, not memory after expulsion, that elevates her to a position of national centrality, and her strength lies in her ambiguity. Katniss is a figure continually surrounded by ambiguity, her popularity described as an "effect she can have" (*THG* 111), a figure whom "no one knows what to do with" (*MJ* 383). Katniss is not an easily codified dead sacrifice, and in *Mockingjay*, Katniss reflects on the puzzle of her political significance, on "those berries that meant different things to different people. Love for Peeta. Refusal to give in under impossible odds. Defiance of the Capitol's inhumanity" (89). Katniss is the living scapegoat, the one whose actions are free to mean "different things to different people," who resonates intimately. She is the tribute who refuses expulsion, the adolescent who ultimately effaces the binaries she moves between, the threat from within that ultimately *does* topple the system.

Katniss's ambiguous position at the trilogy's conclusion reflects the ambiguous subject position she has embraced and forged. She is the active scapegoat, the ontological threat who refuses expulsion, and who works to eradicate "misunderstanding" through the systematic unveiling of the scapegoat. She *has* been dangerous, and continues to be—moving from the girl who "provided a spark" that "[grew] to an inferno that destroy[ed] Panem" (*THG* 27), to the revolutionary symbol who leads regime change. Indeed, Katniss's final execution of President Coin solidifies the danger she presents. As Katniss realizes that Coin is no different than Snow, she again takes action, demonstrating that her loyalty does not fall within party lines, but rather, that she remains committed to ending the system of scapegoating, sacrifice, and misunderstanding once and for all.

In the Epilogue, Katniss is left trapped in the limbo she has created for herself. The adolescent hero has gained power and changed her world through a subversion of the scapegoat's status, emerging as a political figure with an impact innately tied to her status as adolescent, her status as neither wholly tribute nor wholly survivor. However, Prim's death and Katniss's own maiming in the explosion suggest an inescapability of Panem's vision of maturation through the expulsion of childhood. Katniss has still come-of-age through violence, her adulthood won through the survival of traumatic maturations. At the end of the trilogy, Katniss's potency is gone, her political power stripped as she is confined to District 12 in punishment for Coin's assassination. Katniss may never leave her district, and may never take action in her world again, even as her children learn about her in school.

However, her symbolic value remains, and while Katniss is no longer a revolutionary power, she is far from the mute adulthoods that previously characterized Panem. She remains the scapegoat, caught between mechanisms of expulsion and banishment and her own refusal to capitulate. Indeed, Katniss's banishment suggests that despite her status as a symbol of hope, she simultaneously retains the element of danger that the identity of scapegoat carries. The Capitol has scarred Katniss, but not into silence, as her resolution—to tell her children about her traumas—indicates. In this vocal potential, Katniss demonstrates that radical adolescences can open up new forms of adulthood. Adults are still "survivors," but because of Katniss's rebellion, survivors with a degree of political agency; the rebellion returns their voices and frees them from the infantilizing inversions that once crippled their society. Citizens are no longer tied to their districts. Katniss's mother and Gale leave District 12. While Katniss is confined to her home, District 12's newfound self-sufficiency indicates a sustainable, self-contained future, driven, not by the Capitol, but by the adult citizens of the districts themselves.

Ultimately, Katniss has created new, radical identities within her world, which parallels her own construction of social identity, as well as her tenuous narrative conclusion. In a world of free movement, Katniss must remain in her district. Katniss will always be the Mockingjay, will always be a scapegoat, and will always be a potential threat—an uneasy figure of transgression, revolution, intimacy, and power.

Conclusion: Reading Games as Narratives of Maturation

I have utilized notions of scapegoats and political identity to identify a radical potential within adolescence in *The Hunger Games* trilogy, as Katniss Everdeen moves between the socially mandated identities of children as victims and adults as survivors to revolutionize her world. I want to conclude now with a turn outwards, looking at adolescent transformation within the YA genre as a whole. My reading of political maturations is not simply limited to one narrative. *The Hunger Games* marks, and is representative of, a new popularity of YA dystopian texts.[5] Profound violence towards young adult characters is a central feature of YA dystopias that emphasize child sacrifice, adult impotence, adolescent ability and, significantly, an adolescent *responsibility* to "save" their worlds. The popularity of these texts begs questions of why the tropes enjoy such cultural reception. What about these narratives of youth violence, death, and disruption is so fascinating, and how should we feel about their clear titillation?

Eric Tribunella's *Melancholia and Maturation* explores loss and trauma in children's literature and the ways in which trauma is utilized with a "maturing" function for young readers. Tribunella observes that "[i]t is as if loss generates the escape velocity of youth. It is the fuel used to achieve the speed necessary for escaping the gravitational force of childhood" (xi). As Tribunella further examines the function of loss through the vehicle of the children's text itself, his exploration points a way forward. Tribunella writes, "[w]e might imagine the loss of loved objects in children's literature as functioning like a kind of sacrifice. The willingness to make sacrifices is critical to the formation of the disciplined and mature citizen, which accounts for why children's literature often reflects or promotes an ethic of renunciation" (xiv-xv). Tribunella envisions children's literature in itself, the artifact of the book, as acting to induce this loss, introducing child readers to trauma in an effort to mature them through the reading process itself.

Drawing from Tribunella's model of loss in children's literature, I believe that *The Hunger Games*—with its vision of political maturations, and the popularity of this vision among audiences—points to the same notions of maturation as sacrifice and trauma at work within contemporary Western conceptions of childhood. *The Hunger Games* suggests a profound cultural alignment between the child and scapegoat in contemporary society; the trilogy locates real social power in a process of maturation that necessitates the expulsion of the childlike from the community. Adolescent awakening and disillusionment become essential to the process of growing up itself. At the same time, however, as *The Hunger Games* emerges as cultural critique, it points to a cultural desire to interrogate models of adulthood as well. The heroic potential of the dystopian hero is located in the hybridity of radical adolescence—in a figure at once adult and child—and it is this vision of social change and new potential that resonates so profoundly with modern audiences.

The vision of dystopia as cultural critique is not new, and the idea that narratives can inspire an interrogation of contemporary society is touted, often, as one of the defining characteristics of the genre, for both adult and young adult audiences.[6] Dystopias point to "utopian hope *outside* their pages ... for it is only if we consider dystopia as a warning that ... readers can hope to escape its pessimistic future" (Baccolini and Moylan 7). Indeed, the genre of adult dystopias, which tend to be bleaker than those in the YA genre, have traditionally been imagined to contain an implied urge to the reader to take physical action in their own world (Vieira). This emphasis, however, points to more troubling implications in texts geared towards child and adolescent readers.

If we imagine the proximity of the child to violence and trauma as potentially defining to the child character and adolescent reader—shaping the child's growth into adulthood, shaping the child as an engaged and responsible citizen of the state, and shaping the reader's conception of growth and citizenship—then we must interrogate the models of adulthood and actualization within these narratives. In *The Hunger Games* trilogy, nation, community, individuation, trauma, and violence are all intimately connected, and at their core is a defining notion of sacrifice and self with dangerously porous boundaries. As violence forces child characters into political adulthoods, so too can reading the trilogy push the implied child or adolescent reader towards their own "social and political awakening" (Hintz and Ostry 9). The bloody warnings of dystopia, which can be imagined to socially-galvanize the young-reader, are instead imagined to push them towards a maturation similar to those of the central characters within YA dystopian texts—through a loss of innocence and through exposure to violence and trauma within the trilogy.

Thus, the violence of YA dystopias, and indeed, violence within the YA genre as a whole, acts with a disillusioning function, extrapolating from Tribunella's model of loss and melancholia. Trauma and sacrifice within these texts drive maturation forward. Along with Katniss, the reader must learn that the innocent, sweet child represented by Prim, cannot exact social change. Rather, that burden must rest with the scarred, still-vulnerable adolescent, the figure who has experienced and done violence. Represented trauma comes to act with a similar maturing function, and political violence becomes a prerequisite for adulthood. As the violences of dystopia become so closely linked with the process of growing up, the vision of adolescence put forth by these texts becomes highly problematic. The empowered adolescent citizen seems to hold the key to national salvation both intra- and extra-textually, but only after surviving the trials of a traumatic maturation—either in the form of the violence of the Arena, or the violence of reading of the Arena.

As a consideration of the scapegoat enables a new reading of *The Hunger Games*, and *The Hunger Games* points, arguably, to an unarticulated appeal of the conflation of scapegoat and child in contemporary society, the trilogy emerges as torn between these competing impulses. The trilogy acts as a scathing critique of a society that demands these models of sacrifice and trauma. However, at the same time, the narrative issues a similar imperative to its readers to "grow up," figuring trauma as central. *The Hunger Games* represents a world where a politics of maturation demand the sacrifice of childhood for the mute citizenship of adulthood, and as it empowers its readers, urging them to take revolutionary arms against this model of the world, finds itself caught up in similar political impulses. It is a radical text and a reactionary one; one that, in its narrative of powerful adolescent rebellion, recognizes that adolescence must inevitably make way for the demands of adulthood inside and outside of the texts.

The Hunger Games trilogy presents us with a world where children are sacrificed, where adults are infantilized and disempowered, and where social and political change can only be exacted through the adolescent's willingness to defy these boundaries, to take on the role of the scapegoat, and yet, to refuse the violent expulsions of her world. The adolescent emerges as a figure of profound social power, but also, of fearful capacity. Through the narrative of *The Hunger Games*, young readers must confront this dual message of youth empowerment and fear, of child potential and child violence. Real adolescent and child readers see themselves reflected on the page; therefore, we must interrogate contemporary visions of adolescence and what we want adolescent citizens to be. Because she is an adolescent, the YA heroine becomes a force so threatening that her presence possesses the potential to destabilize every aspect of socio-political life, from state to self.

Notes

1. Some examples of this conception can be found in Wordsworth—notably in "Idiot Boy"—and, famously, in Blake's "Songs of Innocence."
2. "Bread and Circuses." Panem's name derives from the famous Latin phrase, hearkening to Ancient Rome where "in return for full bellies and entertainment, [a] people had given up their political responsibilities and therefore their power" (*MJ* 223).
3. See Reynolds and Waller for a more thorough discussion of definitions of "adolescent."
4. Here, it is worth noting the work of Guy Andre Risko, who argues that Katniss is a figure of *homo sacer* following the model of citizenship set forth by Giorgio Agamben (Risko, 2012). Risko views Katniss as existing in Agamben's "state of exception"—stripped of legality and citizenship as tribute, and turned into a simultaneous figure of legal void and legal concern. It is not "murder" when the tribute is killed, but rather, a nationally-mandated sacrifice (Risko 82). For Risko, this notion enables an analysis of Katniss within the politically void "state of exception" that Agamben outlines, allowing a reading of Katniss as a figure whose subjectivity comes to be formed around this idea of the identity-less state of *homo sacer*. In contrast, I argue here that Katniss's identity is in fact laden with significance: the assumption of the role of scapegoat endowing her with identity as "pharmakos," and a fraught identity of "sacrifice" alongside that of "survivor." While the label of "tribute" indeed delineates a politically-mandated identity for Katniss, one which arguably strips her of "citizenship," I envision this identity not as one of void, but as one endowed with a political and social significance which Katniss later appropriates and subverts.
5. While dystopian literature has long enjoyed popularity among adults, dystopia has traditionally been regarded as too bleak for younger audiences. This changed with the publication of Lois Lowry's *The Giver* in 1993, which is hailed as one of the first dystopias for children (Hintz & Ostry 254; Kois 2012). While *The Giver* was met with a great deal of criticism and controversy upon publication, the genre of dystopia for young audiences has since taken off: YA dystopias among some of the most widely-read and popular contemporary children's narratives.
6. See Baccolini and Moylan for a fully discussion of the "critical dystopia," and the evolution of social critique within the dystopian genre.

Works Cited

Baccolini, Raffaella, and Tom Moylan. "Introduction: Dystopia and Histories." *Dark Horizons: Science Fiction and the Dystopian Imagination*. Eds. Raffaella Baccolini and Tom Moylan. New York: Routledge, 2003. 1–11. Print.
Collins, Suzanne. *Catching Fire*. London: Scholastic, 2009. Print.
_____. *The Hunger Games*. London: Scholastic, 2008. Print.
_____. *Mockingjay*. London: Scholastic, 2010. Print.
Eagleton, Terry. *Sweet Violence*. Oxford: Blackwell, 2003. Print.
Fox, Christopher A. "Sacrificial Pasts and Messianic Futures: Religion as a Political Prospect in Rene Girard and Giorgio Agamben." *Philosophy and Social Criticism* 33.5 (2007): 563–595. Print.
Girard, Rene. *Violence and Sacred*. Trans. Gregory, Patrick. Baltimore: Johns Hopkins University Press, 1972. Print.

Hintz, Carrie, and Elaine Ostry. "Introduction." *Utopian and Dystopian Writing for Children and Young Adults.* Eds. Carrie Hintz and Elaine Ostry. London: Routledge, 2003. Print.

Kois, Dan. "The Children's Author Who Actually Listens to Children." *The New York Times.* 3 October 2012. Print.

Reynolds, Kimberley. *Radical Children's Literature.* New York: Palgrave Macmillan, 2007. Print.

Risko, Guy Andre. "Katniss Everdeen's Liminal Choices and the Foundations of Revolutionary Ethics." *Of Bread, Blood and* The Hunger Games. Eds. Mary F. Pharr and Leisa Clark. Jefferson, NC: McFarland, 2012. 80–88. Print.

Tan, Susan Shau Ming. "'Burn with Us': Sacrificing Childhood in *The Hunger Games.*" *The Lion and the Unicorn* 37.1 (2013): 54–73. Print.

Tribunella, Eric. *Melancholia and Maturation.* Knoxville: University of Tennessee Prerss, 2010. Print.

Vieira, Fatima. "The Concept of Utopia." *The Cambridge Companion to Utopian Literature.* Ed. Gregory Claeys. Cambridge: Cambridge University Press, 2010. 3–27. Print.

Waller, Alison. *Constructing Adolescence in Fantastic Realism.* New York: Routledge, 2009. Print.

Zornado, Joseph L. *Inventing the Child: Culture, Ideology, and the Story of Childhood.* New York: Garland, 2001. Print.

Part III
Experiencing Trauma in Safe Spaces

The Privileged Reader as Capitol and Learning Sympathy through Narrative

ANN M. M. CHILDS

All across America, archery clubs and schools are flooded with adolescents, mostly girls and many wearing imitations of the signature braid Katniss Everdeen wears in *The Hunger Games* film.[1] Desperate to be like their heroine, these fans take up as a hobby the skill that the impoverished Katniss uses to keep her family from the brink of starvation. To the fans, it is all entertainment, while for Katniss, it is a matter of life and death. Inside Suzanne Collins's *The Hunger Games*, citizens of the Capitol look forward to the yearly Hunger Games as their favorite form of entertainment. Just as the citizens watch the Games for fun, readers devour the novels for entertainment, consuming the Hunger Games inside the text as an additional spectacle. This puts readers in the paradoxical position of identifying, through a first-person narrative perspective, with the story's heroine, even though they are located, like the Capitol audience of the Hunger Games, on the periphery of the action, at a safe, yet voyeuristic distance from the danger. Ultimately, Collins's readers are one and the same with the Capitol audience, an association that transforms the trilogy into a "safe space" from which privileged readers, neither literally nor physically subjected to the terrors of the Games, can view the action of the Games, with Capitol citizens, from the position of audience not subjected to oppression by a dominant group. I argue that the combination of Katniss's accounts of oppression from a first-person narrative and the readers' dual position of privileged reader and privileged Capitol audience distances the readers from the oppressive system and violence of the Hunger Games Arena. Katniss's narrative intervenes to make possible the reader's identification with her, the social "Other," possible.

Before I develop the ways in which the reader may seem intimately associated with the fictional residents of the Capitol, it is important to establish

Katniss's locality as "the Other" and to define what this means in the trilogy. The concept of the "Other" was popularized by Edward Said's 1978 work, *Orientalism*, which deals with the western created East-West dichotomy and how the familiar is constructed as superior to the Other, but has since branched out from Said's post-colonial studies into many other philosophies and fields dealing with oppression, and is generally used to describe the treatment of any disadvantaged group.[2] Samuel P. Huntington writes in *The Clash of Civilizations and the Remaking of World Order* that "identity at any level—personal, tribal, racial, civilizational—can only be defined in relation to an 'other,'" (129). More recently, scholar Jacqueline Horne has argued that to be an Other is to be excluded from, and subordinated by, the dominant group, so that the dominant group may enjoy advantages that "rely on the *disadvantaging* of other groups" (85). The perks of being in the dominant group cannot exist without the disadvantaged group's oppression. In order for members of the dominant group to justify unequal treatment, they construct Others as subordinate or lesser than themselves because of economic positions, race, and other distinguishing differences that, in *The Hunger Games,* divide the Capitol and districts into dominant and subordinate groups respectively. This hierarchical view, according to the critical race theory of prominent psychologist Janet Helms, results in privileged groups treating Othered groups as objects or as uncivilized sub-humans, and "denies the common humanity of all people" (31).

YA literature in general, and *The Hunger Games* trilogy more specifically, is a fertile ground for discussion of the Other because the adolescent audience's identities are in flux as they come to term with ways they are Othered and ways they are members of dominant groups. Using *The Hunger Games*, this essay seeks to reveal the imaginative potential of YA literature and to suggest that Collins's trilogy provides a roadmap for sympathizing with the Other in a way that also acknowledges the readers' membership in a dominant group.

As readers of Collins's trilogy are positioned as a part of the Capitol audience, a part of the dominant social group, Katniss becomes an Other, a subhuman object of entertainment to audiences both inside and outside of the texts. The Capitol audience enjoys a luxurious and safe lifestyle provided for them by the labor of the districts while they consume entertainment based on the suffering and deaths of others: Katniss and her tribute peers. Katniss's first-person narrative may give readers an even more voyeuristic view of the action than the ubiquitous cameras in the Arena gives her television audience. While the audience gets to see her action the readers have access to the only thing Katniss keeps private from the in-text audience: her thoughts. Still, the readers enjoy her action-packed struggle from a safe distance just as the fictional Capitol citizenry does. The readers' "Capitol perspective" makes it safe for them to identify with Katniss, while her close first-person narrative, which encourages readers to relate to her point of view, persuades the readers to sympathize with someone essentially and dangerously Other from themselves.

There are three major achievements created by this dual identification of readers with both Katniss and Capitol, and each amplifies the trilogy's potential to spark change in the ways readers view privilege and Othered individuals, encouraging them to locate, question and subvert implicit power structures in the real world. First, the juxtaposition of the reader's sympathy with Katniss and similarity with the capitol enables an ambiguous personal space that encourages safe, nonthreatening identification with a disadvantaged Other. Secondly, by encouraging identification with an Other, while also drawing attention to the reader's comparatively privileged position, the novel offers a path of individual development and consequences so that readers may vicariously and more fully explore the nature of oppression. Finally, the vote on whether or not to hold a final Hunger Games in the last third of *Mockingjay* is the culmination of the tug-of-war between identifying with Others like Katniss or with real world privilege, and serves as a Rorschach Test revealing readers' opinions on power and oppression outside of the text.

Identities and Identification

In this section, I seek to investigate the privilege of many, but not all, readers of *The Hunger Games* as members of a dominant real world social group similar to the Capitol audience. I will identify the various forms of Othering that occur within the trilogy because of the privileged reader outside of the text and the oppressed Other—Katniss—inside the text, through a depiction of Katniss and her prep team. This paper investigates a reading of this trilogy that enables the privileged reader to learn sympathy for the Other. The forms of Othering become competing spaces of identification for the privileged reader that constructs a safe place within which they can examine privilege and identity, a space that encourages introspection towards the readership's own identity development. Although reading is a vicarious experience, fiction lends itself to safe spaces because the readers can always remind themselves that the horrors and injustices within the trilogy are purely fictional. YA literature in particular creates a tempered safe space. Not only is the young audience shielded from the textual problems, but an adult author guides adolescents' thoughts, offering some degree of protection from drawing the wrong conclusions about the story. In *The Hunger Games* Collins takes the safe space to another level by avoiding the didacticism common in both children's literature and the dystopia genre. By offering multiple entry points for sympathy throughout the text's power structure, she highlights privilege and oppression while avoiding the kind of radical confrontation that triggers defensiveness. Because *The Hunger Games* does not accuse the reader of privilege or assign direct responsibility or blame, the individual reading experience itself is safe. Additionally, Collins spares readers from the judgment of outside observers as they grapple with their own place in privilege. Therefore, the reading space offers an opportunity to experiment with their identities and see how their own groups may Other, while not feeling personally accused of being part of an oppressive system.

The ambiguous nature of YA literature—a genre that explores the child in an ambiguous and undefined period of life—helps to create the safe space of *The Hunger Games* trilogy that encourages readers to examine contradictions in oppression. The oppression specific to *The Hunger Games* relies heavily on Othering the less privileged class, the rebellious districts, so that those in power, the controlling Capitol, do not have to view them as fully human, but rather as characters on a favorite television show. The YA genre serves as an ideal form in which to address the power and class issues *The Hunger Games* forces readers to confront. As Roberta Seelinger Trites writes in her seminal work *Disturbing the Universe: Power and Repression in Adolescent Literature*, "adolescents occupy an uncomfortable liminal space" where they "are both powerful (in the youthful looks and physical prowess that are glorified)" as well as "disempowered (in the increased objectification of the teenage body)" (xi). *The Hunger Games* reflects this paradoxical adolescent position as Capitol citizens celebrate the strength of the tributes by sponsoring and betting on them, revealing a lack of human empathy that enables the fans to send the tributes to likely death. Because of the adolescent's liminal identity, the adolescent novel as a form is especially conducive to allowing readers to enter and exit identification with Others as well as oppressors, trying out different levels of sympathy and experiencing why sympathy or lack thereof is central to Othering.

According to Charles Sarland, Othering is involved in "the discourses of racism, of xenophobia, of class distinction, of paternalism, of homophobia" (41). In the case of *The Hunger Games,* the racial model of Othering is most useful. At the surface level, the divisions in Panem appear socioeconomic, with wealth concentrated in the Capitol that keeps the poverty-stricken districts at their disposal. However, heritage—being a descendent of a rebellious district's citizens—is more important than wealth: even wealthy merchant and mayor's children are eligible for reaping, because of their ancestral connection to the rebel districts. District residents may be able to improve their station locally by obtaining comparative wealth, even substantially via the riches of a Hunger Games victor for whom "a month of tribute winnings can easily provide for a family for a year" (*CF* 59). Even then, however, the children of the locally privileged are all still entered into the lottery—they cannot buy their way into

Capitol citizenship and exemption from the Games. Like Capitol citizens, the privileged reader is outside of the danger of the oppressive system—free from the danger of selection for the Games as well as free from the guilt of being part of the fictional world's specific oppressive system.

Collins plays with and subverts basic ideas about how identification works in children's literature in such a way that may benefit the growth of the privileged reader. Collins not only uses identification in the traditional sense as defined by Trites, but adds a radical and new dimension to the term by having her readers identify not only with the central character, Katniss, but also with secondary characters like Effie Trinket and the stylists. The rule of thumb for adolescent literature, according to Maria Nikolajeva, "is that young readers should be encouraged to identify with the central, or focalizing character" ("Exit Children's Literature?" 231). In *The Hunger Games*, this character is Katniss Everdeen. Because, as Nikolajeva claims, "first-person perspective encourages the reader to share the character/narrator's point of view," Katniss immerses the privileged readers into her Othered experience, even though it differs drastically from their own (*Power, Voice and Subjectivity* 191). The first-person voice therefore encourages the readers to have sympathy for the focal, yet Othered, character, and that sympathy binds the readers to the character's suffering. According to Freud, "sympathy only arises out of the identification" (440). Freud's notion of sympathy interacts with Nikolajeva's notion of identification in that sympathy allows the readers to reconsider their own privilege and opens their eyes to the suffering of others, namely, the Other, and in this instance, Katniss.

However, there is "evidence that readers take up a range of positions" within the text "of greater or lesser involvement, and of varied focalization" (Sarland 43). For example, readers sympathize with oppressed Katniss's nobility and heroism when she sacrifices herself for her sister, not just because she is the narrator but also because it is pleasurable to identify with nobility and heroism. However, Katniss is not the only noble, self-sacrificing character. Cinna, despite his privileged position as a Capitol fashion designer, sacrifices his life when he uses his art, via the mockingjay symbolism in Katniss's *Catching Fire* costume, in the rebellious act of sympathizing with the Othered group— the rebel districts. By choosing to become a martyr for the districts' cause, Cinna's self-sacrifice is both sympathetic to Katniss as well as accessible to readers, giving them an opportunity to identify with the nobility of eschewing their own privilege to stand with oppressed Others. Thus, Collins's portrayal of noble and heroic Capitol citizens, such as Cinna, encourages reader identification as well, accomplishing the varied focalization Sarland discusses and subverting the simplicity of a Katniss-good/Capitol-bad narrative.

The majority of named Capitol characters are in fact sympathetic to Katniss—just as the reader, privy to Katniss's inner thoughts, may very well be. The readers' identification with, and sympathy for, the Capitol citizens is created through the sympathy Katniss feels for them herself. In *Catching Fire*, when Katniss protests the punishment that befalls her stylist team in District 13, Gale asks her "Are you actually defending them?" to which Katniss struggles "to find a logical position" that would justify her affection and forgiveness towards the trio (54). In their initial appearance in *The Hunger Games*, Katniss thinks, "They're so unlike people that I'm no more self-conscious than if a trio of oddly colored birds were pecking around my feet" (62). Through the course of the trilogy, she initially finds the stylist prep team so alien as to be an inhuman Other, but develops the ability to sympathize with them by finding ways her own experiences and those of her prep team align. For example, in *Mockingjay*, Katniss identifies with the prep team—starved and mistreated for their affiliation with the Capitol—as hunger and punishment are two of the injustices Katniss has great experience with, growing up in District 12. The reader, identifying with Katniss, vicariously identifies with the prep team, being used to satiety and suddenly deprived, just as readers would be if they imagine themselves in *The Hunger Games* world. This multi-layered exercise of identification leads back to a privileged position closer to that which the reader occupies, resulting in a two-way sympathy. The readers sympathize with Katniss when she sympathizes with her prep team, and since the readers occupy a similar space to the prep team, they experience Katniss sympathizing with them in return. The complexity of these relationships guides readers to examine their real world system positions and sympathize with those in positions outside of their own.

So, if many readers are identifying with Katniss, but can relate more to the Capitol audience because of socio-economic similarities, who are the Others in Collins's trilogy? While the Capitol audience and by extension the trilogy's readers participate in Othering, those who they Other can respond by a toothless, non-oppressive Othering of their oppressors. They can also, to various degrees, adopt the dominant positions and dehumanize themselves or members of their own group; they can perform "self-Othering," a necessary practice Katniss must participate in so that she can survive the Capitol's brutality. So, the Capitol Others Katniss; Katniss Others the Capitol and her own fellow Others; and the readers switch in and out of viewpoints, Othering or being Othered based on whom they identify with.

Katniss's status as an Other is hammered in by the Capitol citizens working on her own team. In the same scene when Katniss identifies her prep team as subhuman, Flavius admires her makeover: "Excellent! You almost look like a human being now!" (*THG* 62). Although the statement is a joke, jokes are telling. After all, one of Katniss's introductions to Capitol-style living is Effie's light remark that "the pair last year ate everything with their hands like a couple of savages" (*THG* 44). While she is trying to pay a compliment to Katniss's and Peeta's manners, they have experienced hunger; she has not. They can relate to the starving children. She is, in a roundabout way, complimenting Katniss by being surprised that Katniss is not a "savage" herself. The compliment is that Katniss behaves like a person instead of an Other; it is only a compliment because she is considered less civilized and is expected to behave as such. Even in trying to relate to Katniss, Effie and Flavius reinforce her status as the dehumanized Other.

While both Katniss and her Capitol support team view each other as Others, this does not mean that the way they Other is the same: Katniss is a depersonalized object, a dress-up doll for the stylists to play with, whereas to Katniss the stylists are too alien to relate to, but still living beings rather than objects. The support team's views are backed by the dominant Capitol culture, a dystopia of extreme brutality that encourages its people to disassociate from one another, viewing out-groups as subhuman, so much so that they celebrate the out-groups' deaths. So, when Katniss thinks of her prep team as "an affectionate trio of pets," she is both contradicting the dominant culture by valuing that they are alive, while also conforming to the idea that out-groups are subhuman by affirming that the prep team members are not capable of the full range of human emotions and attachment.

After all, even when Katniss survives the first Games and the team is happy to see her, their gushing is self-centered: "It's funny, because even though they're rattling on about the Games, it's all about where they were or what they were doing or how they felt when a specific event occurred" (*THG* 353–354). To the prep team, the Games are all about themselves, the audience experiencing entertainment, even though their lives are never at risk. Katniss, upon her first arrival in the Capitol as a tribute, recoils, "sickened by their excitement, knowing they can't wait to watch us die" (*THG* 60). The Capitol's joy in the deaths of the tributes relies on viewing tributes as subhuman. Katniss takes on this viewpoint, self–Othering by taking on the dominant group's perspective and dehumanizing her own group. Gale suggests she view the Games like hunting: "[t]he awful thing is that if I can forget they're people, it will be no different at all" (*THG* 40). If the tributes are less than human, killing them becomes hunting, a sport, a means of survival. The idea that Katniss enjoys hunting is reinforced throughout the entirety of the trilogy—by dehumanizing the other tributes, killing them becomes potentially enjoyable, just as watching the Games is only enjoyable if the viewers do not accept the Tribute's humanity. The goings-on in the lives of Capitol citizens do not matter to Katniss. However, the tributes' survival does not matter to anyone adhering to the Capitol's dominant ideology, which positions entertainment over life. Both groups, therefore, Other each other.

The explicit interaction with Othering and self–Othering—Katniss's intellectual exercise of dehumanizing her fellow tributes the way the Capitol encourages, so as to contemplate killing them—results in an interesting position for the readers. Readers are encouraged to participate in Katniss's Othering of her combatants, which means dehumanizing a group Katniss is a member of, while immersed in Katniss's viewpoint. If the readers are identifying with Katniss, this puts them in the position of dehumanizing themselves in the eyes of the dominant fictional culture, the Capitol. However, no matter how close the readers are to Katniss through her narration, their experiences in reading her trials in the Games align them with the prep team, who are also voyeurs into Katniss's narrative—the characters in the trilogy are not real, so the readers' experiences as spectators, much like Katniss's prep team experience the Games as audience, is by definition more real. As the readers experience the trilogy, they are prompted to question out-group privilege systems. The practice of sympathizing with an excluded Other ideally informs the way readers encounter real world oppression, allowing them a point of reference when transferring sympathy towards a fictional Other to real world groups and individuals being oppressed. Ideally, foregrounding how Othering works will help those readers, upon re-reading, to interrogate their beliefs and persuade them against participation in oppressive systems. However, certain current real world oppressive systems, such as racial discrimination, may be blind spots for some readers.

While readers can relate to socioeconomically Othered characters, the visual medium of *The Hunger Games* film forces them to confront that they cease relating to characters once the characters' identity as racial Others becomes visible. Through the marketing of, and responses to, the film version of *The Hunger Games*, real life engagement with these power issues is both complicated and confirmed. The film's casting call for Katniss triggered one of the earliest controversies: "Ms. Zane's staff has posted the single paragraph laying out the filmmakers' broad criteria for Katniss. She should be Caucasian, between ages 15 and 20, who could portray someone 'underfed but strong,' and 'naturally pretty underneath her tomboyishness'" (Jurgensen). Despite Katniss's racially ambiguous description in Collins's texts, the filmmakers want her to be Caucasian, and despite this demand eliminating the opportunity for actresses of all other races to even compete for the role, *The Wall Street Journal* still calls the casting criteria "broad." When Jurgensen labels the racially-narrowed casting criteria as "broad," he demonstrates the invisibility of the Other.

However, at the center of the casting call's intentional disregard of the Other is the cynical belief that privileged audience members will not be able to identify with a character so visibly a member of an Othered group. The cynical belief is unfortunately true for the readers who, upon finding out that Rue is black, took to Twitter to post their dismay in public "outbursts [that] were microcosms of the ways in which the humanity of minorities is often denied and thwarted, and they underscored how infuriatingly conditional empathy can be" (Holmes). One of the most illustrative types of tweets had to do with readers finding that Rue's death "wasn't as sad" because of her race, just as Capitol citizens find Rue's death less sympathetic because she is a district girl (Holmes). The marketing of the film also encouraged the film's audience to dissociate themselves from the district tributes, by selling the tributes as sub or nonhuman. In addition, marketing techniques encouraged the audience to position themselves as the Capitol. The film's trailer, released as part of a carefully plotted campaign to build hype, helped in this purpose, selling *The Hunger Games* as the Hunger Games, a spectacle of entertainment for the audience's viewing pleasure. Editors of the trailer purposefully cut any footage of the Hunger Games in a move that shrunk the distance between film audience and Capitol audience by making them spectators at the same event. Of that decision, Lionsgate's chief marketing officer explained: "[e]veryone liked the implication that if you want to see the games you have to buy a ticket" (Barnes). Just as the Capitol audience must buy tickets to see the ceremonies and action up close, so too must the theater-going viewers of the film buy a ticket. The cutting of the trailer framed the Hunger Games as the main event to be watched by the real audience, an audience in collusion with Collin's Capitol audience inside the text of *The Hunger Games*.

But when the story is translated into a visual medium to be watched instead of read, some members of the audience—now positioned even more explicitly as Capitol citizens—find it harder to sympathize with Othered characters. This lack of sympathy is especially apparent in responses to decisions to cast non–Caucasian actors in important roles in the film adaptation of *The Hunger Games*. I suggest that the reason actors' races in particular have triggered such an outcry is because the readers were strongly identifying with Katniss and the tributes, and so expected the actors cast as tributes to look like them. While part of these complainants' upset comes from viewers' lack of sympathy with the real world Other, another part is the undeniable visual proof that they are part of the Capitol and not the noble, oppressed heroes of this story, and their subsequent discomfort at that fact. But in a way, this is a good thing—it forces readers to reconsider their position. While reading the novels leaves readers sympathizing with an *abstract* Other, their real world failure to sympathize with people they were actively oppressing and dehumanizing proves how difficult and painful identity development can be.

Regardless of the readers' opinions on their place in oppressive systems, the subtle juxtaposition of readers vicariously experiencing the Games with the Capitol citizens, also viewers of the Games—especially those like the prep team with attachments to Katniss—does not explicitly accuse readers of being the Capitol or oppressors gaining at the Other's expense. For example, Katniss never directly accuses the members of the prep team, who occupy a space similar to that of the implied reader, of being her oppressors. Instead, she explicitly addresses their lack of awareness in *Mockingjay* when she defends them against Gale's accusations of their callousness in participating in the oppressive system: "They don't see...I mean, they don't know..." (53). By highlighting the obliviousness of people perpetrating the oppressing and Othering, the story lays out a path for dominant-cultured readers to identify with the less privileged. While "more radical books push readers to identify with the poor, or to recognize their own privilege," *The Hunger Games* encourages identification with non-privileged and oppressed groups and so *persuades* readers that privilege blinds them to the suffering of others (Mickenberg and Nel 462). *The Hunger Games* exhibits a subtlety in its awareness of privilege and poverty, creating a nuanced picture of an oppressive system's participants at each level of the hierarchy, as well as of their varying degrees of privilege and differing amounts of responsibility for the system. Therefore, it is more successful than the "more radical" and more forceful novels that overtly demonize privileged groups, and I suggest that its greater success makes it, actually, the more radical text. *The Hunger Games* trilogy enables readers to identify with the disadvantaged Other enough to sympathize, while also offering up unwitting oppressors who are subject to the internalized ideologies of their society, such as Effie and the stylists. Rather than creating a superficial and obvious critique that oppressing people is bad, the text demonstrates to readers, in a way in which they can easily relate without being accused, the shades of grey inherent in oppression and blameworthiness.

Antagonists and Capitol-dwelling side characters, from Capitol authorities such as the president and head Gamemakers to lower stylists and average citizens, form a cohesive hierarchy above the districts' people, drawing attention to the ways oppression functions throughout the spectrum while offering readers chances to identify with each group. Through this hierarchy, it is possible for readers to critique their own social positioning in relation to the fictional Capitol's elite citizens, and to Katniss, in a natural, nonthreatening way. This critique is no accident. The final question in the ScholasticTeens Youtube.com channel's video, "Suzanne Collins Answers Questions about The Hunger Games Trilogy," asks her, "What would you like young readers to ultimately take away from the Hunger Games Trilogy?" Collins's answers: "Questions about how elements of the book might be relevant in their own lives... Was there anything in the book that disturbed you because it reflected aspects of your own life, and if there was, what can you do about it?" In other words, Collins *wants* her readers to identify forms of oppression in *The Hunger*

Games, such as Othering, in their own lives, and hopes readers will find ways to correct it. And they can, through the radical notion of sympathy.

The Dangers of Sympathy and Identification

The established dual positioning of readers created by the immediacy of Katniss's narration and the socioeconomic vantage point shared with Capitol citizens means that, while vicariously experiencing Katniss's life, the readers also experience an interwoven plot about how one develops personal beliefs about real world power and oppression. But the text does more than offer examples of developmental stages: by demonstrating the consequences that befall members of dominant groups who reject their privilege to sympathize with an oppressed group, the text offers readers an extra taste of oppression. The multiple focalizations offered create a nuanced picture of dominant groups and Othered peoples. Janet Helms's model of racial development can help further clarify and interpret this picture.[3] Helms's model features stages—Contact, Disintegration, Pseudo-Independence—that reveal the invisibility of privilege to those who experience them. I argue that Capitol-born characters experience these stages and that by looking at *The Hunger Games* through Helms's theory, we see that Othering is invisible to the privileged inside and outside of the trilogy, and that readers vicariously experience these stages alongside Capitol characters to whom they might relate. By making opaque what was once invisible, Collins provides readers and characters with the opportunity to examine their own privilege.

One of the earliest stages in Helms's model is Contact. The Contact schema is characterized by a person who "does not consciously think of herself/himself as" privileged, becomes aware of the existence of the less privileged, interacts with "naïveté" towards the Other and "believes that other groups necessarily want to be assimilated" into the dominant culture's viewpoints—a goal the person is more than happy to help the Other with (Helms 41). The first dialogue exchange Katniss has in *The Hunger Games* with her stylist prep team is marked by the characteristics of the Contact schema:

> "Excellent!" You almost look like a human being now!" says Flavius, and they all laugh.
> I force my lips up into a smile to show how grateful I am. "Thank you," I say sweetly. "We don't have much cause to look nice in District Twelve."
> This wins them over completely. "Of course, you don't, you poor darling!" says Octavia clasping her hands together in distress for me [62].

The prep team is comically tone-deaf. They consider it a great travesty that Katniss's status as a citizen of District 12 denies her the Capitol-endorsed value of beauty, and yet remain completely naïve to her greater problems back home, such as staying alive. Katniss forgives them because "they're sincerely trying to help" (*THG* 63). The prep team's pleasant obliviousness best illustrates the Contact schema. By highlighting privileged naïveté in *The Hunger Games*, Collins provides readers a tool they can use to question their own assumptions about shared values. While gently letting the readers know that trying to help, however sincere, sometimes is not enough, the text uses Katniss to allow readers to know what it is like to be on the receiving end of privilege related cluelessness. Ideally, this will encourage readers to listen to Othered or marginalized people in real world situations, rather than assuming the dominant viewpoint as a universal truth.

Once the privileged individual encounters significant evidence contrary to the dominant viewpoint, denial of the oppressive system is no longer an option and she must shift schemas. The individual in Helms's potential second schema, Disintegration, "is caught in the midst of a moral dilemma" where maintaining one's social positioning requires that "he or she must subscribe to immoral social practices, but to conform to them denies the common humanity of all people" (31). Disintegration combines the knowledge that the privileges an individual have are a result of being in a dominant group and participating in an unjust system, with the additional knowledge that the privileges are at risk should the oppression end. It is a place of moral confusion. In *Catching Fire*, the former victors and current tributes of the Quarter Quell manipulate Disintegration during their pre-game interviews. They play up the moral dilemma on whether to send the familiar victors back into the Arena using the crowd's past-established affection towards them until they whip up such a frenzy that "people have been weeping and collapsing and even calling for change" (251). These same people calling for change still tune into the programing and place bets, though, just as the reader continues reading through the horrific situation.

The victors were hoping to settle the internal dispute of Disintegration by playing on the Capitol citizens' emotions to persuade them that their privilege of watching the Games should be cast aside in favor of repairing injustice. If the victors had succeeded, they would be prodding the citizens into the next schema of identity development, Pseudo-Independence. Pseudo-Independence "represents the person's attempt to recapture morality" (Helms 62). Early on in *The Hunger Games*, Effie demonstrates this schema because she quickly comes to like Katniss. When Katniss is upset over her impulsive display during her individual time with the Gamemakers, Effie comforts her by saying, "Well it serves them right. It's their job to pay attention to you. And just because you come from District Twelve is no excuse to ignore you" (*THG* 107). Effie is not taking responsibility for her role as someone who benefits from District

12's oppression, and while she is not criticizing the system for forcing Katniss in the Games, she is criticizing individuals for their personal actions in devaluing Katniss for being part of an oppressed group. Both the lack of acknowledgement of personal responsibility in oppression and the decrying only of "overt" unfair acts are features of this schema (Helms 61–62). Pseudo-Independencefunctions as a comfortable space, both blameless and righteous, enabling readers to see, from outside of the text and system, the unjust system going unquestioned by its fictional participants. By questioning if they benefit from oppression the way Effie does, readers may question their own complacency towards the oppression for which they feel they have no direct responsibility. Additionally, the use of the schema gently opens the readers' eyes to the fact that privileged individuals, as part of an oppressive system, benefit at the expense of Othered people, without actively trying to.

While the Pseudo-Independence schema leads to people like Effie, still an implicit participant in an oppressive system, it does "signal the first major movement toward the development of a positive," non-oppressing identity (Helms 62). Effie is capable of sympathy with Katniss, which reveals a degree of identification. However, Effie's primary mode of helping is correcting Katniss's behavior and manners so that the Capitol may find her more sympathetic, not questioning the Capitol for lack of sympathy. Effie and those like her fail at "recognizing how institution practices that work to their advantage may rely on the *disadvantaging* of other groups" (Horne 85). She "has actual tears in her eyes" upon saying goodbye to Peeta and Katniss as they leave for the Games, but then destroys the moment by adding, "I wouldn't be at all surprised if I finally get promoted to a decent district next year!" (*THG* 138). The Games, had the rules not been changed, would have resulted in the death of someone Effie likes, but Effie does not connect the necessary tribute deaths with her potential advancement. When readers sympathize with Katniss, they see Effie's blindness towards the individual who pays the price for her privilege. If readers simultaneously identify with Effie, though, their knowledge of Katniss's perspective may prompt them to wonder if they ever behave as Effie does, easing them into the uncomfortable position of questioning who pays for the advantages their own privileged groups enjoy.

The act of Othering, "often buried so deep in the dominant culture as to be invisible to those who live within it," creates Effie's oblivious viewpoint (Sarland 39). Readers may not notice ways that society penalizes the poor for lack of money, but will easily see how the foreign, fictional Tesserae systematically leads to "the poor getting the worst of it," punishing people for starving by making them more likely to get selected for the Games (*THG* 13). By using a fictional, nonthreatening space—the clean, harmless pages of a book or the sterile lines of an e-reader—Collins creates a point of reference for readers to use when confronted with real world examples of institutional discrimination, opening up readers' eyes to the possibility of invisible, systematic discrimination in their own lives. I hope that these readers will be less likely to dismiss accounts of real world oppression, and instead will identify with real world oppressed groups in the same way they identified with fictional Others in *The Hunger Games*.

One of the ways that oppressive authorities bolster their worldviews as the only truth is by ensuring that their viewpoints are the only ones heard. So, when a privileged person breaks ranks with his or her group to sympathize with an Other, this person endangers the dominant culture's narrative of reality and must be silenced as punishment and as an example of what happens to those who become dangerously and intimately close to oppression. Readers for whom real life oppression is too well buried to see also will struggle to understand how oppressive structures must silence their opposition in order to avoid the moral dilemmas—such as Disintegration—that prompt exploration of oppression and trigger criticism. Readers may be unable to see the silencing of controversial opinions in their own lives, namely because it does not apply to them. However, they are able to see silencing in *The Hunger Games* when the minor characters—and Capitol citizens in particular, with whom readers share a socioeconomic background—begin to face consequences. Examples of characters and punishments include the missing Effie Trinket or Peeta's stylist, Portia, as well as his prep team who are executed "on live television" in *Mockingjay*— for becoming too close to the oppressed (182). The most obvious example of silencing is the Avox, whose tongue the Capitol has removed as punishment for dissent. The government literally and physically silences dissidents. But more than just words are stolen from an Avox. Katniss notes: "I know any move I would make toward Darius, any act of recognition, would only result in punishment for him" (*CF* 218). To be an Avox is to be the most extreme of Others, an object. Poor Darius's true crime that results in his sentence as an Avox is not trying to stop Gale's whipping, but his sympathizing with Gale. Darius's silencing coincides with the replacement of the familiar Peacekeepers in District 12. Darius was willing to speak up for the District 12 residents, which means he listens to them. Instead of cutting out the tongues of District 12's residents, the Capitol eliminates friendly ears to restore proper silence.

Despite threats and punishments, some people will take the risk of rising above the Pseudo-Independence schema to the higher levels of identity development—Immersion/Emersion and Autonomy—and directly confront oppressive systems while fully knowing the dangers it causes for them. Immersion/Emersion is the self-exploration of a person who "assumes personal responsibility for" his role in an oppressive system, actively looks at ways to confront specific instances of oppression, and "develops realistic awareness of the assets and deficits" he has as a privileged group member (Helms 33). Autonomy, the final schema, is when the individual is at peace with his or her membership in a dominant group while committing to "working toward the elimination of sociopolitical oppression in general" and refusing to participate in it (83). This individual is "aware of the many shapes and shades in which oppression can exist," as well as aware of "how oppression hurts all people even when it is not directly aimed at them" (83). Helms theorizes that these "phases of identity" are "fluid, changeable constructs rather than discrete, linear, stepwise mutually exclusive stages" (34). Therefore, it is logical that the readers can bounce from one schema to another as they identify with different characters.

Cinna is the closest example of a character who achieves the two highest schemas, Immersion/Emersion and Autonomy, in *The Hunger Games*. He personally acknowledges Katniss's humanity and viewpoint when he comments, "How despicable we must seem to you" upon their first meeting (*THG* 65). Even though he is revealed to have been working for the resistance all along, he still includes himself in the "we" that is the Capitol because he benefits from his life of privilege. Culturally, he rejects the Capitol, standing out "by how normal he looks" and by his "quiet voice somewhat lacking in the Capitol's affectations" (*THG* 63). He rejects the frivolousness of Capitol values even while engrossed in one of its most beloved forms of art—fashion—and in its most beloved form of entertainment—the Hunger Games. In these examples, he leans more towards Immersion/Emersion, and so allows the readers to vicariously experience that schema.

Cinna also challenges the institutions of oppression head on. He humanizes Katniss and Peeta in the public eye by suggesting they hold hands in their chariot entrance—"just the perfect touch of rebellion" (*THG* 77). He also willfully subverts President Snow's demand that Katniss wear her wedding dress on live TV by transforming it into a mockingjay costume, a very public "act of rebellion in itself" (*CF* 253). Depending on the reading, these actions could fall into either category—Immersion/Emersion as Cinna tackles the individual level oppression of Katniss or Autonomy as he strategically riles up the rebellion to fight to dismantle the oppressive system. The Capitol deals with Cinna's public rebellion through the brutal beating that ends his life, the first of many executions of those believed to be too sympathetic to the oppressed districts. Readers who sympathize with him as privileged but striving to eliminate oppression, vicariously experience the consequences that befall those who fight for the oppressed group, and reject their dominant positioning in favor of adopting the Immersion/Emersion or Autonomy schema.

Because of the variety in positioning of the secondary and tertiary Capitol characters, readers vicariously experience not only alternate schemas but also moving from one schema to another, as they move from one character to another. Through these experiences, the text helps readers to practice developing their own personal meanings of oppression, identity and privilege. Roderick McGillis maintains that, in children's literature, "each attempt at story is an attempt to understand what it is like to be an 'Other'" (220). *The Hunger Games* magnifies this function of children's literature because of how deeply it explores both the oppressor and the oppressed. Even though Katniss's first-person narrative has the potential to turn the story into a straightforward attempt at getting readers to identify with her directly, *The Hunger Games* creates a richer reading experience that encourages identification with characters other than, and Othered from, Katniss. Hans Robert Jauss and later Michael Benton identify this as "'ironic identification,' where the reader is drawn in and willingly submits to the fictional illusion only to have the author subvert this aesthetic experience" (96). Simply put, ironic identification is "identification and nonidentification at the same time" (Bunbury and Tabbert 120). Collins creates this ironic identification by positioning the Capitol citizens closely to the readers, and by giving them their own hidden plot running parallel to Katniss's narrative.

Rorschach Test

In a Scholastic.com interview on responses to her trilogy, Collins says, "Of all the things I've ever written, I don't think I've ever had a book or a television project that so much of the experience was dependent on the reader's own experience." In other words, readers' understandings of the text and what it means to them are shaped by their own biases and stage of identity development. Never is Collins's quote more relevant than in the pivotal *Mockingjay* scene when the surviving victors must vote on whether or not to hold a final Hunger Games reaping Capitol children. Why, after three novels that critique the evil of a system that creates the Hunger Games, would Collins suddenly reinsert this evil into the burgeoning government? I suggest that it is a purposeful move that helps readers understand their own identities. Collins deftly writes the scene so that Katniss withholds the reasoning behind her vote from readers. In this way, through Katniss's silence, Collins forces the readers to create their own explanation of Katniss's motives, granting them power over the narrative. The tools readers can use to determine their interpretation of Katniss's vote are the previously established ideas of identification development inside and outside of the text. The result is a literary version of a Rorschach Test, the famous projective psychology test where the subject's interpretations of inkblots are used to analyze her. The way readers interpret Katniss's vote reveals their stances on identity formation, identification and the nature of power and oppression. When Collins refuses to tell readers the meaning of Katniss's vote, she is asking them to interpret the answer through their individual ideologies. Sarland explains the centrality of ideology to dystopian works:

> All texts carry ideological assumptions, whether overt or covert, but readers have three options: they can assume the ideology of the text and subsume it into their own reading; they can miss or ignore the ideology of the text and import their own... or they can question the text in order to reveal the underlying ideology [Sarland 43].

The readers' interpretation of Katniss's vote reveals how much of the identification and privilege commentary they have taken in. Their interpretation puts them on the spot, asking them what they find the ideological assumptions of the text to be, what they think of these assumptions, whom they have identified with, and how their identities progress alongside the Capitol characters who initially see Katniss as a pleasant Other but come to hold her dear.

Collins creates this Rorschach Test when she pits dystopian genre conventions against a gap in the text: the silence of Katniss's motives. After spending three novels immersing readers in Katniss's immediate thoughts, she shuts out the readers for the first time:

> The scent of Snow's rose curls up into my nose, down my throat, squeezing it tight with despair. All those people I loved, dead, and we are discussing the next Hunger Games in an attempt to avoid wasting life. Nothing has changed. Nothing will ever change now.
>
> I weigh my options carefully, think everything through. Keeping my eyes on the rose, I say, "I vote yes ... for Prim" [*MJ* 370].

Katniss does not disclose to the reader what options she weighs, what thoughts she considers. Instead, readers are left to fill in the gaps as to the reasons for, and meaning of, her vote.

Haymitch's vote emphasizes the reader's role in creating narrative meaning for themselves. As an authority figure whose reasoning usually aligns with Katniss's thoughts, he is a logical figure for readers to look to for insight into Katniss's motivations in her vote and to confirm the text's ideology. He, however, gives a non-answer—"I'm with the Mockingjay"—instead of a clear declaration of support or opposition for the Games (*MJ* 370). Instead of illuminating readers on how the text asks them to interpret Katniss's decision, Haymitch's non-answer reinforces the gap that readers must fill for themselves. Katniss thinks that his vote will prove how alike he is to her and will reveal "how much he truly understands" her (*MJ* 370). Just as for three novels readers have known Katniss's intimate thoughts, for those three they have also seen and been told how much alike Haymitch and Katniss are. Haymitch's lack of a clear answer means readers cannot depend on him to explain Katniss's sudden hidden reasoning. Instead, Collins leaves readers with two main paths of thought as to what goes through Katniss's mind when she places her vote—one cynical and one subversive. The individual reader's interpretation reveals his or her own perceptions and biases regarding Othering and oppression.

The cynical reading of the text is the straightforward one. It is that Katniss's vote for another Hunger Games means, plainly, that she is in favor of another Hunger Games; it is a vote in favor of brutalizing other children. Readers already familiar with the dystopian genre are especially susceptible to interpreting the text cynically, due to dystopian expectations and conventions. According to Kay Sambell, "The concept of heroism, fatally combined as it is with this dark reading of human nature as predatory and aggressive, is played out ironically and tragically in the dystopia in order to caution readers about its terrible consequences" (249). The "dominant genre model" of dystopia is a didactic warning about humanity, a "serious and daunting comment on where we are really going as a society and, worse, what we will be like when we get there" (Sambell 247). Readers with knowledge of the genre's terrifying and didactic commentary buy into the dystopia's straightforward and fatalistic world presentation, and read Katniss's choice accordingly. They see no cause to suspect Katniss's vote is anything other than her opinion. So, a pessimistic reading latches onto dystopian genre conventions to conclude that Katniss's vote is just another sign that there will always be Othering and oppression.

However, even readers without experience of dystopian genre conventions find a cynical reading compatible with other expectations about YA literature. The trilogy fits Nikolajeva's opinions of general adolescent literature conventions regarding power, and the replication of power: "In a young adult novel, society catches up with the protagonist, depicted in transition from being oppressed to becoming an oppressor—unless he perishes on the way" (*Power, Voice, and Subjectivity* 15). Now that the districts are in power, they will turn around and victimize as the Capitol has victimized them. As Katniss thinks prior to the vote, "Nothing has changed. Nothing will change" (*MJ* 370). Katniss's hopelessness warns against the true nature of humanity, "these monsters called human beings" (*MJ* 377). Therefore, a cynical reading of power in the trilogy would suggest that Katniss's survival—and her vote—denotes that she has become an oppressor, Othering the Capitol citizens as a natural consequence of her group becoming socially dominant.

However, we do not have to read Katniss's choice, or Collins's trilogy, as cynical. I suggest that, instead, both choice and trilogy subvert power hierarchies and oppressive forces. A more optimistic reading is that Katniss's vote is a means to an end, a way to bring President Coin to justice. By the time Katniss casts her vote, she knows, from both Gale and President Snow, that the bomb that killed Prim came from rebel forces instead of the Capitol, and she suspects Prim's presence there was no accident: "...someone had to approve putting a thirteen-year-old in combat. Did Coin do it, hoping that losing Prim would push me completely over the edge? Or, at least, firmly on her side?" (*MJ* 369). When Coin opens the final Games for victor vote, she admits it is her idea. Katniss knows that Coin has no love or trust for her, and has been trying to kill her. The subversive, and thus optimistic, reading is that Katniss's vote of yes is for show; it is a trick to lure Coin into a false sense of security, which enables Katniss to assassinate President Coin instead of President Snow. This reading implies that Katniss rejects Coin's actions and philosophies—from using the rebel medics as martyrs to making Capitol children pay for their heritage as scions of oppressors. Readers taking this viewpoint believe Katniss is punishing Coin. Therefore, these readers' understanding of oppression and responsibility, in the form of punishment, functions at the individual level. To them, the systematic hierarchies that create a class of dehumanized people are less concerning than Coin, as an individual, facing justice for her personal decisions and crimes against a specific person, Prim. In readings that go only this far, the assassination is personal for both Katniss and Coin.

Especially idealistic readers may argue that the assassination was more than an assassination. The Hunger Games serve as "the ultimate entertainment" which in turn is used by Snow as a way to control the Capitol population as well as the districts (*MJ* 223). Coin has proven herself to be just as controlling. Plutarch has a great understanding of *Panem et Circenses*. It is possible to view Coin's assassination as negating the need for a new spectacle by causing chaos, controversy and "the first big televised event" after the revolution (378). This interpretation requires a lot of reading in between the lines. Those who hold this reading embrace the idea that oppression ends through sympathy instead of punishment on a systematic level; they embrace a different view of justice than the eye-for-an-eye view that subjecting the Capitol to the pains of oppression is necessary for equality. This reading suggests reader growth alongside Katniss's own growth, from earlier textual examples of her sympathy for specific Othered characters, such as the prep team, to viewing all members of the group are people, not Others.

By using Katniss's vote for a final Hunger Games to create a situation in which the ideology of the text is ambiguous, Collins demands readers look to their own stances on identity, sympathy and Othering—identities informed, hopefully, through the textual examples of identity schema progression. An individual reader's interpretation, therefore, reveals more about the reader than it does about the novel. One reader may look at this Rorschach Test and assume the dire ideology common to dystopias, and agree that power is a zero-sum game where there will always be oppressors and the oppressed. Another could overlook the text's larger themes of institutional oppression and view the assassination as a personal retaliation strictly between Katniss and Coin. A third could take the gap in the text as a challenge and aggressively interrogate it, looking for institutional change that encourages the development of non-oppressing, positive identities by opposing oppression. These are not the only potential interpretations and ideologies. After all, the Rorschach Test is not about the inkblots on the page, but about the interpreter, and what he or she makes of the blots. In the same way, Katniss's choice to stage another Hunger Games is not about her words, but about what readers make of the unspoken motives behind those words.

Conclusion

Understanding how Othering functions in the text, how the text enables the development of identities and how the development of identities influences personal ideologies, all come together to open up rich intersectional possibilities in *The Hunger Games* to greater scrutiny and exploration by highlighting the importance of having sympathy for multiple viewpoints. While Katniss and the Capitol citizenry are natural positions for readers to assume and identify with, the characters of individual districts (such as favored District 1 and District 2, granted additional privilege) and the socioeconomic divides within a single district offer additional viewpoints for sympathetic identification. Collins knowingly plays with the fact that "engagement is not the same thing as identification" in order to explore oppression from more viewpoints than Katniss's direct perspective as victim (Nikolajeva, *Power, Voice and Subjectivity* 191). Each of these viewpoints encourages specific commentary on the nature of degrees of power, power's relationship to oppression, and how power manifests differently based on the wielders' biases. That *The Hunger Games* allows its readers to fail at sympathizing with the viewpoints of Othered people outside of the text—such as those readers who could sympathize with Rue as a member of an oppressed socioeconomic class but not when confronted with her race by the film—proves it to be a work that challenges assumptions about the didactic nature of adolescent dystopian fiction. And how does *The Hunger Games* allow readers to fail? By presenting subtle narratives about power and oppression instead of delivering an explicit message ordering readers to sympathize with a list of specifically named oppressed groups, Collins lets the readership decide their own opinions on Othering, a radical move considering the genre's propensity towards didacticism. After all, one of the burdens of writing adolescent dystopia is that authors end up with a tendency to "heavily control their narratives in ways that fail to repose trust in implied young readers to think for themselves" (Sambell 251). Collins, however, does not fall into this trap, but allows readers to think for themselves.

One of the multiple ways Collins demonstrates trust for readers is by forcing them to decide why Katniss votes for a final Hunger Games, at the risk of them reaching grim conclusions. By giving readers agency in determining the text's meaning, Collins places an additional responsibility on them—they must develop their identities, questioning where they fit into power structures as participants, bystanders and/or oppressors. They may not get it right the first time. However, by allowing readers to experience, vicariously, viewpoints that have not evolved as far as Helms's final schema, Collins allows the reader's identity development to be the complicated, messy journey that it is in actuality. The result is a novel that empowers readers as they grapple with their own identities and the oppressions of their own worlds.

The same tools that enable readers to develop their understanding of oppression, enhances each aspect of power dynamics in *The Hunger Games*. In the end, the readers' understandings of privilege are deeply personal. Collins navigates this, avoiding a one-size-fits-all approach, through the creation of sympathy. The sympathy she creates is all the richer because the texts are so entertaining. Even while she critiques the use of human lives and suffering for entertainment, Collins work is still engaging enough that reading it is not reading a lesson within a story, but a story that has lessons for those who peel back the layers and examine them. Most importantly, by using the genre of popular fiction to explore the complicated power structures and multiple perspectives and identities within the text, Collins provides readers with a safe space where the pleasures of entertainment protect readers from the painful sting of reasoning through their privilege, preparing them to examine identity and Othering in real life as well as in the future fictions they read. Readers may start as passive members of a Capitol audience, but through a reading of Collins's trilogy, they can potentially transform their own identities, becoming compassionate agents of change.

Notes

1. Courtney Rubin discusses this trend in an article for *The New York Times* entitled "The Odds Are Ever in Their Favor."
2. Feminist theory, in particular, has found the concept of the Other helpful. Simone de Beauvoir's *The Second Sex*, for example, re-positioned the Other as the woman in relation to the dominant man.
3. While the widespread oppression of district citizens is not a one-to-one of the modern day race relations that Helms writes about, the group based oppression in *The Hunger Games* is similar enough to the Othering and identity politics of race that Helms's reasoning can explain the attitudes, behaviors and beliefs of participants at each part of an oppressive system.

Works Cited

Barnes, Brooks. "How *Hunger Games* Built Up Must-See Fever." NYTimes.com. *The New York Times.* 18 March 2012. Web. 19 January 2013.

Benton, Michael. "Readers, Texts, Contexts: Reader-Response Criticism." *Understanding Children's Literature.* 2nd ed. Ed. Peter Hunt. New York: Routledge, 2005. 86–102. Print.

Bunbury, Rhonda, and Reinbert Tabbert. "A Bicultural Study of Identification: Readers' Responses to the Ironic Treatment of a National Hero." *Literature for Children.* Ed. Peter Hunt. New York: Routledge, 1992. 114–125. Print.

Collins, Suzanne. *Catching Fire.* New York: Scholastic, 2009. Print.

_____. *The Hunger Games.* New York: Scholastic, 2008. Print.

_____. *Mockingjay.* New York: Scholastic, 2010. Print.

_____. "Personal Responses to *The Hunger Games*." Scholasticwww. Scholastic. Web. 1 Oct. 2012.

_____."Suzanne Collins Answers Questions about The Hunger Games Trilogy." Youtube-www.ScholasticTeens. Web. 14 April 2013.

Freud, Sigmund. "Group Psychology and the Analysis of the Ego." *Literary Theory: An Anthology.* 2nd ed. Ed. Julie Rivkin and Michael Ryan. 2004. 438–440. Print.

Helms, Janet E. *A Race Is a Nice Thing to Have.* Alexandria, VA: Microtraining Associates, 2008. Print.

Holmes, Anna. "White Until Proven Black: Imagining Race in Hunger Games." NewYorker.com. *The New Yorker.* 30 March 2012. Web. 19 January 2013.

Horne, Jackie C. "Harry and the Other: Answering the Race Question in J. K. Rowling's Harry Potter." *The Lion and the Unicorn* 34.1 (2010): 76–104. *Project MUSE.* Web.

Huntington, Samuel P. *The Clash of Civilizations and the Remaking of World Order.* New York: Simon and Schuster, 1996. Print.

Jurgensen, John. "The Newcomers." Online.WSJ.com. *The Wall Street Journal.* 25 February 2011. Web. 19 January 2013.

McGillis, Roderick. "Self, Other, and Other Self: Recognizing the Other in Children's Literature." *The Lion and the Unicorn* 21.2 (1997): 215–229. Print.

Mickenberg, Julia L., and Philip Nel. "Radical Children's Literature Now!" *Children's Literature Association Quarterly* 36.4 (2011): 445–473. Print.

Nikolajeva, Maria. "Exit Children's Literature?" *The Lion and the Unicorn* 22.2 (1998): 221–236. Print.

_____. *Power, Voice and Subjectivity in Literature for Young Readers.* New York: Routledge, 2010. Print.

Rubin, Courtney. "The Odds Are Ever in Their Favor." NYTimes.com. *The New York Times.* 28 November 2012. Web. 30 May 2013.

Said, Edward W. *Orientalism.* New York: Pantheon Books, 1978. Print.

Sambell, Kay. "Carnivalizing the Future: A New Approach to Theorizing Childhood and Adulthood in Science Fiction for Young Readers." *The Lion and the Unicorn* 28.2 (2004): 247–267. Print.

Sarland, Charles. "Critical Tradition and Ideological Positioning." *Understanding Children's Literature.* 2nd ed. Ed Peter Hunt. New York: Routledge, 2005. 30–49. Print.

Springen, Karen. "The Hunger Games Franchise: The Odds Seem Ever in Its Favor." *Publisher's Weekly.* 22 March 2012. Web. 15 November 2012.

Trites, Roberta Seelinger. *Disturbing the Universe: Power and Repression in Adolescent Literature.* Iowa: University of Iowa Press, 2000. Print.

Recreating the Holocaust
YA Dystopia and the Young Jewish Reader

Adam Levin

Recently, a handful of informal websites and teaching blogs have identified parallels between the narrative of *The Hunger Games* trilogy and the events of the Holocaust, as well as how these parallels can be used to enrich young learners' factual knowledge of the Holocaust.[1] However, none of these resources have paid attention to how reading *The Hunger Games* trilogy as Holocaust literature may be effective in assisting these learners in gleaning an understanding of the Holocaust beyond its significance as a historical event. I speak here specifically of the psychological effects of the Holocaust on those who survived it. This is, perhaps, the most difficult issue to address within Holocaust education, both through literature and in the classroom. This difficulty arises from the fact that it is almost impossible to put the complexity of the emotional responses to the Holocaust into words. These responses are primarily shaped and dictated by the trauma of the Holocaust survivors, a concept which in itself is difficult to get young learners to comprehend. Jewish youths, in particular, struggle to understand this trauma and its origins. This is because, by virtue of their religious and/or familial background, there is a careful hesitancy and sensitivity, on the part of literature and classroom education, towards exposing these youths to questions that may render the trauma narratives of Holocaust survivors problematic, flawed, and/or inaccurate.

This anxiety around introducing Jewish youths to a more complex understanding of Holocaust trauma suggests that in order to access this understanding, these youths need to find a medium that exposes them to trauma in a way that is not shaped and outlined by an overt Holocaust narrative. Such a medium would allow them to continue to learn about the Holocaust in a safe space but, at the same time, would give them a certain amount of freedom to explore the notion of trauma, its implications, as well as its complications. I suggest that if Jewish youths recognize Holocaust parallels in *The Hunger Games* trilogy, and choose to read it as Holocaust literature, this space can potentially be created. The fact that Collins did not intend to write the trilogy as a piece of Holocaust fiction indicates that it has no obligation to provide the reader with an "accurate" reflection of Holocaust trauma and its attached history. Subsequently, the young Jewish reader who reads it as such has the opportunity to engage with an understanding of this trauma without the limitations imposed by its realities, and the representation of these realities, both in the classroom and through conventional Holocaust literature.

Defining Holocaust Literature

Before examining and defining *The Hunger Games* trilogy in relation to the genre of Holocaust literature, it is necessary to establish what the term "Holocaust literature" implies. In truth, to speak of Holocaust literature as being simply literature about the events of the Holocaust is to simplify and, inevitably, misinterpret it. As David G. Roskies states, "Holocaust literature comprises all forms of writing, both documentary and discursive, and in any language, that have shaped the public memory of the Holocaust and been shaped by it" (2). The writing in question has mostly been constructed through the intensely personal narratives of either deceased Holocaust victims or survivors, as opposed to the broader historical narrative. The purpose of emphasizing the personal over the historical in Holocaust literature can be put as follows: it is only through learning of the nature of the victim's and/or survivor's trauma that the reader can fully grasp the true magnitude of the Holocaust, its ineffability and, furthermore, the consequences the Holocaust past has for our present. Alvin H. Rosenfeld observes that Holocaust literature is a literature that acknowledges the Holocaust as being symbolic of "the end of one era of consciousness and the beginning of another" (21). In this new era of consciousness, our familiarity with the term "Holocaust" has exposed us to realities that, in the past, could have never been thought possible (Rosenfeld 22). In reading the personal narratives of Holocaust literature, we are provided with a means through which to comprehend and deal with these realities through the way in which the literature "attempt[s] to retrieve some ongoing life—posit a future tense—for whatever it is of human definition that remains to us" (Rosenfeld 22).

A central concern that arises from reading Holocaust literature is that the concept of trauma itself is a complex and immensely difficult to articulate or define in any medium. In her efforts to define trauma, Cathy Caruth turns to the general definition of post-traumatic stress disorder, which states that trauma is "a response, sometimes delayed, to an overwhelming event or events, which takes the form of repeated, intrusive hallucinations, thoughts or behaviors stemming from the event, along with numbing that may have begun during or after the experience, and possibly also increased arousal to (and avoidance of stimuli recalling the event" (4). Caruth contests this definition, claiming that the experience of trauma is not defined by the event or the distortion of the event (4). Rather, she claims, trauma is facilitated by the manner in which the person, who has experienced the event, takes possession of it. The event is not experienced in its entirety during the period in which it occurs. Instead, it is experienced belatedly. Referencing Sigmund Freud's theories on the connection between history and trauma, she notes that, in this belated context, the event is recreated in a manner that is not distorted but, in contrast, accurate and authentic.[2] Yet, the exact details of the event cannot be accessed or controlled in a conscious state, precisely due to the unwillingness to recall and, essentially, relive it. The truth of the event remains in the forms of dreams, flashbacks, and unconscious thoughts. The fact that the transmission of knowledge, pertaining to the event, cannot be controlled implies that its very truth is often questioned.

Referencing Pierre Janet, a pioneer in studies of traumatic memory, Bessell A. Van Der Klork and Onno Van Der Hart further establish a useful distinction between traumatic memory and narrative memory. Narrative memory, as Janet puts it, refers to ordinary memory processes. In the moment where narrative memory occurs, the subject is fully aware of what is happening and the memory of the experience is integrated into his/her consciousness with ease. In this regard, it also functions as a social act, "an aspect of life [that can be] integrated with other experiences" and can be narrated, easily, from one person to the other. In contrast, the processing of a traumatic memory is delayed (Van der Kolk and van der Hart 163). The subject's memory, in this capacity, is not social, but, rather, solitary in nature. Essentially, it cannot be articulated to anyone. Trauma then, as Caruth deduces, is largely rooted in the inaccessibility of history for the traumatized subject and, therefore, the struggle of decoding this historical enigma. The central question that is raised by the nature of trauma, she concludes, "extends beyond the question of individual cure and asks how we in this era can have access to our own historical experience, to a history that is in its immediacy a crisis to whose truth there is no simple access" (6). These complex characteristics of trauma imply that it is, indeed, impossible for Holocaust literature to reflect accurately on the trauma of the Holocaust experience.

However, though Holocaust literature can never accurately reflect on the trauma experienced by Holocaust survivors, it can indicate the anxieties faced in articulating trauma. It can also demonstrate, more specifically, how the trauma conceived by the past impacts us in the present. In doing so, these works address a further layer of trauma, namely that experienced by the listener (or, in this case, the reader) who gains second-hand insight into the Holocaust narrative. As Dori Laub states in his discussion of the value of Holocaust testimony, "the listener to the trauma comes to be a participant and a co-owner of the traumatic event: through his very listening, he comes to partially experience trauma in himself" (57). Inevitably, Laub continues, the listener "partakes of the struggle of the victim with the memories and residues of his or her traumatic past" (58). Like this listener, the reader of Holocaust literature undergoes a form of trauma, attributed to the impossibility of ever finding a coherent truth in the narrative while, simultaneously, being active in the effort to find this truth. This trauma, as works of Holocaust literature indicate, is necessary to facilitate an ongoing experience and discussion of trauma history.

The Problem of Representing Trauma in Holocaust Education and Youth Holocaust Literature

An understanding of Holocaust trauma and its problematics is particularly necessary to the education of youths who are learning about the events of the Holocaust and their impact for the first time. While Holocaust trauma is probably already a difficult concept for young learners to grasp, it is potentially more problematic for Jewish youths to comprehend, by virtue of both their and/or their educators' religious or familial connections to the Holocaust past. The sensitivities toward learning about the Holocaust, which emerge through these connections, can make it problematic to engage both with the issue of trauma and Holocaust history on a general level. Geoffrey Short and Carole Ann Reed point out that in secular schools, many educators have commented on how teaching Holocaust history with Jewish children in the class requires caution because (as one teacher puts it) "some [of them] have found it very difficult to cope with the lesson" (60). Furthermore, Jewish parents in these schools have objected to the teaching of the Holocaust in a classroom setting, suggesting that this teaching "should be done at home" (Short and Reed 60).

A clearer example of this dilemma is outlined in Simone Schweber's study of the Holocaust education received by an eighth grade class of Lubavitch[3] Girls' yeshivah[4] in the Midwestern United States. As Schweber details, the community of this particular yeshivah conformed to ultra–Orthodox religious practices, implying that their knowledge of real-world events was consistently informed and monitored by their religious beliefs. This proved greatly problematic when the students were introduced to Holocaust education, particularly because their inquiries about the finer details of events (such as why the Holocaust came into being in the first place) went unanswered by their educator who generally remarked "why not?" In other words, for the educator, exploring historical nuances of the Holocaust was secondary to framing a heroic narrative around the plight of the Holocaust survivor and the Nazi perpetrator. This narrative assisted in creating a favorable impression towards the power of the Jewish faith and belief in Hashem (G-d). As one girl remarked in response to her teachings, she believed that "Hashem used the Holocaust as a testament to both the endurance and enduring nature of the Jewish people" (Schweber 171). Yet, when asked about their understanding of the Holocaust beyond these faith issues, the girls failed to respond beyond expressing the belief that the motivations of the Nazis were "beyond reason, beyond explanation, and fundamentally abnormal" (Schweber 171).

The historical gap in the students' knowledge extended to their restricted exposure to issues of Holocaust trauma. In an effort to personalize Holocaust events for the students, the educator invited Holocaust survivor Marion Lazan, author of the Holocaust memoir *Four Perfect Pebbles*, to speak to them about, amongst other things, her childhood experiences at the Westerbork and Bergen-Belsen concentration camps. Schweber notes that Lazan presented her story in an immaculate fashion, "as though she had memorized the script of her story. Every sentence was complete, every image, poetic" (164). Although Schweber does not address this directly, the certainty and artfulness of this narrative potentially erased any questions towards the subject of traumatic memory and its possible influence on its articulation. Indeed, many of the questions asked after Lazan's presentation pertained, once again, to issues of faith, specifically in relation to her brother who, she claims, lost his faith during his time at the camps. Many of the students were shocked by this declaration, choosing to continuously believe that religious faith was stable and infallible, despite the atrocities of the Holocaust.

The reluctance towards engaging with Holocaust history and, more specifically, trauma beyond its moral and/or its religious implications extends to youth Holocaust fiction. A central concern here is the ongoing debate of what youth Holocaust literature should be.[5] In "Reading the Shards and Fragments: Holocaust Literature for Young Readers," David L. Russell claims that Holocaust art is a "necessarily didactic art" (267). He continues by noting that "stories of the Holocaust are like cautionary tales, warning us of the danger of complacency, reminding us of the tenuous thread in which human decency is at times suspended" (267). Although it is questionable whether this claim applies to adult Holocaust literature, which is not inherently preoccupied with producing a moral message, it is certainly a necessary consideration in youth Holocaust literature.

As critics such as Eva Tal and Adrienne Kertzer have identified, this emphasis on morality has proven to be problematic for this genre because it inevitably softens Holocaust realities. Tal notes that this softening is achieved by a reliance on the naiveté of the child protagonist that is conventionally at the center of a youth Holocaust narrative. The protagonist's often limited grasp of Holocaust realities provides a medium of expression through which the adult writer's anxieties about putting these realities into a sensitive and accessible form are resolved. This is because, as Tal suggests, "the young character's incomprehension serves to indicate the incomprehensibility of the catastrophe [of the Holocaust]" (4). She further observes that "the child's failure to understand can act to filter the disclosure of the horrifying truth that is taking place, or can serve to underscore it" (Tal 5).

Adrienne Kertzer observes that "to suggest that the narrator [or protagonist] has problems of believing, comprehending, and narrating her own story, that the sensations and memories accessible only through dreams are fortunately not accessible through ordinary language, goes against our understanding of the [didactic] function of historical children's literature" (n.p.). The question then is this: if youth Holocaust literature is incapable of exploring the complexities of trauma, how does a young reader access these complexities and the implications they have for the narrative the reader has experienced?

Perhaps, I would like to suggest, the solution is to turn to a text that is not restricted by issues of Holocaust representation and didacticism. Such a text would possibly require a very loose connection to the tradition of Holocaust narratives or, perhaps, no overt or intentional connection at all. By not being rooted in an obligation to serve a historical narrative accurately, such a text could create an alternative space for young readers (most especially young Jewish readers) to explore and question the nature of Holocaust trauma and its impact. *The Hunger Games* trilogy, I argue, is a series that prospectively opens up this alternative space.

Defining The Hunger Games *Trilogy as Holocaust Literature*

On a surface level, it appears problematic to identify *The Hunger Games* trilogy as Holocaust literature. This is particularly because the dystopian genre, under which the trilogy is classified, is a literature that does not address Holocaust literature's preoccupation with the past and its impact on shaping the present. As Raffaella Baccolini and Tom Moylan put it, the dystopian genre "has served as a prophetic vehicle, the canary in a cage, for writers with an ethical and political concern for warning us of terrible socio-political tendencies that could, if continued, turn our contemporary world into the iron cages portrayed in the realm of utopia's underside" (2). This implies that dystopian literature is focused specifically on the impact our present will have on the future. Hence, the kind of Holocaust which occurs predominantly in dystopian literature is a nuclear one which is part of our impending future as opposed to our historical past.

As Carter Kaplan notes in "The Advent of Literary Dystopia," there is an element of the past in dystopian literature. However, the past in question is one grounded in myth, as opposed to real world events, and serves a different purpose to that of Holocaust literature. He states that "dystopia uses fiction to portray institutions based on intellectual mythology and essays prophecy and prognostication" (200). Furthermore, "it examines the possible effects intellectual mythology can have on individuals and society" (Kaplan 200). Mythology, as Kaplan's analysis suggests, is important to shaping the content of a dystopian narrative. However, because this mythology is interpreted in a futuristic form, its roots in the past are mostly unrecognizable. An understanding of the past echoes in a work of dystopian literature. Unlike with Holocaust literature, is not essential to engaging with the text and its commentary. It is likely, for instance, that readers of *The Hunger Games* trilogy are unaware that the series, as author Suzanne Collins has stated, is based on the Greek myth of Theseus and the Minotaur and may not be familiar with the elements of Roman mythology to which it frequently refers. However, this knowledge is not necessary to comprehend and engage with the trilogy's narrative.

Despite its adherence to the thematic and plot concerns of dystopian literature, there are certain aesthetic and stylistic narrative elements that create links between *The Hunger Games* trilogy and the features found in Holocaust narratives. In *Representing the Holocaust in Children's Literature*, Lydia Kokkola observes that young readers identify Holocaust narratives by "build[ing] on specific images that are easily recognizable" (68). Kokkola, citing Kertzer, observes that the most recognizable and iconic of these images are "the star of David, cattle trucks containing people, chimneys, grey striped shirts and bunks" (68). She further notes that these narratives can also be identified in cases where the protagonist is seen "constantly travelling to avoid capture" (Kokkola 68). The summary of John Boyne's Holocaust novel *The Boy in the Striped Pyjamas* suggests that an additional detail that young readers may recognize as being applicable to a Holocaust narrative is the image of a fence. The summary states that as, readers journey with the protagonist, they will encounter a fence and warns "fences like this exist all over the world. We hope you never have to encounter such a fence." It is questionable whether young readers will easily recognize that a fence image, as it is relayed here, is associated specifically with a ghetto or concentration camp environment. However, the feeling of entrapment that this structure creates could indicate to these readers that it represents captivity, the kind of which they can link to the imprisonment of Holocaust victims.

Fence imagery is, in fact, perhaps the primary means through which young readers can identify allusions to the Holocaust within the narrative of *The Hunger Games* trilogy. As Katniss describes it, the fence that surrounds District 12 is barb-wired and has the potential to be electrically charged (*THG* 4), presumably to keep the district safe by keeping out wild animals. However, the presence of predatory Peacekeepers, stationed at the fence, who constantly monitor the movements of the district's citizens, may make young readers realize that the fence image here does not denote a protected space but, rather, a restricted and imprisoning one, much like the fences and walls of the ghettos and concentration camps.

The second fence image that can be located in the trilogy is the metaphorical one that surrounds the Hunger Games Arena itself. This particular image may be recognized when considering the mode of transportation that Katniss and Peeta take to the Capitol. Katniss describes the tribute train as being fancy and in immaculate condition, a sharp contrast to the cattle trucks used to transport the Jews to the concentration camps, it is used with a similar intention, namely to transport the tributes (victims) to their place of death. If young readers notice this association, they may then identify the Hunger Games Arena as being symbolic of a concentration camp environment, with the force field and cameras that surround it, substituting for the barbed-wire fence.

On another level, some young readers might be able to identify subtle parallels between Katniss's present-tense narration and the method of diary writing employed in *Anne Frank: The Diary of a Young Girl*, a text many of these readers may have encountered in some form or another while learning about the Holocaust.[6] The diary details the teenage Anne's final two years of life, during which she, her family, and some of their acquaintances hid from the Nazis in a secret annex. Anne speaks to the reader through her engagement with the fictional Kitty, whom she addresses with each diary entry. As Barbra Chiaello suggests, Anne consistently protects Kitty, using her words to disguise both the extent of her knowledge about her potential fate, as well as her fear of death. In doing this, she constructs (what Chiarello terms) a utopian fantasy which protects both her and the reader from acknowledging the uncertainty of her future.[7]

Like Anne, Katniss presents information to the readers of *The Hunger Games* trilogy in a manner that shields both them and her from the terror she is experiencing as events unfold. As Katniss herself suggests, when she refers to her relationship with her mother, she tends to "put up a wall to protect [herself]" (*THG* 153). This emotional wall is inevitably placed between her and the reader (her "Kitty") in that, when she is allowed the opportunity to make herself vulnerable and express the true extent of her fears, she stops herself. For instance, on her first journey to the Capitol, she thinks of her home in District 12 and is overcome by loneliness. When she attempts to express this loneliness through tears, she is unable to, claiming that she is "too tired or numb to cry" and that she only feels "a desire to be somewhere else" (*THG* 54). The only moments in which Katniss makes herself, to an extent, vulnerable to the reader is when she reflects back on her past memories of her father, noting particularly how his singing voice was "so filled with life it made [one] want to laugh and cry at the same time" (*THG* 43).[8] In these moments, she expresses a longing for the return of an unobtainable past in a way that mirrors Anne's desperate desire for a utopian future.

Identifying these parallels between Katniss's narration and Anne Frank's diary entries is particularly useful for young readers, because it helps them to identify the narrative of *The Hunger Games* trilogy as one that they not only can read as Holocaust literature by virtue of its aesthetic elements, but also through the way in which it addresses the complexities of trauma. In this regard, it also alerts them to the notion that the trilogy's narrative is defined and shaped by the protagonist's trauma. Engaging in a reading of the trilogy, with this trauma centered framework in mind, provides these young readers with an entry point through which to begin assessing the construction and complications of post–Holocaust trauma.

The Problem of Faith in the Epilogue

Of course, what differentiates the trauma narrative of *The Hunger Games* trilogy from that of conventional Holocaust trauma narratives is not only that the trilogy has no overt connection to events of the Holocaust, but also that it is set in a world that is purely fantastical. Although the Capitol, District 12, and the Hunger Games Arena may be allegorically linked to real-world locations and the events that occurred within these locations, they remain grounded in a fiction of which the reader is constantly aware. As part of this fiction, neither Katniss nor any of the other characters in the trilogy have any reality-based political or religious affiliations. For young Jewish readers who choose to read the trilogy as Holocaust literature, an awareness of this fact is vital for two specific reasons. Firstly, it suggests that, unlike with an authentic work of youth Holocaust literature, these readers are not required to attach any didactic meaning to the trilogy's text. Secondly, by virtue of its non-didactic qualities, it provides them with a space to probe into questions of trauma, without the anxiety of grappling with the sensitivities of Holocaust history and their possible familial ties to it.

With this in mind, Katniss's link to the persona of a Holocaust survivor is purely allegorical. It implies that it is easier for young Jewish readers to critique her trauma narrative and, in doing so, question its particular stylistic attributes, consistencies and accuracy. These questions, as they evolve from reading the trilogy, can subsequently lead into and be contextualized within an analysis of the narratives of Holocaust survivors. This process of contextualization, I suggest, could be facilitated through an exercise whereby these readers consider their critique of Katniss's narrative in relation to how they themselves (in their capacity as her "listeners") would narrate her trauma. Through engaging with this trauma of the "listener"/reader, these readers may then translate and map the observations they glean from this critique onto their interpretations of a Holocaust survivor's narrative, leading to a more complex understanding of trauma within this narrative.

Mockingjay's Epilogue provides a useful entry point through which to develop this critique. In it, an adult Katniss is introduced to us as a fragile and timid woman, trying desperately to escape her past, while, simultaneously, grasping onto her happier memories of this period. No longer able to emotionally distance herself (and, indeed, the reader) from her trauma, she details her difficulties in articulating the stories of her past to her and Peeta's two children, whom she observes playing in the Meadow, both unaware that it is, in fact, a graveyard site. As she watches them, Katniss states:

> Peeta says it will be okay. We have each other. And the book. We can make them understand in a way that will make them braver. But one day I'll have to explain about my nightmares. Why they came. Why they won't ever really go away.
>
> I'll tell them how I survive it. I'll tell them that on bad mornings, it feels impossible to take pleasure in anything because I'm afraid it could be taken away [*MJ* 390].

Engaging young readers in a close-reading of this passage potentially opens up a space through which to begin to examine the notion of healing as it is expressed in the trauma narratives of Holocaust survivors. It may, in some instances, be considered problematic and inauthentic. To facilitate this examination, a useful starting point is to consider the manner in which Katniss seeks to avoid the responsibility of telling her children about the full extent of her trauma by relying on "the book" to articulate the narrative for her. The book, as is established prior to the Epilogue, is a scrapbook compiled by Katniss, Haymitch, and Peeta and contains images and writings that are connected to Prim, Katniss's parents and her tribute friends. The motivation behind this, she explains, is to "[record] those things you cannot trust to memory" (387). The "things" in question, however, are not crucial to maintaining the authenticity of her trauma narrative. Rather, they are brief memories of happier moments such as "Lady [the goat] licking Prim's cheek" and her "father's laugh" (387).

These memories are possibly selected because they are suited to creating the utopian vision of the future Katniss strives to create as she chooses to pursue a relationship with Peeta, as opposed to Gale, because Peeta represents "the promise that life can go on" and "that it can be good again" (388). More importantly, they soften her trauma narrative, disguising and distracting from the painful details that she cannot possibly express through language. The game Katniss plays as she makes "a list in [her] head of every act of goodness [she has] seen someone do" (390), in this instance, can be read as furthering her efforts to find the right language through which to package the sensitized narrative she desires to relate to her children.

Because they have had intimate access to Katniss's thought processes and experiences, and are, therefore, fully aware of the trauma she has undergone, young readers may use this passage to initiate a discussion on how they themselves would articulate Katniss's narrative to her children. Would they necessarily be able to access and describe this narrative with the words that Katniss cannot permit herself to find? Or would they too struggle to find these words, choosing instead to lessen the heightened moments of trauma by concealing and counterbalancing them with a sensitive utopian-like narrative?

The method in which young readers pose these questions, through their reading of *Mockingjay*'s Epilogue, when read in relation to the content of Holocaust survivors' narratives, may provide them with an appropriate entry point through which to question the way in which the utopian notions of hope and faith are utilized in these narratives. For instance, are the messages of hope and faith that so often underscore these narratives really followed and believed by the survivor? Or are they a means of softening the painful truths and realities that cannot possibly be expressed through language? Because, in reading the Epilogue, young Jewish readers are not required to directly ask these questions in relation to their religious faith, they are provided with a space to potentially take these questions a step further by inquiring into how the faith of the listener/reader is instrumental in forming the narrative of the Holocaust survivor. In *Catching Fire*, Katniss (albeit indirectly) comments on this question when, in considering her plans to ensure Peeta's survival, she states:

> [If] I could really save Peeta ... in terms of a revolution, this would be ideal. Because I will be more valuable dead. They can turn me into some kind of martyr for the cause and paint my face on banners, and it will do more to rally people than anything I could do if I was living. But Peeta would be more valuable alive, and tragic, because he will be able to turn his pain into words that will transform people [244].

Established in the first novel of *The Hunger Games* trilogy, Peeta's strength lies in his ability to manipulate his words and behavior in a manner which plays to the desires of those around him. Katniss herself notes this when she observes how he seamlessly appeals to the sensibilities of the Capitol audience by "waving and smiling at the gawking crowd" (68), and infusing his interview with Caesar Flickerman with witty anecdotes that immediately capture the audience (130). She is quite right then to suggest that, if given an opportunity, Peeta would be able to seamlessly create a survivor narrative that could heal people. Yet, Katniss does not imply that this act of communal healing in any way could represent the extent of his trauma. Rather, just as with the image she has of her face on banners, fulfilling the role of the deceased martyr who rallies people together, Katniss perceives Peeta's role in his potential narrative as one that primarily performs a moral obligation to the people, easing them into a version of reality where their desire for hope and faith can be realized. Hence, this narrative, when considered in this context, would be one that would be mainly expressed by the communal voice of the people, rather than by the true nature of Peeta's trauma.

If young Jewish readers apply this interpretation of the passage in *Catching Fire* to their reading of *Mockingjay*'s Epilogue, they may interpret Katniss's own efforts to create a communal faith narrative, through the story she attempts to construct for her children, as a reflection on the tension between a communal faith narrative and a singular survivor narrative. Perhaps the clearest example of this tension is evident in the manner in which she shifts from speaking about her and Peeta's presumably shared belief that they can relate the events of the past to their children in a way which "will make them stronger" (390), to a gesture towards her private nightmares that she is reluctant to share. The fact that, as she states, these private nightmares "will never really go away" (390) indicates that the message of the narrative she intends to teach her children is not one that she can bring herself to fully comprehend and believe. Interestingly, however, her efforts to recollect "every act of goodness [she] has seen someone do" (390) suggest that, despite her hesitancy in believing it, Katniss is trying to find some way to connect with this narrative. This is perhaps because shaping her narrative to conform to the demands of the communal faith narrative may, indeed, be her only way of (at least partly) putting her trauma into words.

In interpreting the conflicts Katniss encounters in formulating her faith narrative, young Jewish readers could raise two particular questions, in relation to the link between faith and trauma, while continuing with the exercise of relating Katniss's narrative through their own words. On one hand, these readers could question how their own belief systems could influence the manner in which they choose to interpret and relay Katniss's narrative. In doing so, they may consider to what extent a dependence on these beliefs could, firstly, ease the harsh realities of the narrative and, secondly, provide them with an accessible means through which to explain the trauma they are detailing.

On the other hand, they may question how their awareness of the beliefs of those whom they are relaying the narrative to could possibly impact on the way they choose to shape it. As they pose these questions, young Jewish readers may then turn their attention to a Holocaust survivor's narrative and examine if and where they may find a similar conflict between the faiths of the narrator and the listener/reader at play. As an entry point to their analysis, they may consider deconstructing the survivor's narrative in the same manner as the *Mockingjay* Epilogue, noting possible areas where notions of faith (more specifically religious faith) act a mechanism through which the survivor relates his or her trauma.

In doing so, they may firstly, keeping both their own and Katniss's personas and viewpoints in mind, examine to what extent this faith acts as a crutch for the survivor, filling gaps where moments of trauma cannot be put into words. Following this, young Jewish readers may then consider whether (as with Katniss's narration and their own efforts at formulating her narrative) there is evidence of the survivor using faith to sensitize the listener/reader and, in so doing, play on the nature of his or her beliefs. On another level, they could turn their attention more specifically to the question of how they, in their capacity as listeners/readers, apply their faith to their interpretation of the survivor's narrative. Here, they could take an introspective approach, contrasting the ways in which their faith may potentially influence their interpretation of the *Mockingjay* Epilogue to the ways in which it could influence their interpretation of a Holocaust survivor's narrative. This aspect of their analysis could facilitate a discussion on the possibility that, in taking a specifically faith-based perspective in interpreting the Holocaust survivor's narrative, they may be neglecting to consider subtle elements of narrative which may give them more comprehensive insight into the aspects of the survivor's trauma which he/she fails to articulate. Perhaps here, they could also attempt to imagine themselves in the position of Katniss's children who, through their exposure to "the book," may be encouraged to continuously interpret her words through the lens of the faith narrative, omitting to consider the hidden layers of trauma that only we as readers are aware of. Through taking on this position, young Jewish readers may then begin the process of examining the aspects of trauma which lie behind the faith narrative.

Katniss and the Problem of Memory

Exploring the emphasis on conceptions of faith in the narratives of Holocaust survivors, via their reading of the *Mockingjay* Epilogue, may then lead young readers (most specifically young Jewish readers) to pose the central question of how a survivor's memory is complicated by his/her trauma. *The Hunger Games* trilogy potentially provides access to this question. What is most interesting about the trilogy is the way that the narrative is presented primarily in the present tense. Yet *Mockingjay*'s Epilogue suggests that this narrative is, in fact, comprised of a record of Katniss's past memories. A unique interpretation young readers may choose to adopt, in this respect, is that the narrator throughout the trilogy is not, in fact, the teenage Katniss. Rather, it is the adult Katniss who chooses to retell her narrative by allowing herself to, essentially, experience the events of the past as if they were occurring in the present moment. The motivation for this could be that Katniss is, perhaps, aware that the only way in which to effectively produce a narrative memory for her children is to reconnect with her traumatic memory where the most crucial elements of this narrative exist. Subsequently, observing her past as if it is her present provides her with a medium through which to access these memories which have escaped her.

It is, ultimately, in *Mockingjay* where Katniss's memory of events is at its most faulty, particularly in the scene in which she is set on fire while battling with the citizens of the Capitol. In this scene, Katniss questions whether what is happening to her is "real or not real?" (348) before descending into a utopian-like fantasy, mirroring the way she presents her past memories of her father, as she imagines both herself and her deceased friends and family members as "birds in the open sky" (348). Within this fantasy, Katniss avoids the experience of watching Prim die in reality by envisioning her as a "small white bird tinged in pink" who attempts to "keep [her] afloat" (349). The bird, however, has to let go of Katniss and fly away with the other birds to avoid capture by Katniss's enemies who, in this fantasy, become "horrible scaled things that tear [her] salty flesh with needle teeth" (349).

Symbolically, of course, this memory represents Katniss's return to the hellish reality of earth and Prim's flight to heaven. On one hand, by concealing the realities of this incident, through this fantasy, Katniss is possibly protecting both us (and, perhaps, her children) from learning of the true magnitude of events that leave her "a badly burned girl with no wings. With no fire. And no sister" (350). On the other, however, the trauma of this event may be too severe for her to recognize through memory. From this perspective, it is particularly convenient that, via her memory, Katniss constructs a fantastical image that prevents her from engaging with this trauma.

In identifying these various instances where Katniss's memory fails her, young readers can then move onto the second layer of their narrative exercise. In this case, their task as "listeners"/readers could be to attempt to fill in her memory gaps, perhaps through a particular focus on the above mentioned scene in *Mockingjay* where the realities of the incident in question are at their most unclear and obscure. In deciphering this narrative, these readers may begin to pose questions in relation to, firstly, Katniss's method of using an allegorical fantasy to represent her trauma and, secondly, how they themselves would choose to remember this trauma and, by extension, represent it through words. Would they, for example, feel confident remembering and expressing it in a precise or accurate form? Or would they, like Katniss, prefer to have this memory distorted and buried? Attached to this could be the question of what kind of memory they would want this trauma replaced with, and how they would want this replacement memory to be represented through thought and language. A further issue to address would be if these readers' chosen memories can, like Katniss's memory, be symbolically linked to and, therefore, representative of the trauma they have undergone.

Through addressing these concerns, these readers could then proceed to consider and contextualize them in relation to a Holocaust survivor's narrative. In this case, they could focus on detecting where the memory gaps in this narrative are and, subsequently, how both Katniss's and then their own methods of handling and covering these gaps reflect on the ways in which Holocaust survivors choose to do so. Young Jewish readers may choose to focus specifically on the use of birds in Katniss's replacement memory as a symbol of faith, which they can link to symbols of their religious faith. The Star of David, for instance, acts a symbol of the unity between the Jewish people, in the same way as the united formation of the birds act as a united symbol of "the ones [she] loved" (348). Therefore, they could perceive the use of this image in both the Holocaust survivor's narrative, and, perhaps, their own narration of Katniss's trauma, as a potential mechanism through which to disguise and suppress the memory gaps.

In this case, considering how Katniss's fantasy begins as a utopian vision but then transforms into a devastating nightmare highlights for them both the stability and instability of relying on these faith symbols to define the replacement memory. The irony for Katniss is that even though the image of peaceful, flying birds in this memory does, indeed, represent a symbol of hope and freedom for her, it also symbolizes an unobtainable way of being, both in her present and in her future. This is because the impact of her trauma implies that her efforts to access elements of faith in this memory will forever be intercepted by the "horrible scaly things" (349). Even if the true reality of these monsters remains in Katniss's (to return to Caruth's Freudian reference) unconscious thoughts, dreams and flashbacks, they are, in fact, instrumental in shaping and defining her conscious faith narrative.

Keeping this analysis in mind, young Jewish readers may consider, for example, how their and, more significantly, the Holocaust survivor's image of the Star of David as a faith symbol is, in fact, shaped and informed by the significance this symbol adopted during the Holocaust and the devastating reality that it set in motion. This form is namely that of the yellow star which, when worn by the Jewish people, acted as a symbol of Nazi control and their oppression. Therefore, if these readers choose to read Katniss's suppression of the reality of the scaled monsters, in relation to what may be their and then the Holocaust survivor's own suppression of the yellow star image in the construction of their respective narratives, they may gain a vital entry point through which to begin considering and assessing how this suppressed association and its reality underlies the way in which the Holocaust survivor constructs his/her faith narrative.

The Continuity of Trauma

One of the central lessons that young readers should take away from their reading of *The Hunger Games* trilogy in the context of a trauma narrative or, more specifically, a Holocaust trauma narrative, is that the act of dealing and reconciling with trauma is an ongoing one which, in the long term, may never have a clear resolution. The trilogy clarifies this point in two ways. Firstly, Katniss's inability to retrieve her lost memories and, more overtly, the fact that we are not informed whether or not she is ever able to turn her traumatic memory into a narrative memory for her children, suggest the possibility that her efforts will be continuous, difficult, and potentially unsuccessful. The present-tense narration, in itself, indicates this in that Katniss's inability to shift to past-tense in the Epilogue, as she fully assumes the role of her adult self, implies that she may never be able to psychologically ground her narrative in the past and, in doing so, may never be able to disassociate from the psychology of her teenage self. Secondly, the Epilogue comes to an abrupt end as Katniss refers to her work of listing good acts as a tiresome game, but then cautions that "there are worse games to play" (390). The manner in which we are impulsively pushed away from the narrative after these closing words could be read as Katniss's effort to push us away in order to return to the solitude of her traumatic memory, where she can protect herself from dealing with the realities of this narrative which she so desperately wants to avoid.

If young readers closely consider this interpretation, they may address two concerns in relation to their function as "listeners" of Katniss's trauma. First, they can assess whether their own efforts at formulating Katniss's narrative into words have successfully grappled with the complex questions on the nature of faith and memory, as they have arisen in their reading of the trilogy. Secondly, if they do believe they have been successful at this effort, they could consider what narrative choices they have made, with regards to these questions, that have made their articulation of Katniss's trauma effective. Conversely, if they do not believe they have been successful, they could question how the complex intersection between faith and memory may have an impact on their difficulty in putting Katniss's trauma into words.

This could lead to a question of whether they believe that they could ever find an appropriate and effective means through which to turn a traumatic memory into a narrative memory, or if they believe this process to be ongoing and possibly irresolvable. In posing this question, they may return their attention to the Holocaust survivor's narrative, specifically focusing on the manner in which it concludes. In examining this conclusion, they may consider whether it attempts to reach a point of catharsis. If so, they could explore whether this catharsis appears stable and authentic, or if the survivor, in fact, makes a subtle attempt, like Katniss, to push us away so he/she can return to the realm of his/her traumatic memory, forever leaving a crucial gap in the narrative. This, I think, may potentially open up young Jewish readers to explore the notion of post–Holocaust trauma as an ongoing process, not only in relation to their understanding of a Holocaust survivor's narrative, but also, potentially, in connection with how this process affects their own efforts to define their narratives as the post–Holocaust generation.

Introducing The Hunger Games *Into Holocaust Youth Literature Scholarship*

Throughout this essay, I have claimed that although *The Hunger Games* trilogy is not intentionally written as youth Holocaust literature, it possesses particular literary parallels that may easily acquaint it with this genre. The most obvious of these parallels is evident in the settings used and narrative style employed throughout the trilogy. However, on a more complex level, these parallels are particularly evident in the way in which the trilogy explores issues of post-war trauma, which can be linked back to the complexities of post–Holocaust trauma. Reading the trilogy as post–Holocaust trauma literature is particularly useful for young Jewish readers who are exposed to the subject of post–Holocaust trauma in scarce detail, both in their schooling and through the literature they read. The resistance towards exposing youths to this subject, on a general level, is that trauma, in itself, questions the authenticity of a narrative, complicating the notion that these youths are meant to perceive the narratives of Holocaust survivors as accurate reflections on the events of the Holocaust. For Jewish youths, learning about this subject is further complicated by the fact that they may have familial connections to the

Holocaust, as well as that the fact that it is inherently and crucially linked to the history of their faith.

Because *The Hunger Games* trilogy can be linked to Holocaust narratives, purely on an allegorical level, undergoing a reading of the trilogy as Holocaust literature does not require these youths to directly address the familial, historical, and religious anxieties they are ordinarily made to grapple with, both in their classroom teachings and in the literature they read. Therefore, the trilogy provides a unique alternative space through which to begin engaging these youths in a discussion of post–Holocaust trauma. The process through which this engagement can occur, I have suggested, involves young Jewish readers engaging with the trauma of the listener/reader as they become involved in an interactive relationship between the young Jewish reader, Katniss's narrative and, by extension, the narrative of the Holocaust survivor. Within this process, these readers, through a close-reading of how issues of trauma are explored in Katniss's narrative, could be given an opportunity to articulate her trauma in their own words. Through engaging with the trilogy in this way, they open themselves up to exploring questions on two particular aspects of trauma narratives. The first of these is how the notion of faith is used in constructing a trauma narrative and whether this faith can be considered authentic within this context. The second concerns the ways in which traumatic memory affects the construction of this narrative, particularly in relation to the issue of faith.

Considering trauma narratives in relation to these concerns of faith and memory, as well as involving the reader in the experience of narrating trauma, provides ideal scaffolding for beginning to consider and analyze how conflicts surrounding faith and memory are evident in the trauma narratives of Holocaust survivors. By opening up young Jewish readers to experiencing the complexities of faith and memory within Holocaust survivors' narratives from a complex and multi-faceted perspective, *The Hunger Games* trilogy not only enriches their understanding of post–Holocaust trauma, but also, through the interactive process it facilitates, makes these issues of trauma accessible to them on a personal level, emphasizing the importance of post–Holocaust trauma in the construction of our present day selfhoods. In doing this, the trilogy provides a unique platform from which young Jewish readers can begin to learn about the Holocaust, beyond its historical and faith-based contexts.

Notes

1. Of these few web resources, the one that is most specifically focused on the connection between *The Hunger Games* and the Holocaust is a website called "*Hunger Games* vs. the Holocaust." The site focuses on the first novel in the trilogy, outlining the symbolic similarities and differences between its narrative and the events of the Holocaust for young learners. In one section, Alice Chudnovsky, the educator who compiled the website, makes an intriguing

observation as she suggests that District 12 represents what the world would have been like, had Hitler's Final Solution succeeded.

2. Caruth specifically references Freud's final work, *Moses and Monotheism*. In this text, Freud used the example of a child's memory to explain, what he termed, "the return of the repressed" (124). He claims that the memories of a child at two years old remain misunderstood, and as he gets older, they "need never be remembered by [him], except in dreams" (Freud 124). However, Freud continues, at a later stage in life, the memories "will [inevitably] break into [his] life with obsessional impulses, [they] will govern [his] actions" (124).

3. The name of this school, as represented in the article, is a pseudonym, in order to protect the school and the participants in the study.

4. A yeshivah, in this context, is an institution primarily dedicated to the study of Jewish biblical texts.

5. It is worth noting that most of the literature available on the subject of youth Holocaust literature, does not deal specifically with the readerly concerns of Jewish readers. It focuses more on the perceptions of readers from non-denominational backgrounds.

6. Illana Abramovitch notes that *Anne Frank: The Diary of a Young Girl* has been recognized as required reading in American schools since 1960. A 1996 survey on the Anne Frank Museum website, she states, indicated that the diary was being studied in fifty percent of American schools.

7. The term "utopia" itself is complex and often difficult to define. In this context, it is best to refer to Nell Eurich's definition of utopia as "man's dream of a better world" (vii). As J.C. Davis elaborates, this pursuit for the "betterness" in question, arises from "existing circumstances" (13). It is created through either an escapist fantasy which provides a mental distraction from an undesirable reality, or (as Davis puts it) "a blueprint for action, providing a model of what should replace the existing state" (13). Utopia may be further conceptualized through "a satiric reflection of what exists" (Davis 13).

8. As a further point of comparison, it is worth noting that Anne too had a particularly close relationship with her father (whom she affectionately referred to as Pim) and a distinctly antagonistic relationship with her mother.

Works Cited

Abramovitch, Ilana. "Teaching Anne Frank in the United States." *Anne Frank Unbound: Media, Imagination, Memory*. Eds. Barbra Kirshenblatt-Gimblett and Jeffrey Shandler. Bloomington: Indiana University Press, 2012. 160–177. Print.

Baccolini, Raffaella, and Tom Moylan. *Dark Horizons: Science Fiction and the Dystopian Imagination*. New York: Routledge, 2003. Print.

Boyne, John. *The Boy in the Striped Pyjamas*. Oxford: David Fickling Books, 2006. Print.

Caruth, Cathy. "Introduction." *Trauma: Explorations in Memory*. Ed. Cathy Caruth. Baltimore: Johns Hopkins University Press, 1995. 3–12. Print.

Chiarello, Barbara. "The Utopian Space of a Nightmare: The Diary of Anne Frank." *Literature of the Holocaust*. Ed. Harold Bloom. Broomall: Chelsea House Publishers, 2004. 153–170. Print.

Chudnovsky, Anne. *Hunger Games vs. Holocaust*. Feb 2012. Web. 4 February 2013.

Collins, Suzanne. *Catching Fire*. New York: Scholastic, 2009. Print.

_____. "A Conversation: Questions & Answers." Scholastic. n.d. Web. 30 April 2013.

_____. *The Hunger Games*. New York: Scholastic, 2008. Print.

_____. *Mockingjay*. New York: Scholastic, 2010. Print.

Davis, J.C. *Utopia and the Ideal Society: A Study of English Utopian Writing 1516–1700*. Cambridge: Cambridge University Press, 1981. Print.

Eurich, Nell. *Science in Utopia: A Mighty Design.* Cambridge: Harvard University Press, 1967. Print.
Feldman, Shoshana, and Dori Laub. *Testimony: Crisis of Witnessing in Literature, Psychoanalysis and History.* New York: Routledge, 1992. Print.
Frank, Anne. *Anne Frank: The Diary of a Young Girl.* 1947. London: Puffin, 1995. Print.
Freud, Sigmund. *Moses and Monotheism.* 1939. Trans. Katherine Jones. New York: Vintage, 1967. Print.
Kaplan, Carter. "The Advent of Literary Dystopia." *Extrapolation* 40.3 (1999): 200–212. *ProQuest.* Web. 4 February 2013.
Kertzer, Adrienne. "'Do You Know What "Auschwitz" Means?': Children's Literature and the Holocaust." *The Lion and the Unicorn* 23.2 (1999): 238–256. *ProQuest.* Web. 7 December 2012.
Kimmel, Eric. "Confronting the Ovens: The Holocaust and Juvenile Fiction." *Horn Book Magazines* 53.1 (1977): 84–91. Print.
Kokkola, Lydia. *Representing the Holocaust in Children's Literature.* New York: Routledge, 2003. Print.
Laub, Dori. "Truth and Testimony: The Process and the Struggle." *Trauma: Explorations in Memory.* Ed. Cathy Caruth. Baltimore: Johns Hopkins University Press, 1995. 61–76. Print.
Rosenfeld, A.H. "The Problematics of Holocaust Literature." *Literature of the Holocaust.* Ed. Harold Bloom. Broomall: Chelsea House, 2004. 21–48. Print.
Roskies, David G., and Naomi Diamant. *Holocaust Literature: A History and Guide.* Brandeis: Brandeis University Press, 2012. Print.
Russell, David L. "Reading the Shards and Fragments: Holocaust Literature for Young Readers." *The Lion and the Unicorn* 21.2 (1997): 267–280. *ProQuest Central.* Web. 10 August 2012.
Schweber, Simone. "'Here There Is No Why': Holocaust Education at Lubavitch Girls' Yeshivah." *Jewish Social Studies* 14.2 (2008): 156–185. *JSTOR.* Web. 21 January 2013.
Short, Geoffrey, and Carole Ann Reed. *Issues in Holocaust Education.* Aldershot: Ashgate, 2004. Print.
Tal, Eva. "How Much Should We Tell the Children?: Representing Death and Suffering in Children's Literature About the Holocaust." *The Holocaust Martyrs' and Heroes' Remembrance Authority*, n.d. Web. 21 January 2013.
Van Der Kolk, Bessel A., and Van Der Hart, Onno. "The Intrusive Past: The Flexibility of Memory and the Engraving of Trauma." *Trauma: Explorations in Memory.* Ed. Cathy Caruth. Baltimore: Johns Hopkins University Press, 1995. 158–182. Print.

Part IV
Popular Responses in Actual Spaces

"I have a kind of power I never knew I possessed"
Transformative Motherhood and Maternal Influence

Katie Arosteguy

> "If a mother had deserted us ... the child in us, the small female who grew up in a male-controlled world, still feels, at moments, wildly unmothered. When we can confront and unravel this paradox, this contradiction, face to the utmost in ourselves the groping passion of that little girl lost, we can begin to transmute it."
> —Adrienne Rich, *Of Woman Born*

For most readers and fans, Katniss Everdeen brings to mind a spirited, smart young woman whose skill, bravery, and rebellious nature propel her into a leadership role in the fight against the Capitol in Suzanne Collins's dystopian *The Hunger Games* trilogy. Katniss is rarely, if ever, conceived as a mother. However, the series is framed by the overarching meta-narrative of mothering, as a constant thought on Katniss's mind in the first novel, an imaginary event that undergoes hyper-surveillance in the second novel, and a real-life event some "five, ten, fifteen years" (*MJ* 389) later in the third novel. In an effort to contribute to the recent critical maternal research aimed at discovering how "mothering and being a mother are political, personal, and creative" (Podnieks and O'Reilly 10) acts, I examine here the complex portrayal of mothers and motherhood in the trilogy. I read the trilogy as a "matrilineal narrative"—a story that, according to Tess Cosslett, "shows how the identity of a central character is crucially formed by female ancestors" (7–8). Katniss's development, survival, and journey to motherhood depend on her reconciliation with her mother—a process fraught with betrayal, negotiation, and resistance. Through the character of Katniss, Collins challenges traditional conceptions of motherhood and confronts a multi-faceted maternal identity.

Mothers have rarely been subjects in their own right throughout history; instead, their identities and meaning have been defined by others in relation to their socially-constructed roles as wives and mothers. Since the 1990s, motherhood studies as an academic discipline has concerned itself with recovering and documenting the vast and meaningful maternal literary traditions that have developed despite this silencing. In their groundbreaking 2010 work, *Textual Mothers/Maternal Texts: Motherhood in Contemporary Women's Literature,* Elizabeth Podnieks and Andrea O'Reilly contend that "[n]ot only has the mother been lost to the broader traditions of literary history that have privileged narratives by and about male figures, but also she has been lost within the daughter-centric literatures that do depict the mother" (12). *The Hunger Games* opens up ways to think about maternal absence, ambivalence, and agency that depart from "age-old dichotomies" that narrowly define the good mother as "selfless, sacrificial, and domestic" and the bad mother as "selfish for seeking autonomy beyond her children" (Podnieks and O'Reilly 4). Characters who mother and act as mothers, a process known as "othermothering," are significant in this trilogy because their acts broaden societal discourse on what motherhood is and who can be a mother.[1]

Because motherhood has been co-opted by other, more dominant, voices and subjects through time, contemporary maternal discourse struggles to grapple with the complexities that mothers face. While genres that allow for women to express authentic accounts of motherhood have exploded in the last couple of decades (i.e. parenting blogs, mothering advice literature, "mommy lit," etc.), a "new momism" ideology has gripped the national consciousness and, while masquerading as a critique of patriarchal motherhood, convinces modern mothers that they have natural capacities and instincts to nurture children, that they must be their children's primary caregiver, and that mothering should be their full-time job (O'Reilly 206). The "quality time" mothers are expected to spend with their children has reached unattainable new heights as mothers who "choose" to do other things with their time (i.e. work) are often criticized, and the important role of husbands/fathers in childrearing is largely ignored. The mother is also expected to be the moral compass in her child's life.

As such, topics that *The Hunger Games* deals with—children killing other children perhaps being the best example—prove to be problematic and uncomfortable in discussions where real world modern mothers are involved. Researching mothers' reactions to *The Hunger Games,* however, reveals a dangerous cocktail of pent-up feelings of tension, guilt, and blame that modern day mothers carry with them as a result of continued narrow definitions of motherhood. The trilogy ultimately opens up a space for mothers to express these emotions and work through the haunting realization that we will have to explain the content of the novels to our children and, to effectively do so, we must talk about motherhood—in all of its shades.

A Guilty Pleasure for Mother Readers?

I have to admit that I probably would have never read *The Hunger Games* if a woman in our book club did not pick it one month for our upcoming discussion. I am glad I read it, however, because I was pleasantly surprised when this *New York Times* best-selling, YA trilogy triggered interesting and complicated thoughts about motherhood for me. What hooked me from the beginning of this reading experience was the strong reaction some mothers in my book club (and many online) had against the subject matter of the novel. Some said they could not read it because, being mothers, they could not stand the thought of children killing children. This was curious to me. Was I a cold-hearted, unfeeling mother who enjoyed reading about the cruel slaughtering of children?

In my research the next day, I found several blog posts, news articles, and reviews written by mothers that confirmed this feeling of maternal discontent expressed by women in my book club. Most ran something like the following from Jane Roper's blog titled "How Can a Mother Love *The Hunger Games*?":

> I mean, ever since I became a mother, I can't get within ten feet of a movie wherein a child or teenager dies. There have been times when I've been in tears after hearing about a bombing or natural disaster or *anything* that has killed kids. Losing one of my children, at whatever age, is my worst fear, hands down [Roper "How Can a Mother Love *The Hunger Games*?].

Palo Alto Software CEO and mother of three, Sabrina Parsons, titled her Forbes blog, "How Being a Mom Ruined *Hunger Games* For Me." In it, she describes her experience of viewing the movie as "horrific" and reports having nightmares afterward where her children were sent to the Games. She writes, "I [woke] up crying and need[ed] to go check on my kids and give them kisses" (Parsons). British mother Shona Sibary, in her review titled "Why I Feel I'm a Bad Mother for Taking My Girls to *The Hunger Games*," reveals that "every maternal nerve in my body was telling me to turn around and take my daughters home. I mean, what mother in her right mind voluntarily takes two impressionable, sensitive young girls to a film ... involving children hacking each other to death in cold blood?" (Sibary) Of course, to be fair, positive reviews that pointed out the novel's ability to raise questions of class, nation, gender, media, and violence in American culture—all things you would want to talk about with your children at some point—balanced these out. But the pangs of guilt many women felt made me think about what *The Hunger Games* has to do with mothers and mothering. Why were mothers blaming themselves for the potential negative consequences of exposing their kids to this subject matter? What was underlying this intense fear? I had a sneaking suspicion that no father who had read the trilogy or saw the movie was being kept up at night with the same fears.

Even more interesting were the numerous accounts I found of mothers who admitted they were *secretly* enjoying the novels. A mother on the babble.com site confesses, in a comment response to Roper's blog, that "I read the whole trilogy in three days! I could NOT put it down. Every now and then I'd think, 'WHY isn't this bothering me more?' But then I'd stop asking because the question was interfering with my reading" (Hanh-Burkett, Blog Comment). A woman named Christi jokingly writes:

> I loved them so much that my own children lived their own Hunger Games for the days it took me to read them and do literally nothing else. I would randomly throw some Cheerios or graham crackers down on the floor, much like a little silver parachute floating to the ground. Luckily, nobody died during my version of the games. May the odds be ever in your favor, kids [Christi, blog comment].

While clearly an exaggeration, there is something telling in this humorous confession. According to dominant maternal rhetoric in the blogosphere, a mother is good if she is bothered by the content of *The Hunger Games*. If she likes it or, worse yet, willingly exposes her children to it, she is a bad mother. When mothers do like the trilogy, they qualify their enjoyment as aberrant and deviant, suggesting that this is the only safe way to express maternal dissent.

Family historian Stephanie Coontz explores maternal blame in her discussion of post–World War II America and the construction of the nuclear family. She argues that "[a]long with the refrain that smothering homemakers created homosexuality, narcissism, and neurosis—was the drumbeat of claims from politicians, psychiatrists, social workers, and judges that working mothers were the cause of all other childhood ills, including delinquency, insanity, and all forms of criminality" (68). Coontz locates the source of this maternal blame in the popular media and in societal structures that are often thought of as neutral spaces. The shameful feelings of guilt these mothers feel for engaging in pleasureful acts of reading indicate complicity with patriarchal motherhood, an institution that makes mothers believe they are fully responsible for their children's moral development.

The very resistance to reading *The Hunger Games* as a mother and the guilt-ridden anxiety exhibited by so many women who do read the series convinced me of one thing: as a mother myself, *I had* to read *The Hunger*

Games. If a trilogy was having such a strong reaction from mothers, I wanted to see if the novels themselves offered any meaningful discussion of maternal identity. Katniss's reality by the end of the trilogy is that she will have to be exactly the mom that these mom-bloggers abhor. The Epilogue to *Mockingjay* ends with Katniss in deep contemplation about how she will explain the Games to her children, how she will make them understand. In ending the trilogy this way, Collins reimagines the role of the mother and suggests that it is exactly our ability to admit and explain evil, violence, and oppression to our children—not just the kinds that appear in *The Hunger Games* but the kinds our children witness every day—that makes us mothers. While somewhat taboo in circles of modern mothers, the novel series is deeply concerned with a search for the maternal, a quest to discover what it means to mother in difficult times where the old rules cannot and do not apply.

Reimagining the Mother-Daughter Relationship

In the narrative conventions of young adult literature, parental relationships wherein the adolescent protagonist finds that s/he must break away from an overbearing, absent, or otherwise "bad" parent (often the mother) are common conflicts. Hillary Crew, in the first-ever book length study of mother-daughter bonds in YA literature, points out that mothers in these novels have mostly served as obstacles the hero/ine must overcome to achieve autonomy. According to Crew, the daughter needs to "fracture her identity with her mother" to differentiate herself and explore her growing maturity (65). What is more, mothers are often confined to strict binaries of good or bad depending on the extent to which they prohibit the "daughter's progress toward being independent and morally and socially responsible" (86). Mickey Pearlman further contends that "missing mothers" are often depicted as "dependent and confused" or "repressed, depressed, or obsessed" in much writing by contemporary women authors (2). A mother's mothering, or failure to mother, often becomes a key focus in mother/daughter texts, and the conflict that ensues serves to center the story (103).

While Katniss's story does echo that of the daughter breaking away from the mother to some extent, *The Hunger Games* departs in interesting ways from both the traditional discourse of maternal absence and the depiction of the mother as angry, controlling, or invasive. Katniss's mother is far from absent; rather, she is very much present, and it is this present-ness that Katniss must learn to navigate. There is a rich and complicated storyline that runs through the trilogy concerning Katniss's relationship with her mother. If we agree with Adrienne Rich that "the cathexis between mother and daughter—

essential, distorted, misused—is the great unwritten story" (225) then we must consider how Collins's treatment of the mother/daughter bond is part of a "larger discourse on mother-daughter relationships and on mothering" (Crew 8).

Even though Katniss attempts to reject and cast aside her mother in *The Hunger Games*, Collins resists the urge to follow typical YA narrative conventions of the mother-daughter relationship. Instead, Katniss needs and desires her mother's knowledge in *Catching Fire* and *Mockingjay* as she realizes her own weaknesses. In this way, Collins insists on making Katniss's mother present. Katniss's quest to understand her mother informs and guides her decisions in the Games and in her life afterwards. At the beginning of *The Hunger Games*, Katniss acknowledges that her mother was supposed to be "very beautiful once" (3). Clearly, there are pieces of her mother's life that Katniss is not privy to or simply cannot understand, and this seems to frustrate her, leading to her decision to reject her mother. However, as she desperately attempts to uncover her mother's knowledge during the Games, the reader sees that Katniss's identity (as a young woman and, increasingly, as a mother) is bound up in discovering who her mother is. Casting her mother aside, Collins seems to suggest, is not an option for this modern-day heroine who ultimately must reconcile with her mother in order to save herself and those around her from the perils of the Capitol.

In *Stories from the Motherline*, Naomi Lowinsky defines this quest as a search for the "motherline," "a looking backward to th[e] mother" as a way of "looking forward to th[e] daughter" (4). She describes this process as "a cord, a thread, as the yarn emerging from the fingers of a woman at the spinning wheel...Each thread is tied to others to create a complex, richly textured cloth connecting the past to the future" (12). While Katniss's father teaches her how to hunt and bargain in the Hob—skills that ultimately allow Katniss to keep her mother and sister alive following her father's death—it is her mother's "dead eyes" that haunt her because she cannot, at the time, understand them (28). From the beginning of the novel, her mother's mental absence during a time of crisis, her very inability to mother, angers Katniss. These angry thoughts become doubtful ruminations about her own maternal future. She repeats several times throughout *The Hunger Games*: "I never want to have kids" (9). Katniss's disinterest in children seems in part to stem from a fear of exposing them to the horror of the lottery and the Games, but there seems to be a deeper reason here, one that is rooted in her mother. She is unable to imagine an effective maternal role for herself because she has no example. The lottery, the Games, hunger—all are made worse by the fact that she has no active parent or provider. She is doing the work of both the parent and child. Her inability to understand her mother's actions or to access maternal understanding prevents her from being able to conceive of herself as a mother.

From the beginning, Katniss has a difficult time connecting to her mother and seeing herself as her mother's daughter. She draws attention to how her physical attributes differ from Prim's and her mother's. She notes that Prim and her mother have light hair and blue eyes, but she does not (*THG* 8). She also acknowledges that one time when an unconscious boy was brought to her mother's kitchen table and she saw the wound, she ran off in fear (178). Prim, conversely, "who is scared of her own shadow," stayed and helped (179). Katniss believes that Prim has inherited her mother's healing abilities while she has not. When she is faced with the challenge of healing her burned leg in the Games and, later, her tracker jacker stings, she admits that she cannot remember which herbs would help heal her (179 and 198). She realizes that her life depends on her ability to retrieve the information her mother possesses that, up until this point, she seems to have actively rejected in an effort to be more like her father. She needs to understand her mother and access her knowledge in order to live and make sense of the world around her.

One tangible item exists that allows Katniss to access her "motherline" and engage in the process of "looping." Lowinsky defines looping as "an associative process by which we pass through our own experience to understand that of another" (21–22). Because Katniss seems to partly believe that she has been denied a certain biology that would allow her to access her mother's knowledge and because the reader senses that she has in part actively refused this information, the existence of something physical that allows her to locate her mother is critical to her development as a woman and a mother. The plant book, started by her mother's family and added to by her father, outlines the medicinal uses of plants that Katniss strives to remember in the Games. When Katniss served as her mother and sister's caretaker, this book saved their lives several times because it helped Katniss to identify potentially lethal plants when she foraged for food or for supplies for her mother. Her first use of the plant book was to keep her immediate family alive. In the Arena, she is faced with the challenge of remembering and applying formulas to save someone else. She recognizes that her mother's knowledge can save Peeta and herself and, hence, aid in her rebellion against the Capitol. Looping from herself to her mother and back to herself through this matrilineal artifact allows Katniss to know and understand her mother.

When she is faced with the task of saving Peeta and healing his infected injury on his thigh toward the end of *The Hunger Games*, Katniss realizes she must attend to "what I have neither the skill nor the courage to face" (256). At one point, she despairs: "I'm no good at this. I'm not my mother" because she cannot recall the images and explanations from the book (257). However, she "tr[ies] to capture the calm demeanor" her mother exhibited during difficult cases in an effort to heal Peeta (*THG* 256). This is not an easy task for her, and indecision and uncertainty mount. Katniss validates her mother's experience in this moment, a monumental event that is accompanied by Katniss's further revelation that it was her mother's unsurpassable love for her father that precipitated her mental breakdown. Up until this point, Katniss has seen her mother as outside of herself, as unreachable, and as unnecessary. In one of the few passages where Katniss reflects on her own bravery, performing the mother becomes an act of valor. Whereas in most YA literature the daughter breaks away from an absent, overbearing, or crazed mother, Collins suggests that recognizing the maternal and performing mothering afford one the most growth. In this moment, Katniss realizes that she needs her mother in order to heal her best friend. It is the first time she demonstrates an understanding (and forgiveness) of her mother's ambivalence and equates her own travails with her mother's. Prior to this point, she saw herself as separate from her mother, and here they become one.

At the end of *Mockingjay* when Katniss and Peeta begin their married life together back in District 12, Katniss decides to create a book that she will model after her "family's plant book" (387). This new book will contain pictures and information about all of the people "it would be a crime to forget" (387). The plant book, like this new book, serves as a place to "recor[d] those things you cannot trust to memory," but which must ultimately be remembered (*MJ* 387). The plant book originated with her mother and father and contains the secret to her survival, much as the new book will infuse her children with the wealth of lived history they will need so they can "understand in a way that will make them braver" (390). While her mother cannot return to District 12 because of the possibility of another mental breakdown, Collins notes that she starts a hospital in District 4 and that Katniss will be in touch with her. Because this new family book is modeled on the one her parents started and because it records the memories and thoughts Katniss needs to "come back to life," the book can be read in part as an homage to Katniss's mother (387).

Maternity here is complexly defined and extends beyond one woman's knowledge or experience. The small memories, noted "strange bits of happiness," sketches, pictures, scents, etc. broaden our understanding of motherhood to be not just a person, but a way of life, an enriched culture, and a hopeful future. The book, in addition to fueling her mental recovery, will be Katniss's guide to help her in her new role as mother since her own mother will not be physically present. When she considers how her children will fare and how she will raise them, she concludes: "Peeta says it will be okay. We have each other. And the book" (*MJ* 390). As Sheila Hughes points out: "[t]he original mother's absence remains as powerful as any physical or spiritual presence," and it is Katniss's desire to make her mother present, albeit through a book, that demonstrates the versatility and importance of maternity—which "is always open for disintegration, contestation, remaking" (79 and 80).

Collins complicates the mother/daughter relationship by giving the mother a much more significant role than she is afforded in other YA literature. Real-world mothers seem to get caught up in the action of the series (and movie) and fail to read between the lines for what Collins is saying about maternal realities. Rather than feeling guilt for exposing one's kids to *The Hunger Games*, Collins suggests we use the texts to open up understandings of what it means to mother and what a critical role mothering has in society. While the action of the Games is disconcerting for anyone to think about, *The Hunger Games* is broadening societal discourse surrounding motherhood if one is willing to listen. In opening up a literary space to explore other, more complicated, ways of viewing the mother/daughter relationship, *The Hunger Games* challenges those mothers most concerned with epidemics of violence and dystopic futures that threaten traditional relationships.

Othermothers Empowering Mothering

In addition to complicating the relationship between Katniss and her mother, Collins explores the meaning and function of motherhood/mothering outside of biological motherhood in this transformative, dystopian space. These acts of mothering, known in motherhood studies as "othermothering," enrich the maternal narrative and further work to unmask motherhood. Situating her novels in a dystopian future allows Collins to create a more egalitarian society that can explore (at least in a literary space) alternate forms of mothering. Even though the president, head Gamemaker, Games host, and head Peacekeepers are male, the Games do not discriminate based on gender and set the stage for a society to exist outside the paradigm of patriarchy. With Katniss as the story's heroine, her mother as a harbor of knowledge, and her sister as the ultimate sacrifice for the revolution, Collins imagines a society where women factor in as critically important agents. This society makes possible a "lived reality" of mothering, defined by motherhood scholars as an empowering discourse that

> [s]eeks to challenge the dominant ideology of motherhood and change the various ways that ... patriarchal motherhood is limiting or oppressive to women ... the central aim of [which] is to confer to mothers the agency, authority, authenticity, and autonomy denied to them in patriarchal motherhood [Podnieks and O'Reilly 18].

Podnieks and O'Reilly point out that, in patriarchy, examples of maternal agency—"mode[s] of mothering that mitigate[e] the many ways that patriarchal motherhood ... regulates and restrains mothers"—are rare and difficult to find and document (17). In *The Hunger Games*, however, Katniss, through acts of "othermothering" with Prim, Peeta, and Rue, reimagines maternal roles.

While the third novel ends with Katniss becoming a biological mother, she spends most of her time in the role of "othermother" for various characters, among them Prim, Peeta, and Rue. While most YA literature deals with the theme of losing mothers, matrilineal narratives are more concerned with the concept of finding mothers. Podnieks and O'Reilly note that, in these texts, "Mothers find themselves as mothers, as well, engaging in dialogue with multiple facets of their own identities as they may or may not come to terms with their maternal roles, desires, and needs" (20). Through her various acts of mothering, Katniss expands the definition of mother and allows for multiple and varied maternal voices to speak. In her role as "othermother," she grapples with the realities, expectations, and triumphs of mothering—all of which seem to reach outside the constraints of patriarchal culture and culminate in both personal and political empowerment and activism.

Because of her mother's mental absence when her father died, Katniss takes on the role of mother to her sister, Prim. Prim usually sleeps beside her at night, and when Gale proposes his ingenious plan at the beginning of *The Hunger Games* to escape District 12, his one hesitation is that they (he and Katniss) could make it "if [they] didn't have so many kids" (9). Katniss's internal narration continues: "They're not our kids, of course. But they might as well be" (*THG* 9). All of Katniss's actions toward her sister are in an effort to protect and provide for her, qualities she finds lacking in her own mother. When she volunteers in place of her sister on reaping day in *The Hunger Games*, Katniss both saves and loses Prim. When the Games are over and she returns home, Katniss notes that reaping day, along with "the cruelty in the district, the parade of sick and wounded that she often treats by herself now if my mother's hands are too full—these things have aged her years" (*CF* 181). Katniss is disturbed by how quickly Prim has had to mature in her absence. While at the Games, Katniss displaces her motherly affection onto Rue, who reminds her of Prim. Referring to her as "this wispy child," "a simpleminded child," and "a baby animal," Katniss takes on a motherly role to Rue, declaring: "Rue has only me" as she holds her in the last moments before her death (*THG* 201, 204, 236, and 213).

Contenders in the Games are not supposed to form friendships, so Katniss's devotion to Rue and her courageous action to hold and sing to Rue before she dies evolves into political activism. As we later find out, her actions inspired an uprising in District 10 against the Capitol. Katniss associates singing to Rue with singing to Prim when she is sick. At one point, she even mixes up the reality of Rue with the absence of Prim. She thinks to herself: "If this is Prim's, I mean, Rue's last request, I have to at least try" (*THG* 234).

This thought conflates the two girls in Katniss's mind as people she must care for and foreshadows Prim's death in Book Three. Rue's District 11 sends Katniss a parachute to recognize her efforts and to demonstrate solidarity against the Capitol. Katniss knew she was responsible for Rue, and her death haunts Katniss through the end of the trilogy. Near the end of *Mockingjay*, when Katniss notices her sister among the Rebel medics who have come to help the children, her first instinct is to run after her and save her, much as she did on reaping day. This time, however, she does not make it. The relationships Katniss develops with Prim and Rue are genuine attempts to cultivate a maternal identity. While qualities such as being protective, caring, and nurturing might, in contemporary American society, seem stereotypically maternal, in *The Hunger Games*, Katniss's mothering acts are political choices, as society is slowly stripping away her ability to be cared for and to care for others.

Collins writes into her books a rich script of "othermothering" whereby Katniss is able to tease out and explore personal qualities of herself that she has not had the opportunity to explore through her relationship with her own mother. In this way, Katniss "finds" mothering outside of a patriarchal reality and discovers agency and authority through the political ramifications of her mothering. Her relationship with Rue acts as the catalyst for her mockingjay status of leader of the rebellion, and Prim's death is representative of a mother's greatest sacrifice. In this case, however, Prim was sacrificed for largely political reasons—that of the revolution. Collins's exploration of "othermothering" allows for multiple and layered understandings of mothering and adds to a reality of "lived mothering."

Ironically, the tension that real-world mothers exhibit in response to the main storyline of *The Hunger Games* is similar to the tension that Katniss experiences throughout the trilogy. She is terrified of being a mother because of the world her children will inhabit and she fears she will not successfully navigate the maternal role. But Katniss does not give up (like some of these mommy bloggers do); she does not reject the maternal role altogether. Instead, she makes carefully calculated decisions that show her ability to embrace the complex shades of maternity. The real-world mommy bloggers could take a lesson from Katniss and appreciate the multi-dimensionality she affords mothers. Choosing to mother, to expose one's children to content that explores our deepest societal fears, can also be a political act.

"Five, Ten, Fifteen Years" Later: Katniss as Mother

What starts out as a haunting premonition in *The Hunger Games* undergoes hyper-surveillance in *Catching Fire* and comes to fruition in *Mockingjay*.

Some "five, ten, fifteen years" later, Katniss becomes a mother (*MJ* 389). Her first experience at the Games, coupled with her inability to understand her mother, seem to solidify her opposition to mothering in *The Hunger Games*. In *Catching Fire*, as a result of her and Peeta's pretend relationship, and now pretend engagement, all of Panem believes her to be pregnant. At the age of seventeen, Katniss is encouraged to play to the cameras and the public and go along with the mock pregnancy. At one point, Peeta, known for his ability to perform for the crowds, puts a locket on Katniss's neck, places his hand on her stomach, says, "You're going to make a great mother, you know" (*CF* 353). The reader, as well as Peeta himself (we can infer), wonders at the sincerity behind this comment. What kind of mother would Katniss be? Immediately afterward, Katniss admits that if one of them could be a parent, "it should be Peeta" (*CF* 354).

Throughout the trilogy, the decision about whether or not to have children plagues Katniss. The decision has far greater implications, and carries much more weight, than we can imagine. Katniss's maternal ambivalence is rooted in her concern about bringing children into a world where the Games exist. As she states several times throughout the books, the Games do not discriminate. As Podnieks and O'Reilly point out, "motherhood itself is an ambivalent concept and identity" (16) and her fears about mothering seem to hinge on a fear about how one is supposed to mother in a world like this. However, her acquiescence to Peeta's desire to have kids demonstrates an acceptance of herself and her role in the Games. After all, creating the book is preparation for explaining the history of Panem and the Games to her children—the ultimate challenge she faces as a mother. Accepting the challenge to parent and explain the world to them demonstrates a desire "to resist, subvert, and change the discourses" that commonly define mothering (Podnieks and O'Reilly 18). Katniss makes this decision very consciously and purposefully. Determined to "make them braver," her final decision to have kids proves to be a political act that stands in the face of oppressive societal regimes (390).

Mothers and critics alike have to this point failed to critically interrogate *The Hunger Games* for its representation of motherhood and the important cultural and societal questions it raises about the complexities of mothering; therefore, I have attempted to perform such an analysis here. Katniss's development in the trilogy hinges on coming to an understanding of her own mother's ambivalence and an acknowledgement that mothering is a deeply personal, and sometimes political, act. Because the books break traditional YA literature representations of the mother-daughter bond in important and telling ways, the series has the potential to deepen conversation on the topic of mothering. Discussing the books with other real-world modern mothers can open up a space to explore the stifling effects of narrow definitions of motherhood that so easily get embedded in our minds. Instead of approaching the book with fear, guilt, or extreme pleasure, why not approach it as an opportunity to examine what we should be examining every day—what it means to mother, how that is defined, and what it might mean if it was taken away?

Note

1. While I only deal with Katniss as an "othermother" in this essay for sake of space, it would be interesting to analyze how other characters act as "othermothers"—in particular, Peeta and Haymitch.

Works Cited

Blasingame, James. "An Interview with Suzanne Collins." *Journal of Adolescent and Adult Literacy* 52.8: 2009. 726–727. Print.
Christi. Blog Comment. "How Can a Mother Love *The Hunger Games*?" Babble.com. 10 February 2012. Web. 13 September 2012.
Collins, Suzanne. *Catching Fire*. New York: Scholastic, 2009. Print.
_____. *The Hunger Games*. New York: Scholastic, 2008. Print.
_____. *Mockingjay*. New York: Scholastic, 2010. Print.
Coontz, Stephanie. *A Strange Stirring: The Feminine Mystique and American Women at the Dawn of the 1960s*. New York: Basic Books, 2011. Print.
Cosslett, Tess. "Feminism, Matrilinealism, and the 'House of Women' in Contemporary Women's Fiction." *Journal of Gender Studies* 5.1: 1996. 7–17. Print.
Crew, Hilary S. *Is It Really Mommie Dearest? Daughter-Mother Narratives in Young Adult Fiction*. Lanham, MD: Scarecrow, 2000. Print.
Hanh-Burkett, Tracy. Blog Comment. "How Can a Mother Love *The Hunger Games*?" Babble.com. 10 February 2012. Web. 13 September 2012.
Hughes, Sheila Hassell. "'Red Mother': The Missing Mother Plot as Double Mystery in Louise Erdrich's Fiction." In *Textual Mothers/Maternal Texts: Motherhood in Contemporary Women's Literatures*. Eds. Elizabeth Podnieks and Andrea O'Reilly, 79–93. Waterloo, Ontario: Wilfrid Laurier University Press, 2010. Print.
Lowinsky, Naomi Ruth. *Stories from the Motherline: Reclaiming the Mother-Daughter Bond, Finding Our Feminine Souls*. Los Angeles: Jeremy P. Tarcher, 1992. Print.
O'Reilly, Andrea. "The Motherhood Memoir and the 'New Momism': Biting the Hand that Feeds You." In *Textual Mothers/Maternal Texts: Motherhood in Contemporary Women's Literatures*. Ed. Elizabeth Podnieks and Andrea O'Reilly. 203–214. Waterloo, Ontario: Wilfrid Laurier University Press, 2010. Print.
Parsons, Sabrina. "How Being a Mom Ruined Hunger Games for Me." Forbeswww. Web. 13 September 2012.
Pearlman, Mickey. *Mother Puzzles: Daughters and Mothers in Contemporary American Literature*. New York: Greenwood, 1989. Print.
Podnieks, E., and A. O'Reilly, eds. "Maternal Literatures in Text and Tradition: Daughter-Centric, Matrilineal, and Matrifocal Perspectives." *Textual Mothers, Maternal Texts: Motherhood in Contemporary Women's Literatures*. Ontario: Wilfrid Laurier University Press, 2010. Print.
Rich, Adrienne. *Of Woman Born: Motherhood as Experience and Institution*. New York: W.W. Norton, 1986. Print.

Roper, Jane. "How Can a Mother Love *The Hunger Games*?" Babble.com. 10 February 2012. Web. 13 September 2012.

Sibary, Shona. "Why I Feel I'm a Bad Mother for Taking My Girls to *The Hunger Games*." *Dailymail.co.uk*. 29 March 2012. Web. 13 September 2012.

Yu, Yi-Lin. *Mother She Wrote: Matrilineal Narratives in Contemporary Women's Writing*. New York: Peter Lang, 2005. Print.

Performing the Capitol in Digital Spaces
The Punitive Gaze of the Panopticon Among Fans and Critics

DEIDRE ANNE EVANS GARRIOTT

In an interview about her best-selling young adult trilogy, Suzanne Collins reveals that the idea for *The Hunger Games* came to her late one night while watching television. At one point, she alternated between channels covering the United States's war in Iraq and those showing reality television.[1] Collins reflects in this interview that the two seemingly disparate genres—news and reality television—conflated in her mind until she could not tell them apart (Collins "Contemporary Inspiration"; Dominus "War Stories for Kids"). This conflation ultimately sparked the creative process that resulted in *The Hunger Games*. These kinds of programs may not seem similar to one another in the minds of most audiences, because they tout vastly different agendas within the world of television programming. News is supposed to be factual, credible, and informative. It reports the real. Most audiences of reality television, even those who are fans, would admit that they realize that reality television is sensational and even, to an extent, scripted. Despite its association with "reality," it is not necessarily a view into the real world. Despite these differences, these two genres are commonly characterized by the investigative, and sometimes judgmental, gazes of the camera and the audience.

In her trilogy, Collins explores how the gaze can be used punitively. In doing so, she evokes imagery of the Panopticon. According to Michel Foucault in *Discipline and Punish: The Birth of the Prison*, "the gaze is alert everywhere" (195) and creates a system of surveillance working from the bottom up: citizens watch each other, are watched by official police, who are watched by other officials, who are watched by and report to a central figure (196). In very obvious ways, Collins writes about a world in which the panoptic gaze is alert and active. Because of her various uses of panoptic imagery, I read Collins's *The Hunger Games* trilogy as a rhetorical text that provides insight into the use of the gaze in our present reality rather than as a text that warns readers about a potential future.

While some readers may resist thinking about "rhetoricity" and the notion that Collins's trilogy and the film adaptations are rhetorical, understanding these texts as rhetorical is essential to the arguments that drive this collection's scholarship. In addition, such an understanding informs the functions of the trilogy as it is read in non-academic communities. The majority of authors in this collection are concerned with the novel as a source of commentary and as a text that has the potential to change or impact the world— *our* world—outside of itself. Both functions—making commentary and effecting change—make the text rhetorical and consequential. By "rhetorical," I mean that any text, particularly *The Hunger Games* in its various incarnations, can and is used by its audiences for civic purposes, or purposes that extend beyond (but may still be included in) a strictly academic, strictly literary sphere. Moreover, a text is rhetorical when it is "consequential," as Carole Blair argues (18). A text is consequential when it is affective and effective. When it responds to a situation, when it causes a change, and/or when it prompts a response, then it is affective and effective.

Collins's discussions of the trilogy suggest that she wrote with purpose, or rather, for consequences; if nothing else, she sought to investigate and explore Western culture's relationship with the media and war, and she wanted to expose young adult readers to the horrors of warfare and how those horrors affect children. Investigating problems and informing readers about civic issues through the medium of fiction suggest a desire for the text to produce a change, even if it is simply to raise awareness in readers. Furthermore, the popularity of products related to *The Hunger Games* suggests that some of these messages, or at least Katniss's story, have resonated with readers. This essay in particular considers how this resonance has manifested in popular culture, particularly in the ways that fans—whether or not scholars would classify these readers as "YA"—have begun to use the novel to better understand the world around them and, at times, as a means of political and social entry. Because *The Hunger Games* has had such an impact in popular culture, the editors and contributing authors of this collection believe it is important to analyze the varied responses of the trilogy's fans, readers, and critics.

In this essay, I look at one particular consequence of *The Hunger Games*: the way readers, fans, and critics have appropriated the texts to support and forward their own political and social ideologies, both in positive and in regressive, negative ways. Specifically, I analyze how these audiences have responded on the Internet, mostly on the micro-blogging site Twitter, as well as on professional blogs, to the casting of actors to portray characters in the film adaptation of the first novel, *The Hunger Games*. I focus on the popular responses of both fan culture and critics.

This essay begins with a brief discussion of Collins's own fear of the Panopticon. I provide this close reading and analysis to supplement Collins's own commentary about the way the gaze is used. I pair this close reading with an explanation of Michel Foucault's theory of discipline and punishment that emerges from his analysis of the Panopticon, a prison system. Then, I summarize the interactions between social media users, bloggers, and online film critics concerning casting for the film adaptation of *The Hunger Games*. What follows is an analysis of the texts and popular discourse, based on these arguments: that *The Hunger Games* has provided fans with an entry into the civic, public sphere, since the texts are sites of rhetoric, and that the interactions on the Internet among fans of *The Hunger Games* resemble Foucault's Panopticon, a conceptual system of discipline and punishment intended to modify behavior, in action. In other words, I argue that the fans' racist Tweets and the critics' comments about Jennifer Lawrence's body are modes of social commentary. The authors of these digital texts seek to police the filmmakers' casting decisions, to criticize those decisions, and then to punish all those involved in the movie by publishing their political positions about the film online. I also argue that these writers—regardless of whether or not they write professionally—are unaware that what they are doing is policing and enact the kind of use of the gaze and societal fracturing that Collins critiques in the novels. Finally, I argue that the Panopticon created in the discussion of race and bodies of *The Hunger Games*'s cast, as a form of rhetoric or public discourse, is problematic because of its real world manifestation of what Collins critiques in her trilogy: surveillance and oppression.

Collins's Fear of the Panopticon in the Trilogy as Social Commentary

Like our world in which the ever-present gaze of the news and reality television functions, Collins writes about Panem, a post-apocalyptic political entity that exists on the North American continent.[2] When readers encounter Katniss, Panem has survived a rebellion during which thirteen districts rebelled against the oppressive and elitist Capitol. Readers learn, eventually, that the Capitol emerged victorious. All of Panem believes that District 13 was destroyed, and the Capitol has reasserted control over the remaining districts, in at least two dominant forms: the presence of Peacekeepers and the annual Hunger Games. Both forms of control utilize a punitive gaze. The Peacekeepers, Capitol-empowered law enforcement, monitor the district citizens. Should the Peacekeepers observe (or claim to have witnessed) any kind of disobedience or signs of insurrection, they can enact punishment. This gaze is local, internal.

The annual Hunger Games, however, are nationally televised, and so the gaze operates at the national level. All citizens—the elite residents of the Capitol as well as the oppressed laborers in the districts—watch while a boy and a girl from each district are selected to compete in a fight to the death. The last child standing is the victor, and the victor's survival of the Arena promises wealth and food to his/her district of origin. The Capitol uses the Hunger Games to remind the districts of the Capitol's power and to punish them for their rebellion less than a century ago. The Capitol requires the district citizens to watch the Hunger Games in their houses and in their public squares. Watching their children killing each other and dying is an ongoing punishment. Thus, the gaze becomes punitive and something to be feared. A child being watched in the Hunger Games is both being punished by the Capitol and is performing the Capitol's punishment.

When readers first meet Katniss in District 12 on Reaping Day as she sneaks outside of the fence to hunt, she "glance[s] quickly over [her] shoulder" (*THG* 6). She explains that "[e]ven here, even in the middle of nowhere, you worry someone might overhear you" (6). Her use of the word "worry" here signals that being watched and being heard are threats. Katniss's worry persuades the reader to be worried as well. Shortly after Katniss muses about her fear of secretive surveillance, she worries about its oblique form. After she volunteers to replace her sister Prim in the Games, Katniss is aware that she is now the subject not only of District 12's attention but also the cameras' attention, which will broadcast her to all of Panem. Prim panics as Katniss moves toward the stage, clinging to her older sister to keep Katniss from sacrificing herself as a tribute. Katniss affects a cold, distant demeanor with her sister, because "[w]hen they televise the replay of the reapings tonight, everyone will make note of my tears, and I'll be marked as an easy target. A weakling. I will give no one that satisfaction" (23). Katniss has been reared in a society that has grown accustomed to being watched, so she does not need time to adapt to surveillance; however, she does need time to adapt to being noticed, as she has struggled to remain unobserved and unnoticed for her own safety. Now that she is the object of the gaze, she realizes that she has to adjust her behavior accordingly to appear to be a fitting tribute, one who is not a weakling.

Katniss's awareness of the potential of being watched as the trilogy opens and later her very conscious adjustment to being in the frame of the gaze demonstrates how the Panopticon functions as a means of discipline and punishment. In *Discipline and Punish*, Foucault analyzes a prison system that

Jeremy Bentham envisioned. Bentham conceived of a prison circular in shape. All the cells faced the interior center of the prison toward a tower. At any given time of day, someone could be in the tower watching the inmates, waiting for the prisoners to misbehave, so that the prison guards could punish them. However, the prisoners never knew if or when someone was in the tower watching them. The potential was always there. Additionally, because of the circular shape of the structure, the prisoners could watch each other (201–2). Katniss's worry about being overheard is similar to the concern about being watched: the potential is always there. As in the prison, Katniss knows that there is a watcher and that if the watcher catches her doing something wrong, she will be punished. This fear of punishment is implicit in her worry.

Foucault argues that the Panopticon—both in terms of the actual structure and as enacted civically in cities and villages—divides individuals, and breaks down communities, because each person is a potential watcher and therefore has the potential to enact punishment on a person. Because of this, no sense of unity and community can be achieved because "individuals are inserted into a fixed place, in which the slightest movements are supervised, in which all events are recorded, in which an uninterrupted work of writing links the centre [sic] and the periphery, in which power is exercised without division, according to continuous hierarchical figure" (197). Most importantly for this essay, Foucault argues that the Panopticon created individual divisions of segmentation rather than binary divisions (198). In other words, in this form of discipline, all individuals are confined, monitored, and expected to report, and this division segments individuals from each other so that no imagination of community or identification exists, because each person is a threat.

Collins's Panem is the result of a large-scale panoptic society. Motivated by the gaze of the news and reality television cameras, Collins writes about a world in which all citizens fear being watched, perceive they are being watched, and are watching each other as a result of that fear. Collins's immediate inclusion of surveillance and its ongoing presence in the trilogy indicate her own fear of it. Because news and reality television in the present called such concerns about the camera's gaze to her mind, I argue that her use of panopticism in *The Hunger Games* is not a warning about the future but rather a criticism of the present. Granted, the kind of surveillance in Panem is heightened. Most people in the United States are not as worried and aware of being watched as is Katniss. However, the potential for being watched is increasing—from cameras at stop lights to businesses monitoring our online activity. Panem is not a distant future. It is happening now, and increasingly, we are aiding in it by watching each other, disclosing our watchfulness online, and seeking ways to punish those whose behavior we deem inappropriate.

The Internet as a Public Sphere and Online Discourse as Rhetoric: Fan Culture and Fandom as Civic Engagement

Before I summarize the online activity surrounding the film adaptation's publicity and the way these actions are dialectical, or responsive to each other, it is necessary that I first argue that fan culture and fandom can be serious rhetorical activities that deserve critical attention and should be analyzed as civic discourse. I argue that fan culture is a kind of popular critical response and rhetorical appropriation of the text because fan culture, or fandom, has achieved new and sometimes exciting levels of visibility and agency that it has not before enjoyed. Because of the Internet and the rise of social media, blogging as a career, and online formats of traditional periodicals, fan culture has more (digital) sites where fans may discuss the texts that excite them, present their own critical assessments, and produce and share art or fiction inspired by the text.[3] These activities seem benign at worst and positive at best. After all, who would be troubled by people being excited about reading, being inspired by reading to create their own art, and to engage in civic or academic activity? The problem with this ambivalence regarding fan culture is that it ignores the activity's political and rhetorical potential, and ignores its capability to forward social, civic arguments that represent some shared ideologies and that can influence others. Because fan culture's influence is growing on the Internet and is becoming newsworthy, it requires critical attention to understand the influence of texts on the world and how they motivate and provide entry into political and civic discourses.

Critical Responses to the Casting for The Hunger Games Film: Popular and Scholarly

In the midst of news about the casting of actors for the film *The Hunger Games* and in reviews immediately preceding its release a trend of discourse emerged: a focus on the actors' appearances. In some cases, the focus on appearance spearheaded honest and much-needed conversations about race and the way Hollywood often "whitewashes" films adapted from novels. Still others seemed to "concern-troll" the lack of hungry-looking bodies, turning Jennifer Lawrence's figure into a case study in what hunger does *not* look like.

These kinds of reviews disturbingly lingered on descriptions of Lawrence's breasts and hips, before arguing that she is too robust to play a tribute who had, on occasion, feared dying from hunger. The reviews often admitted that portraying excessively thin bodies can be problematic in a culture already unhealthily obsessed with size. To portray the often-starving citizens of the districts on film, actors would have to starve themselves to achieve an emaciated appearance. In her blog "The Imminent Whitewashing of *The Hunger Games*' Heroine" on *Jezebel*, Sarah Seltzer reports that a casting call for actresses auditioning to play Katniss needed to be capable of "portray[ing] someone 'underfed but strong.'" Seltzer notes, "Seeking actresses who look 'underfed' is fraught for obvious reasons" ("Imminent"). While some actors have lost extreme amounts of weight for film roles, such practices are unhealthy for the actor.[4] However, despite such allowances for difficulties adapting the film, these bloggers and reviewers seemed unaware that they, too, were contributing to the various ways in which women continue to be objectified in the media.

Despite these comments, both the concerns about the absence of racial diversity and criticisms about fuller-figured bodies often comprised productive discourses that invited readers and fans to consider what gets lost, emphasized, or minimized when Hollywood gets a hold of a text. Seltzer reflects in her conclusion, "Hollywood will be sending a message, and in this particular case, a message that is inherently directed at our youth. Which, depending on what way things go, could be a wonderful thing" ("Imminent"). Seltzer represents one particular kind of blogger, one who comes from a feminist perspective, and who is clearly disappointed in what was, at the time, simply a casting rumor regarding Jennifer Lawrence and the film adaption of Collins's trilogy. Her article on *Jezebel*, however, emphasizes to readers a problem in Hollywood—namely, casting white actors in roles that were originally written about characters who are described as representing other ethnicities. Thoughtful discourses like Seltzer's most often occurred in more traditional online sites, such as blogs or, even more formally, film reviews for traditional media outlets like *The New York Times*, which were published both in print and online.

However distasteful some of these reviews were, occasionally, they were tame compared to some of the reactions to casting African-American actors in key roles. Many fans were prompted to respond online using social media and micro-blogging outlets to express their opinions about the casting of non-white actors in certain roles. What is interesting here is the motivation by these fans to make their opinions public through writing, especially when they were using writing outlets that do not pay for the text in the manner that a formal publishing house would. These fans do not have careers that depend upon publishing, but "publish" they did by using Twitter to make public their discontent with the casting.

The problem is that these social media discussions were not innocuous. Here, I focus on Twitter updates, or "Tweets." Primarily, the fans most upset with the casting focused on the actress playing Rue, Amandla Sternberg. Rue, the eleven-year-old female tribute from District 11, forms a brief, touching alliance with Katniss in the Arena. In the novel, Katniss frequently muses that Rue reminds her of her sister Prim, whom Katniss saved from going into the Arena by volunteering to be the female tribute when Effie Trinket calls Prim's name from the lottery. Thus, in the novel, Rue and Prim are frequently associated with each other, at least in Katniss's internal narrative. In general, these fans argued that the novel portrays Rue as white and that "changing" her race in this casting decision undermines the integrity of the story.[5] Fans often attacked Sternberg by using racial slurs.

Perhaps the most important part of this activity was that it prompted bloggers—the same ones who were already sensitive to the portrayal of race in the film and had criticized the filmmakers for choosing a white actress to play Katniss—to address these racially-charged Tweets directly. Bloggers on the Gawker-site *Jezebel,* specifically, saved and published screenshots of these Tweets before their account owners could delete them, and then proceeded to write articles that discussed the problems associated with white imagination as the dominant public imagination in the United States, the reality of racism in a world that often claims to be "over" race, and other issues. In other words, these Tweets prompted *discourse.* A conversation was happening across the Internet.

As a teacher and scholar of rhetoric who is interested in civic discourse and practices, I too was upset about these Tweets, then encouraged by the nuanced discussion they raised, and later disturbed by the amount of social policing in which I observed all parties participating. I interpreted the policing as evidence of surveillance, and I was concerned with the "body-trolling" on the part of activist bloggers and film critics. I was disturbed, also, by the perpetuating of racism on Twitter and the implied argument that diversity is unfavorable by these Twitter-users. While I found myself agreeing whole-heartedly with the activist bloggers, I was also aware that despite their advocacy of diversity, they were sub-textually criticizing the appropriateness of Jennifer Lawrence's body. This criticism was less sub-textual and more direct in some film reviews. I was disturbed by how this criticism, although well-intentioned in some cases, objectified the female form. I interpreted even then more sensitive texts as a form of monitoring and policing.

Like the activist bloggers on *Jezebel,* I supported a diverse cast, and I was concerned that the casting did not reflect Collins's descriptions of her characters. Unlike some of the professional film critics, I was less worried that Jennifer Lawrence does not look emaciated, because, like many feminists, I am attuned to the problems of objectifying a female body in a way that makes a starved body—or rather, one single body type in particular—desirable, in the name of literary or cinematic "integrity." Furthermore, I applauded the bloggers who directly and indirectly addressed the racism associated with the film.

But I was and am also disturbed that as "netizens" took to digital sites to discuss the film, they engaged in a communal and self-policing that I associated closely with the Panopticon described in Foucault's theories about how its threat of punishment modifies behavior. Many of the Tweets suggested awareness of being watched. The bloggers responding to the Tweets confirmed it, as did the comments responding to the blogs and the formal film reviews. But while these writers seem to address an unidentified watcher, they seemed unaware that in doing so, they were being disciplinary enforcers as well—they were watching and being watched simultaneously. I am most disturbed, however, that we—fans of *The Hunger Games* trilogy—were engaging in discussions about race and body image without the meta-cognition that we are, actually, self-policing like the Capitol does in Collins's trilogy.

I do not want to suggest that I do not support directly calling into question, confronting, and correcting unethical and racist discourse. On the contrary, I eagerly support it and seek to uplift it in much of my scholarly research. These are, indeed, fruitful discussions of race and diversity. Like Sarah Seltzer earlier and two other *Jezebel* bloggers whom I will discuss later, I not only abhor racism but also seek to change these ideas. I believe that the more we—advocates of diversity and a more just world—confront racism, the more we construct a world in which it will be unacceptable to espouse such ideologies and advocate for exclusionary social and civic practices. Thus, I shared with Seltzer the desire to discover and disclose practices that seemed racist. Furthermore, while I do consider this kind of effort—finding and making more public racist behavior—a civic responsibility, I also consider it a way of enacting the Panopticon when it seeks to target and punish through isolation and exclusion rather than correct through other more productive means. However, I would argue that because in the United States we are still fighting against forms of racism, this is a kind of policing that is necessary and that is also still subversive. I perceive it as challenging a previous status quo and a previous panoptic gaze.

What concerns me is not so much that we are policing each other; it is that we, as fans and sometimes critics, seem to be unaware that we are enacting behaviors not that dissimilar from those that the characters in the Capitol of Panem enact: surveillance, discipline through publicity, and finally correction. Ultimately, what this does, I argue, is that we all—netizens—suffer when we are unaware that we monitor each other and use our digital gaze as a form of policing. When we do this, we have internalized the civic of surveillance, and I argue that we need to resist such thoughtlessness, and rather than stopping altogether, we need to be aware of what we are doing. Thenceforth, this essay will examine the rhetorical texts eliciting concerns like those of Sarah Seltzer on *Jezebel*: the Tweets, the casting calls, the newspaper articles, that espoused and affirmed racial and diversity discrimination. These Twitter feeds, blogs, and respected articles in renowned newspapers, like *The New York Times*, criticizing the actors on the basis of race or body type, are examples of Foucaultian self-policing, a digital Panopticon that Collins manifests in her trilogy. Western society's focus on the actors' bodies demonstrates a way that we—digital citizens—perform the Capitol through media.

Reactions to Jennifer Lawrence/Katniss Everdeen

When word came that Gary Ross would direct the film adaptation of Collins's *The Hunger Games*, many fans and bloggers speculated about which new or rising young stars would portray Katniss Everdeen, Gale Hawthorne, and Peeta Mellark. However, fan reaction, in general, was negative to the casting. When Oscar-nominated actress Jennifer Lawrence was cast as Katniss, several blogs pointed out that Lawrence's whiteness seemed to undermine the suggestions in the novel of Katniss's non-white, unspecified ethnicity. Additionally, other voices, including film critics, remarked on Lawrence's body, particularly noting her feminine physique and using their notice as a way to criticize the film's authenticity to its source material. In other words, rather than commenting on the quality of acting, most people who took to the Internet focused on the actors' physical appearances, though the quality of these reactions ranged from serious discourse about whitewashing the film, to body-snarking, to more disturbing trends.

My first exposure to Suzanne Collins' post-apocalyptic trilogy *The Hunger Games* was not through direct contact with the novels but rather through a blog post on *Jezebel*. The overwhelming majority of bloggers on *Jezebel* are female, and topics range from gossip, fashion coverage, and responses to news. Despite the trilogy's popularity and even one "Jezzie" blogger's pronouncement that "[t]he enduring lure of the YA is no secret to the Jez community" (Stein), the *Jezebel* community virtually ignored the trilogy until 2010. Although some *Jezebel* bloggers referenced the trilogy in posts about YA literature, Collins's trilogy did not come under scrutiny until Rich Juzwiak, who is most recently a regular blogger for the father site, *Gawker*, posted his blog, "How a Kid-lit Favorite Is Really About Trash Television" on August 26, 2010. Juzwiak opens his article with a description of Katniss: "Katniss Everdeen is not here to make friends—she's here to win" ("Trash Television"). Of course, he's not incorrect. In the novel, Katniss balks when her mentor Haymitch demands that Peeta and Katniss act friendly during training (*THG 97*). Like many early critics of the trilogy (myself included, upon my initial reading), Juzwiak arrests on the similarities between the broadcasts of the Games and our current exposure to competitive reality television.

Jezebel did not publish much about *The Hunger Games* until March 2011, when Sarah Seltzer responded to recent casting news. In her blog post "The Imminent Whitewashing of *The Hunger Games* Heroine," Seltzer writes about the rumors circulating circa March 2011 about casting Academy Award nominee Jennifer Lawrence as Katniss: "If Lawrence is indeed cast as Katniss, it's a missed opportunity, but there are still plenty of chances left for the filmmakers to honor the diversity in Collins' fictional world and, in turn, in our own". The trilogy does imply some racial diversity, but its language contains no explicit racial qualifiers beyond adjectives describing characters' skin tone and hair color, so, the question is: What casting opportunities were being missed? As Seltzer points out, Collins's narrator describes herself and Gale as having "the Seam look": olive skinned, with brown eyes and dark hair. Meanwhile, Peeta, Prim, and Katniss's (unnamed) mother look more like those District 12 residents who are not from the seam but rather who are associated with the merchant class: pale skin, blond hair, blue eyes. While Collins does not categorize race or ethnicity in her novels, her description of people with darker color laboring in the mines compared to the lighter-skinned residents experiencing a less physically-demanding and dangerous existence recalls images of the intersection between racial and economic distinctions that are, unfortunately, still familiar in the twenty-first century.

Seltzer is careful in her criticism of Jennifer Lawrence. She respects Lawrence's proven talent, noting, "Lawrence is unquestionably a talented actress" ("Imminent""). Instead, Seltzer takes to task the filmmakers, pointing out their casting call for Katniss. Seltzer dissects this casting call: "it's the blunt 'Caucasian' requirement that comes as a surprise" because Katniss does not describe herself in ways that are specifically Caucasian or that exclude other non-white contributions to her genetic makeup ("Imminent"). Thus, calling for a Caucasian actress clearly excludes other capable actresses and privileges whiteness in Hollywood. Seltzer's critique here deliberately avoids focusing on Lawrence. Her problem, indeed, is not with Lawrence herself; rather Lawrence's casting is symptomatic of problems in Hollywood. This casting choice over an actress who may look more like the Katniss Collins describes— and who may or may not self-identify as Caucasian—may challenge traditional ideas of beauty, and how Western society associates beauty with heroism. Moreover, Seltzer alludes to Collins's own symbolic use of race and class as suggestive commentary on our current social hierarchies and privileges ("Imminent"). Seltzer asserts here that the integrity of the complex political and social messages in *The Hunger Games* are compromised when we impose traditionally Western standards of beauty and heroism.

Seltzer's critique, however, is not an evaluation of the film. In a film review for *The New York Times*, Manhola Dargis criticizes Jennifer Lawrence for not looking starved and young enough to play Katniss. Disturbingly, this writer lingers on Lawrence's body, much in the same way as the Tweets above focused on race: "A few years ago, Ms. Lawrence may have looked hungry enough to play Katniss, but now, at 21, her seductive womanly figure makes a bad fit for a dystopian fantasy about people starved into submission" (Dargis "Tested by a Picturesque Dystopia"). Dargis, unlike Seltzer, takes issue with Lawrence's body, arguing that her "seductive womanly figure" contradicts the issues of hunger that are present in the film. Seltzer mentions this issue in her article, but she does so by taking issue not with Lawrence but once more with the casting call demanding an "underfed" appearance. Seltzer approaches this issue with concern, observing that such an appeal is "fraught for obvious reasons" but that the call is consistent with the novel's intense interrogation of hunger and oppression. Dargis is even on track to point out that this film is supposed to make us more aware of hunger as a war tactic. But doing so by lingering on and policing Lawrence's body and its appearance on screen is both voyeuristic and misogynist. This is especially alarming, considering Dargis is a woman.

Dargis does not so much call into question the film's authenticity but rather Lawrence's ability to play Katniss because she looks too "womanly" and is "a bad fit for a dystopian fantasy" ("Picturesque Dystopia"). Upon an initial reading, it might seem that Dargis is indirectly complimenting Lawrence. Yet, Dargis criticizes Lawrence for the body she has and how she chooses to maintain it rather than directly attack Ross or his casting directors for selecting Lawrence for the role. Thus, Dargis's reference to Lawrence's figure implies criticism of actresses' bodies that are not underfed, when literary source material seems to call for this kind of casting. Even though she does not explicitly state this, Dargis's emphasis of her "seductive womanly figure" suggests that Lawrence's body is one that we cannot trust. It is seductive, and therefore has power over the audience. Adding Lawrence's gender here as a descriptor indicates an added criticism, that there is something wrong with Lawrence, not because she *is* a woman but because she is bold enough to *look* like a woman, one who is seductive, powerful, and thus scary to those who might be intimidated by her beauty. Finally, her commentary seems a code for calling Lawrence "fat," because she is not as thin as some other actresses, and because she does not hide her body as though she is ashamed of it. Dargis's commentary on Lawrence's body and disregard of her performance—which is central to the film's success, since Katniss is the way the audience accesses the Games— is a way of policing bodies and the power associated with them.

Dargis, writing for *The New York Times*, inhabits an authoritative place that neither Seltzer nor the fans whose Tweets I will discuss later enjoy. She is the head film critic of the *Times*, which is a publication that exerts a certain authority on culture, so she speaks with authority and without self-critical qualifiers. From her position, she may criticize Lawrence's body freely. Frankly, she also chooses a body that is safer to criticize: Lawrence is white and conventionally attractive. And even before receiving an Oscar for best actress at the 2013 Academy Awards, she had also received a great deal of acclaim for her acting. Her body, though female, and therefore more vulnerable to objectification, is white and beautiful and therefore less oppressed by public criticism than was Sternberg's body—which is subject to oppressive, racialized critiques. However, implicit in this criticism is a creation of a system of determining and policing of what is acceptable and unacceptable in terms of body image, a system that excludes evaluations of acceptable and unacceptable performances.

Dargis's position of authority lent to her by her association with *The New York Times* affords her a place to police. She becomes the voice of an unseen authority on how women, in particular, should look and how that appearance complies with appropriate behavior. Dargis's commentary on Lawrence makes an example of her, veiling criticism in faint praise. Implied in this commentary is a public commentary on public bodies. Lawrence's body becomes a paradigm of any woman who chooses not to conform, whether it is conformity to a script or to expectations. This is not simply criticism of Lawrence's body but any woman who would approve of Lawrence's kind of figure portraying this role. Furthermore, it ascribes nefarious underpinnings to women's bodies: it suggests that they are capable of impeding the agency of others, and so Dargis's criticism seeks to undermine Lawrence's agency by objectifying her. This objectification seeks to bring Lawrence down to size, symbolically speaking, and render her an object to be directed, watched, measured, and judged.

Criticism as Racial Policing

The filmmakers of *The Hunger Games* certainly made conservative casting decisions when they employed white, blonde actors Jennifer Lawrence and Liam Hemsworth as Katniss and her friend Gale; however, director Gary Ross and his casting crew incited controversy when they cast Lenny Kravitz and Amandla Sterberg as Katniss's stylist Cinna and her ally from District 11 Rue, respectively. Both actors claim multiracial backgrounds, including Caucasian, Jewish (in Kravitz's case), and African-American ancestries. Both performers have self-identified, predominantly, as African-American or black. Some fans, myself included, celebrated Kravitz's casting, mostly because of the prior fame and talent he brought to the role. Not much was known about Sternberg at the time of casting.

What was known, however, is that both actors identify with an ethnic group that is not white. While some fans were excited, others were despondent and even irate because they expected white actors to play all the roles. In her essay "Black Writing, White Reading: Race and the Politics of Feminist Interpretation," Elizabeth Abel interrogates the kind of expected whiteness that white readers imagine, and the kind of expected whiteness that I suggest these angry Twitter-users of expressing. Abel analyzes her own experience as a reader to suggest the dominance of "white imagination." When reading Toni Morrison's "Recitatif," Abel imagined Twyla as white, although others interpreted her as a black character (471). Abel attributes her interpretation first to the absence of "signifiers of racial difference (such as skin color)" (471). While Abel focused on historical signifiers to identify race, Lula Fragd (the other reader in Abel's essay) focused on cultural, economic, and maternal politics informed by Fragd's own cultural context, which includes her African-American milieu (475).

Like Abel, these particular readers of *The Hunger Games* used textual signifiers to imagine the characters. These signifiers, however, were influenced by their own racial, social, and political contexts. The casting of the black actors in two prominent roles both challenged their imaginations but also their interpretations. It also challenged their world view, because it tells them that they were wrong and that their world view is not the only world view or even the view of Panem. And they took to social media to express their feelings.

I am now going to share a series of Tweets that respond to Cinna and Rue's race and ethnicity in the film. In the interest of preserving Twitter users' anonymity, I will not disclose their handles. Some of these Tweets have also been deleted, though screenshots published on *Jezebel* still exist. Furthermore, I do not intend to attack any individual Twitter-user but rather discuss how these members perform the Capitol when they Tweet about the casting of *The Hunger Games*. I have preserved spelling, capitalization, and punctuation in order to maintain the voice of each Tweet. Finally, I want to warn my readers that these are extremely offensive and contain disturbing uses of racial slurs:

User 1: "why does rue have to be black not gonna lie kinda ruined the movie"
User 2: "cinna and rue werent supposed to be black" "why did the producer make all the good characters black smh"
User 3: "EWW rue is black?? I'm not watching"
User 4: "KK call me racist but when I found out rue was black her death wasnt as sad #ihatemyself"
User 5: "HOW IN THE WORLD ARE THEY GOING TO MAKE RUE A FREAKIN BLACK BITCH IN THE MOVIE?!?!?!?!?! lol not to be racist buuuuuuuut.....I'm angry now ;O"

These offensive Tweets came to my attention when I was, again, reading *Jezebel* on March 26, 2012. *Jezebel* blogger Dodai Stewart asserts in a post that these Tweets and other public declamations of race in the film "[reflect] a level of idiocy that we weren't expecting" ("Racist *Hunger Games* Fans Are Very Disappointed"). Stewart preserved many more Tweets, but I chose to include just these few, because the rest of them are very similar, and because it is difficult to continue reading them.

In the novel, Katniss describes Rue as having "bright, dark eyes and satiny brown skin" who reminds Katniss of her sister Prim (*THG* 98). Meanwhile, she does not indirectly associate a race with Cinna, noting mostly that he does not look like the other flamboyant citizens of the Capitol and that his most ostentatious feature is his gold eyeliner. Collins never describes characters using our contemporary racial identifiers such as "black," "African-American," or "Native American." Because Collins avoids these identifiers, I think she tries (and fails) to depict a post-racial world where concerns about survival take priority over racial prejudice, although some ethnic diversity seems to exist among Panem's citizens. Thus, it is possible to cast anyone in these roles, regardless of the ways in which they identify themselves ethnically or otherwise in the "real" world.

As much as I love the trilogy, I must say that she does not succeed, because the districts of Panem suggest racial segregation. Additionally, Toni Morrison argues in *Playing in the Dark: Whiteness and the Literary Imagination* that criticism that removes issues of race from a literary text cheapens both the text itself as well as the knowledge that emerges from critical engagement with the text. She asserts, "A criticism that needs to insist that literature is not only 'universal' but also 'race-free' risks lobotomizing the literature, and diminishes both the art and the artist" (12). Collins, as an artist, cannot free herself from her context: a white woman living in the United States in the twenty-first century, where and when race still matters. While *The Hunger Games* is a trilogy with broad appeal, I would not say that it is "universal," because a reader's context will change the reading and rhetorical situation. Furthermore, to say that it is race-free or post-racial would ignore some of the nuanced ways in which race and racism enter the text.

In Katniss's District 12, Katniss assigns certain physical traits to the economic classes. She and Gale come from the Seam and have "the Seam look," including black hair, olive skin, and dark eyes. Peeta, the other District 12 tribute, Katniss's mother, and Katniss's friend Madge, the mayor's daughter, all come from the merchant class, and have the merchant class look: fair skin, or at least not olive, and blond hair. While Collins seems to deliberately avoid familiar racialized terminology, she still depicts a world whose economic classes are racially defined. Regardless, the Capitol draws its tributes for the

Hunger Games from all socio-economic classes, because those in the Capitol intend the Games to discipline all the districts. However, despite the seeming egalitarian drawing of tributes, Collins depicts a world not entirely free from racial segregation, but the ethnic and racial terms seem so forgotten in the world of Panem that actors from a variety of backgrounds could fill the roles easily. In other words, although we see evidence of racial segregation in Collins's text, particularly in District 12, it's not enough evidence to "prove" these characters *had to be* white on screen, so the criticism seems to stem from internal or social exigencies rather than textual ones.

In my previous examples of Internet discourse concerning *The Hunger Games*, the authors wrote in isolated, less situated circumstances. These Tweets seem to be addressing some unidentified audience, but one whose imagined complicity with or judgment of the racist attitudes is infused into the forms the racial comments took on. For example, the Twitter user I have labeled "User 4" seems to invoke an audience, and even seems aware of this audience's judgmental presence, by assuming guilt from the unnamed presence, "call me racist." By invoking someone who might call the user racist, User 4 expresses a sense of self-awareness but also positions her or himself in an inferior position to someone with the authority to criticize. User 4 also seems concerned that he or she will be judged, but this does not censor the statement.

For fans like the ones I have quoted above, *The Hunger Games* has provided them entry into civic discussions on race, imagination, and memory. By criticizing the actors' races, they are also criticizing how Hollywood imagines the United States. When they read *The Hunger Games*, they imagined all the characters as sharing their own identifications: namely, as white. Identification is essential to empathizing with the characters, so that the stakes are higher as the tributes dies. For these readers in particular, identification and empathy depend upon racial sameness. Their imagining of the novel is definitive to them. User 2's Tweets reveal this authority when she or he argues that the Rue and Cinna "werent [sic] supposed to be black," as though Collins intended race to suggest importance or for her descriptions in the text to signify very strict and exclusive ethnic possibilities. These Twitter-users are using their imagination of the novels and their racialized disappointment to enter into larger debates about cultural memory and race, even if those of us who are also engaging in those discussions do not like their contributions. They have appropriated and amplified certain details from the texts to forward political, social arguments about race, authority, and social value—as disappointing and unsettling as these may be.

More importantly, I would point out the consequences of these racist attacks. In forwarding their disapproval of casting non-white actors, these Twitter users are not seeking to create or foster a community of like-minded people. Instead, they are excluding people. First, they most demonstratively exclude non-white critics, fans, or respondents from this discussion. They do this by saying, more or less, that black people are less important and significant to the world and should be excluded from popular imagination by being isolated from the film. Their criticism of the actors in the film is also criticism of a world view that promotes diversity, and so people of diverse backgrounds are excluded by the criticism itself. Secondly, by attacking the actors and filmmakers, they seek to divide themselves from the community that supports the film or supports diversity in the imagined world of Panem. Finally, they seek to isolate themselves by rejecting feedback or responses. By turning criticism on themselves through self-admonishing hashtags or phrases such as "call me racist," they seek to deflect or reject any participation in a larger debate or fruitful discussion. This is the result of the Panopticon. It seeks to divide rather than unite, to turn people against each other rather than to foster identification by overcoming perceived (or real) differences. It does this, in part, by punishing, which is silencing by controlling discourse.

While some Twitter-users invoked an unnamed audience in their isolated expressions about memory and imagination, Dodai Stewart and Lindy West—bloggers for *Jezebel*—directly address these Twitter-users. They do this by including screenshots, like Stewart, or hyperlinks, like West, to these Tweets. In her article "Racist *Hunger Games* Fans Are Very Disappointed," Stewart mostly reports that these Tweets exist, although she occasionally punctuates her article with some editorial moments. For example, she asserts, "[t]here's an underlying rage, coming out as overt prejudice and plain old racism....It's as if that ["that" being African American] is the worst possible thing a person could be."

Lindy West, meanwhile, seeks to explain why these posts are so problematic. First, like some readers of the trilogy, she expresses confusion about the role race plays in the novels, particularly because Collins does not use racialized terminology with which Western readers are familiar ("White People"). She observes that because of such racial ambiguity and the ubiquity of whiteness in Hollywood, "I would guess that the majority of white people and a significant number of non-white people automatically assume that the characters are white" ("White People"). She argues that these criticisms of casting black actors in roles that could be filled by white actors suggest a fear of change, namely that America's appearance is changing in ways that frighten viewers and readers.

Beyond the explicit racism of the Tweets and then the impassioned responses from two *Jezebel* bloggers, I would like to draw our attention to how the use of the Internet has engaged the Twitter users and bloggers into a conversation characterized by meaningful uses of punctuation and pithy epithets. For the Twitter users, the conversation is implied when they use hashtags that suggest the presence of a scrutinizing or sympathizing audience. Stewart and West, however, directly address these users, at times confronting their racist view points, and at others challenging hegemonic discourse. But both contributions—racist and anti-racist—are seeking to correct a wrong. They are policing each other, while they are also aware of being watched by others who may support or challenge their points of view. This awareness, however, does not invite a conversation but rather seeks to stop it, which stops efforts toward community building. This kind of policing is a digital version of Bentham and Foucault's Panopticon, where we watch, attack, and punish rather than talk and communicate.

Enacting the Capitol by Becoming the Panopticon

Foucault imagined real places when he wrote *Discipline and Punish*: towns dealing with plague and, of course, the aborted Panopticon prison project. The digital world had yet to challenge his and our conceptions of space or how it extends the gaze beyond physical place to virtual worlds. But I argue that the way many digital citizens use the Internet has turned it into a Panopticon. First of all, let me clarify that I am not calling the Internet a Panopticon. The Internet has provided the means to extend surveillance into the virtual world. Really, this is not a radical claim. For decades, theorists have argued that the Internet's technological predecessors—the television, reality TV, CCTV, electronic bugs, and the like—are new means of panoptic endeavors. Furthermore, contemporary theorists of digital studies and digital rhetorics have already staked this claim. I argue here that social media and traditional media, both as they are used digitally, are often panoptic.

According to Foucault, the Panopticon and its effects rely on monitoring and separating bodies: "Two ways of exercising power over men, of controlling their relations, of separating dangerous mixtures" (198). These criticisms of race and bodies, I argue, are ways of controlling relations and of separating dangerous mixtures. For the racialized Tweets, we see white readers so ingrained in their whitewashed culture that "dark skin" is code for "tanned" white skin, and so during their reading, the text is still socially safe because the races ostensibly do not mix. Katniss is not black, Rue is not black, but both are white, and when they ally and cuddle in Katniss's sleeping bag, this is safe. When Katniss kisses Peeta, this is not miscegenation, because Katniss is just, maybe, Mediterranean in appearance, so the (racist) readers still interpret her as white. The Tweeters' compulsion to criticize the filmmakers for using black actors is one use of the corrective gaze, both outwardly toward Ross and inwardly at themselves as they engage in behavior they know may not be accepted by the ever-present watchful gaze of the cultural authority. As Foucault notes argues, "[T]he major effect of the Panopticon...[induces] in the inmate [or Tweeter, confined to social media] a state of conscious and permanent visibility that assures the automatic functioning of power" (201) but also that the prisoner is always being seen and regulates the behavior as such, which some of the Twitter uses note. Those who used the hashtag "ihate-myself" or a qualifier such as "call me racist" appeal to the watchful gaze of an authority—but in this case, the authority is other Twitter users, some who might not like racism or who may share these racist sentiments but may, also feeling watched, apply criticism to correct each other's disobedience of social convention. At the same time, however, these Twitter-users are seeking to apply corrective action to Gary Ross, the director, by reminding him of other social conventions that still challenge inter-racial relationships. This dance—criticizing Sternberg and Ross, then self-criticizing—reveals the strange fluidity of the Panopticon, as inmates seek to approach the authority as a means of aligning with it, but at the same time, still moving within the periphery.

Dargis's comment in the *New York Times* review is less self-aware than some of these Tweets, I argue, because she inhabits a periphery near the watch-tower in the center of the Panopticon. Most of the Tweets I have discussed originate from teenagers, whose power in society is questionable, so they orbit peripheries farther from the watchful gaze and are, perhaps, more aware of being watched and judged. Despite their privileged positions as white teens or adults in a nation that still uses racial discrimination to create divisions, some of the teenagers and young adults seem aware of their own limited power to make these claims.

In the text, Katniss frequently mentions being watched by other districts citizens, including the Peacemakers, who we learn typically come from District 2 and not the Capitol. The districts are bounded by electrified fences, where no one can get in or out, and trying to leave is an offense punishable by death. The Arena, too, is a bounded area, full of cameras watching the tributes. Additionally, not only does the Capitol watch the Arena, but so do the districts, watching this punishment and monitoring their own children, re-learning the rules each year.

In *Catching Fire*, Katniss is keenly aware that she is being watched, particularly by her own people, after Gale's whipping, and she in turn monitors herself and her actions. Sometimes this monitoring is self-reflective in her narrative, much in the same attitude as the Twitter-users applying self-reprimanding hashtags. Katniss, however, rarely reprimands herself. Instead, she allows her own self-policing to aid her in appealing to the audience. For example, in *The Hunger Games*, after Katniss learns that Peeta has partnered with the Careers, she realizes that she may seem weak or lose sponsors because of this sudden rupture in the star-crossed lover narrative that Haymitch and Peeta constructed. She realizes that despite her own actual physical weaknesses, she needs to perform strength and resiliency for the cameras. Emerging from the trees that kept her hidden during the night when the Careers and Peeta were hunting tributes nearby, Katniss tells us that she "cock[s] my head slight to the side and give[s] a knowing smile. There! Let them figure out what that means" (*THG* 164). Later, after collecting game she's trapped, she muses, "I'm glad for the cameras now. I want the sponsors to see" (164). Katniss alters her behavior to appeal to the gaze, to earn its approval rather than disproval, much in the same way that the racist Twitter-users appeal to social conventions of hiding or apologizing for "appearing" (rather than actually admitting that they are) racist by including self-deprecating hashtags and remarks. These kinds of performances signal the way that these micro-bloggers are aware of the gaze and have adjusted their behavior to appeal to it. This is the evidence of the Panopticon and of bloggers' own complicity with the Capitol.

Moreover, I would argue that these kinds of ways of talking about *The Hunger Games* or any kind of public imagination—ways that seek to discover, discipline, and correct—are ways that we are actively engaging in behaviors that Collins fears and critiques in her trilogy. Although it can be useful to challenge and correct racist or other prejudiced behavior, it seems equally important to my ethos to confront these panoptic practices. What I am challenging is how we—fans and private citizens—have begun to monitor each other and "out" each other when we encounter behavior we do not like, or which can be, in actuality, counter-productive toward real change. I am doing this because we need to be aware of how we have at times misappropriated Collins's text and how we are also the very social system that Collins fears. By pointing out our own problematic engagement in Capitol-esque behavior, I also seek to underscore the ways that Collins writes social and political commentary about the present and not a speculative novel about a potential future.

I applaud Seltzer, Stewart, and West for confronting hegemonic discourses and practices that perpetuate sexism and racism. However, I am troubled by how Stewart and the *Tumblr* user who supplies her with this collection seek to disclose identities so that other people might witness their transgressions and then attack them in return. Granted, these users were short-sighted in not monitoring their own privacy settings and wrong in espousing such racism, but these are not bloggers or critics whose work is intended for commercial public consumption. Thus, what Stewart and the *Tumblr* user are doing carry some potential for social harm, like the racist Tweets, because they are encouraging panoptic practices of surveillance, discipline, and punishment. They are doing this by searching for, discovering, and disclosing behavior that they find wrong. However, what is most harmful is that they seek to publicize this behavior to incite more attacks on the racist Twitter users rather than to engage these people in debate and open discourse that may lead toward a change in perception. They punish rather than educate. I am not suggesting that Stewart should have engaged each user in an open chat that she would disclose; what I am arguing, however, is that her gaze is panoptic and shuts down discourse by punishing through disclosure. Thus, they too seek division over efforts toward community building that could result in changing the world and even these Twitter users.

As Kelly Wenzer points out in her essay "Perhaps I Am Watching You Now: Panem's Panopticons" in the book *Of Bread, Blood and* The Hunger Games*: Critical Essays on the Suzanne Collins Trilogy*, public consumption of discipline and punishment are essential features in Collins's fictional world, since the entire conceit of the Games is based on ongoing punishment for a past revolt (149 and 152). According to Wenzer, the Capitol's power is achieved partly because members of the public watch each other's punishment, and this act of watching constitutes participation in the punishing of others. In fact, as Wenzer reminds us, a tribute in the Games prior to Katniss's participation in the 74th Hunger Games found himself conveniently killed off by the Gamemakers when he cannibalized his fellow tributes (152). Wenzer and Katniss muse that the tribute's death in this case was a response to viewers' taste, to those watching whose gaze provides judgment.

Being made public—visible to the citizenry for critique, judgment, and punishment— means being subject to correction. The Panopticon's gaze means that we both fear being watched, but we are watching in return because it grants us power. We watch with the fear that we will be watched and judged. The Internet and fan culture have provided outlets where we can watch and be watched, but it has increased the stakes because it extends the reach of the gaze. The gaze, at this point, can be global and also timeless, because an error published online can be immortalized. Internet data can exist forever, if a savvy gazer saves and publishes a screenshot. Thus, content a user deletes can be preserved forever and always be searchable. Thus, the watching is always possible, as is the correction.

In engaging in direct and indirect conversations about things such as casting, we are watching and correcting others' choices, behaviors, and identities. Additionally, as evidenced by the self-deprecating Tweeters, we seem aware of the potential of being noticed outside of our circle of friends or social media contacts. I argue that this awareness of the potential of being watched is a way that netizens have internalized the digital Panopticon. Conscious that they could become the object of the gaze and therefore the subject of correction, these users turn the gaze onto themselves as though such a turn will satisfy our audience's need to correct them. Clearly, however, fans have not satisfied their audiences, as we see reports and responses to Tweets growing in popularity not only on blogs such as *Jezebel* but also on news broadcasts.

But the correction here often does not seek to align us but to separate. Foucault argues that the Panopticon divides us from each other. It makes identification impossible and therefore the imagining of a community weak. I believe that writers like Stewart, Seltzer, and West—and even myself—would like their correction of the filmmakers and Twitter-users to change racist attitudes and lead to a more harmonious community. However, what it does is create a hierarchy—those who are judges and those who are judged. It divides rather than aligns and unifies, despite best intentions. Thus, while bloggers like Stewart and West rightly attack racism, they also engage in the same separation that Foucault notes occurs in a situation that resembles the Panopticon, and which we see separating the people in the districts in Panem.

More troubling, the Tweets are even more divisive in their social policing, because they advocate for racial exclusion. It is difficult to discern these users' goals in their corrective expressions. While Stewart and her (current and former) colleagues seem to intend their gaze to change unacceptable behavior and bring it into more socially and politically appropriate expressions, the racist Twitter users do not seem to be motivated by any illusion of goals toward unity. Instead, they seem to be advocating for social division, and they accomplish this by offending some of their audience.

I would argue that regardless of motivation or intention, the Panopticon in action as I have discussed never results in any social unity. Instead, despite best intentions, it divides us from each other by constructing social hierarchies. This is, I argue, what Collins seems to fear: the way the panoptic gaze turns us against each other. We are doing this now—and even doing it using her own social commentary as our entry point into these practices. The problem is that we do not seem aware that our practices—both those good natured and those less so—are the very reasons why we hate the Capitol when we read the trilogy.

Conclusion

Collins's trilogy about war looks at how putting individuals at war against each other establishes power, which happens through the panoptic gaze, and how it turns us against each other, so that we begin to perform the watchful gaze ourselves. But often when we read the trilogy, we focus on the binary of Capitol versus District. But the panopticon breaks down those binaries so that there is a system of power exerted by the Capitol that watches and segments society, that creates districts that watch each other, and that is so pervasive that individuals within districts monitor and punish each other out of fear of being watched. This is not something Collins simply created. This is not simply fiction. This is reality, which Collins herself has hinted at when she discussed her own inspiration for the trilogy. The violence we face today does include real war, with real casualties and long-term consequences. But it also includes the ways we hurt each other by monitoring each other for social transgressions, pointing them out, and declaiming each other for flaws, for being black, for not being hungry enough, for not being sensitive enough, for being transgressive, for not monitoring ourselves.

This, to me, is why YA literature is so important—it is picking up on how teens begin to apply the social warfare of the Panopticon. *The Hunger Games* trilogy and other recent dystopian YA novels have used panoptic imagery to introduce readers to various means of social warfare. Teens reading these texts are reading social and political commentary. They are engaging with socially-aware ideas, and this seems to bring these readers into some early form of social awareness. The problem is that the way we—teen readers and adult critics—are using this social awareness is a mirror of the problematic fictional institutions we read about and hate.

Notes

1. Collins has not disclosed which reality show or shows she was watching. While her critics and fans might be curious about which reality program may have contributed to her creative process, I think it is irrelevant. Reality television has a range of genres: competition (romantic, talent, and obstacle courses), "real" lives (such as *The Real World* or the *Real Housewives* variants), those that cover subcultures (*Toddlers and Tiaras* or *My Big Fat Gypsy Wedding*), and those that follow businesses (*American Pickers* or *The Cake Boss*). I would also point out that this is not an exhaustive list of the genres but that it is a broad generalization of the kind of reality programming in the United States. Most of these shows claim to provide insight into individuals' lives and promote internal (and I would argue scripted) conflict between "cast members," even outside of the transparently competitive genres. In other words, most reality shows use authentic or fabricated conflict to attract an audience.

2. The gaze of the news has become more pervasive and even invasive because of the 24-hour news cycled that emerges in part because of the popularity of online news outlets and, I would argue, as a result from how the media covered the September 11th terrorist attacks in the United States. News consumers demand constant and immediate access to updated information, so news media have complied through their 24-hour news channels, ticker banners, websites, and use of Twitter.

3. This kind of writing is called "fanfiction." The *Fifty Shades of Grey* trilogy is one of the most popular examples of fanfiction. Author E. L. James reportedly wrote these novels, first, as *Twilight* fanfiction, which became hugely popular online. She revised the texts to minimize the similarities to Stephanie Meyer's *Twilight* series, and the novels were published. This phenomenon suggests that fan products and fan activity have a power and agency that deserve critical attention, even if scholars criticize the quality of the products.

4. Christian Bale and Matthew McConnaughey are two actors who have received media and positive critical attention for losing dramatic amounts of weight for roles. I have observed

that while men are lauded for losing muscle mass and fat for roles, women are paid similar attention for *gaining* weight for roles, such as Rene Zellweger for her portrayal of Bridget Jones. An additional complication in this gender difference is that women are also scrutinized for how quickly or slowly they return to their pre-role weight. Anne Hathaway, however, famously dieted unhealthily to lose weight for her performance in the film adaptation of *Les Miserables*. She won an Academy Award for her portrayal.

5. When Collins describes her characters in the trilogy, she avoids using racialized language that her readers would find familiar, such as "Latin" or "Latin-American" or "African-American." Instead, she describes the characters' appearance in terms of skin, hair, and eye color. Thus, Rue's race could be described as indeterminate. I am not, however, advocating that it is indeterminate. I read Rue as a Black character based on Collins's description.

Works Cited

Abel, Elizabeth. "Black Writing, White Reading: Race and the Politics of Feminist Interpretation." *Critical Inquiry* 19.3 (1993): 470–498. Print.
Blair, Carole. "Contemporary U.S. Memorial Sites as Exemplars of Rhetoric's Materiality." *Rhetorical Bodies*. Eds. Jack Selzer and Sharon Crowley. Madison: University of Wisconsin Press, 1999. 16–57. Print.
Collins, Suzanne. *Catching Fire*. New York: Scholastic, 2009. Print.
_____. "Contemporary Inspiration. Interview by Scholastic." Scholasticwww. Scholastic, n.d. Web. 1 September 2012.
_____. *The Hunger Games*. New York: Scholastic, 2008. Print.
Dargis, Manhola. "Tested by a Picturesque Dystopia: 'The Hunger Games' Based on the Suzanne Collins Novel." *The New York Times*. 22 March 2012. Web. 23 March 2012.
Dominus, Susan. "Suzanne Collins's War Stories for Kids." *The New York Times*. 8 April 2011. Web. 1 September 2012.
Foucault, Michel. *Discipline and Punish: The Birth of the Prison*. Trans. Alan Shepherd. New York: Random House, 1997. Print.
Juzwiak, Rich. "How a Kid-Lit Favorite Is Really About Trash Television." *Jezebel*. N.p. 26 August 2010. Web. 1 September 2013.
Morrison, Toni. *Playing in the Dark: Whiteness and the Literary Imagination*. New York: Vintage, 1992.
Seltzer, Sarah. "The Imminent Whitewashing of *The Hunger Games* Heroine." *Jezebel*. N.p. 14 March 2011. Web. 1 September 2012.
Stein, Sadie. "We Are All 14-Year-Old Girls." *Jezebel*. N.p. 24 April 2009. Web. 1 September 2012.
Steward, Dodai. "Racist *Hunger Games* Fans Are Very Disappointed." *Jezebel*. N.p. 26 March 2012. Web. 1 September 2012.
Wenzer, Kelly. "Perhaps I Am Watching You Now': Panem's Panopticons." *Of Bread, Blood, and* The Hunger Games*: Critical Essays on the Suzanne Collins Trilogy*. Eds. Mary F. Pharr and Leisa A. Clark. Jefferson, NC: McFarland, 2012. 148–57. Print.
West, Lindy. "I See White People: *Hunger Games* and a Brief History of Cultural Whitewashing." *Jezebel*. N.p. 27 March 2012. Web. 1 September 2012.

Creating a New Ethics
Student Responses, Reality Television, and Audience Awareness

LINDA J. RICE *and* KATIE WRABEL

> "But ... what if everyone just stopped watching?"
> "But they won't, Gale."
> "But if they did. What if they did?"
> "Won't happen."
> "It's like a train wreck, Katniss. You may not want to watch, but you do. That's how they win... If no one watches, then they don't have a game. It's as simple as that."
> —Gale Hawthorne and Katniss Everdeen, *The Hunger Games*

As the passage above illustrates, audience is crucial to the very existence of the Hunger Games. Suzanne Collins makes clear throughout her trilogy that the only functions of the Games are to remind the twelve Districts of Panem that the Capitol is all-powerful and to deter citizens from inciting another rebellion. Therefore, without an audience, there would simply be no purpose for the Games. Indeed, as Collins succinctly states: "If there's not an audience, there's not a [...] game" at all (qtd. in Egan 9). Although set in an unspecified future North America, the imagery used throughout *The Hunger Games* echoes the gladiatorial contests of the Roman Colosseum. From the use of ancient Roman names (e.g. Cinna, Flavius, Cato), to the procession of chariots, to the Arena itself, Collins keeps the allusions to Roman culture ever present throughout the dystopian Panem—the name of which, incidentally, Collins derived from "panem et circenses," meaning "bread and circuses," a Latin phrase referring to Roman citizens exchanging their political power and freedom for bread and entertainment (Egan 9).

Although we no longer travel in droves to the Colosseum to watch Roman gladiators fight to the death, contemporary fascination with this form of combat is evident in the wild popularity of *The Hunger Games*. By August of 2012, only months after the theater release of the film adaptation, there were over 50 million copies in print in the United States alone (Bosman). The trilogy not only reveals our society's continued enthrallment with these competitions, it also creates a modern context for an ancient pastime in a scenario that is not difficult to fathom. This is because the spectatorial consumption of the barbaric Hunger Games by the population of Panem is a thinly veiled, even conspicuous, modification of the contemporary phenomenon of reality television. By coupling this modification with the tension between ancient imagery and a futuristic setting, Collins suggests that society has not evolved as far from the gladiator days as we may like to think. Perhaps we have merely exchanged the sand and grit of the physical battles fought in front of 50,000 cheering fans at the Colosseum for the carpet and studio lighting of psychologically and emotionally damaging competitions televised for upwards of 15 million viewers. Because of the importance of audience in *The Hunger Games* and the reality television it critiques, both are socio-cultural artifacts that we should examine in the contextual moment to learn about the audience and, therefore, our social environment.

Rather than approaching this analysis of *The Hunger Games* solely through a scholarly lens, this essay blends traditional academic scholarship and popular discourse on reality television with a group of Integrated Language Arts methods students' (i.e., future middle and high school English teachers) responses to the trilogy. This combination of approaches highlights the many layers of meaning in the trilogy, and emphasizes the important uses of different audiences of readers who find *The Hunger Games* relevant to their lives and to our current social consciousness. In a critical context, more specifically, the voices of students, particularly those who are still adolescents or who are transitioning from adolescence to adulthood, are frequently spoken for or about, but their voices themselves are often silenced. In the interest of intellectual and discursive integrity, scholarly communities must incorporate students' voices and value the quality of the knowledge they contribute to conversations about the literature that represents the adolescent stages that students may still be going through. For example, much of the controversy surrounding *The Hunger Games* concerns the extreme violence and what this violence communicates to children, the intended audience, even to the point that some critics and school administrators warn parents not to allow their children to read or attend screenings because of its "repugnant premise" (Bartlett 17). However, since the role of audience is crucial in *The Hunger Games*, why have we not sought input from an audience for whom this text was written? As they are on the verge of leaving their own adolescence, this particular generation of students, as future teachers, occupies a unique threshold—a nexus of adulthood and adolescence, of teacher and student—giving them a distinct, rich perspective on the text. Because these students grappled with the themes and issues in *The Hunger Games* in a teaching methods course, they approached the text meta-cognitively and pedagogically, and were challenged to think beyond themselves as the intended audience in order to devise teaching strategies that engage and examine the impact this literature will have on their students as well as themselves.

This essay is a short, initial entry way into the kind of YA scholarship that could combine traditional research with solicitations of students' (or other pre-professionals') input. A more extensive undertaking of this sort might be based on long-term qualitative research, through interviews and other field methods, into the impact of *The Hunger Games* and other texts on readers who are as invested in their futures and in literature as this project's participants are. This essay defines "parasocial relationships" that form between the audience and those whom the audience is watching. Several sections that combine traditional scholarship and student responses analyze what the audiences and creators of the Games mean for today's audience of readers and teachers.

Making Connections: The Hunger Games *and Reality Television as Evidence of Parasocial Relationships*

> "The world loves to watch the stars go through problematic, humiliating, or horrific events because they do not think of the people as real; they see them as pure entertainment. It shows a lack of compassion and even a lack of understanding for fellow people."
> —Rebekah Rittenberg, student

The specific connections that Collins's fictional depiction of reality television makes to *our* experiences with reality television largely involve parasocial relationships, or the feelings or relationships viewers assume or imagine themselves to have with television characters. In their research on the appeal of reality television, Patino, Kaltcheva, and Smith's "The Appeal of Reality Television for Teen and Pre-Teen Audiences: The Power of 'Connectedness' and Psycho-Demographics" examines "connectedness," which they define as the "level of intensity of the relationship(s) that a viewer develops with the characters and contextual settings of a program in the parasocial television environment" (289). In *The Hunger Games* trilogy, the construct of connectedness is visible through the involvement of the audience—the citizens of the Capitol, in particular—in the fate of the tributes and in the outcome of the Games. For example, considering the drama created when Katniss tells

Hunger Games master of ceremonies Caesar Flickerman "[Prim] asked me to try really hard to win ... I swore I would" (*THG* 129), it is no surprise that the Capitol audience responds with an enthusiastic applause. This phenomenon of parasocial relationships that exist between the audience and the tributes parallels reality television show patterns with which we may be familiar. For example, Coyne, Robinson, and Nelson's "Does Reality Backbite? Physical, Verbal, and Relational Aggression in Reality Television Programs" specifically examines programs that encourage the viewers to participate "by either voting for the characters they want evicted (e.g., *Big Brother*), or those they wanted to stay (e.g., *American Idol*)" (286). The authors assert that this sense of interactivity and connectedness "persuades the audience to be explicit accomplices in the aggression viewed" and, therefore, blurs "the line between viewer and television characters" (286), a blurring of roles clearly reflected in the increased sponsorship of Katniss and Peeta as they manipulate the media and portray themselves as star-crossed lovers.

The environmental and psychological manipulation rendered in *The Hunger Games* is also present in reality television. Coyne, Robinson, and Nelson, who conducted research on physical, verbal, and relational aggression in reality television programs, found that while reality television "has very little scripting by nature, and purports to highlight real interaction among people... [the settings] lend ammunition to the relational and social warfare that occurs" (295). Coyne, Robinson, and Nelson's research also reveals that producers and editors artificially produce relational aggression more than it is naturally produced; this idea is taken to the extreme in *The Hunger Games* where the Gamemakers control the weather, physical environment, and, therefore, the action in the Arena. Compared with the horrifying muttations and scenarios of Collins's imagination, strategies used to intensify reality television are relatively mild; however, the psychological effects of storylines that thrive on lies, cruelty, and betrayal are an equally grotesque core of reality entertainment.

From Adolescents to Professionals: The Responses of Teacher Education Students

> "The public likes the idea of watching other people whom they actually feel superior to, so producers [of reality shows] and television executives manipulate and humiliate people to ensure the success of their programming. It doesn't end in death like the Games, but often those involved are embarrassed and humiliated, and the audience enjoys their downfall... It is a disturbing aspect of our culture."
> —Katrina Hewitt, student

Our students' responses toward the role of the audience in *The Hunger Games* ranged from commentary on the shallowness of the Capitol to expressions of horror at the "reality" the premise reveals about the underbelly of our own culture. Although some critics have shown concern regarding the trilogy's supposed appeal to adolescents' attraction to violence, these responses divulge an awareness of the psychological and emotional damage of the Games and suggest that Collins's message and clear parallels to American culture may not be lost on her audience of adolescents, young adults, and pre-professionals.

Students responded to the following questions: (1) *What aspects of the real world do you see in* The Hunger Games *series?* (2) *How might* The Hunger Games *be seen as a critique of reality television?* (3) *What might Suzanne Collins be cautioning us, as a society, about through her trilogy?* and (4) *What else would you like to say about* The Hunger Games *and its connections with modern society and/or entertainment?*

Based on their responses, it seems that a primary concern of students regarding the audience in *The Hunger Games* was dehumanization and objectification of the tributes, which subverts the empathy characters have for one another. One student, Mallory Kessen, observes that "Collins cautions against objectifying people to the point that they become shiny toys for us to watch." Kessen's notion of objectified "shiny toys" emphasizes Collins interest, in *The Hunger Games*, with celebrity status and appearance, a perversion of the survivalist and communal values of District 12. Katniss reflects on these warped values in the following passage from *The Hunger Games*:

> They do surgery in the Capitol, to make people appear younger and thinner. In District 12, looking old is something of an achievement since so many people die early. You see an elderly person, you want to congratulate them on their longevity, ask the secret of survival. A plump person is envied because they aren't scraping by like the majority of us. But here it is different. Wrinkles aren't desirable. A round belly isn't a sign of success [124–25].

The social commentary above is undeniable; Katniss's rumination serves as a direct critique of American culture and obsession with appearance and youth, and it also illustrates that social environment and circumstance shape what a culture deems valuable. Because of the grotesque surplus and wealth of the Capitol, these citizens have the luxury to be solely concerned with appearance and sources of entertainment, unlike the citizens in the Districts living in poverty. Katniss articulates this clearly herself: "How would I spend the hours I now commit to combing the woods for sustenance if it were so easy to come by? What do they do all day, these people in the Capitol, besides decorating their bodies and waiting around for a new shipment of tributes to roll in and die for their entertainment?" (65). Katniss critiques the hollowness of the Capitol's existence and objectification of human beings, which in turn gives readers pause to evaluate the contemporary values of the American culture that the Capitol parallels.[1]

The comical depiction of Katniss's introduction to and makeover by her styling team emphasizes the fascination with the physical as well, but it also reveals the dehumanizing nature of the Games. Both Katniss and her stylists (with the exception of Cinna) seem alien to each other. In fact, to Katniss, Flavius, Octavia, and Venia do not even appear human. As they study her naked body to determine how to approach her makeover, she reflects on the disconnect between their worlds: "I know I should be embarrassed, but they're so unlike people that I'm no more self-conscious than if a trio of oddly colored birds were pecking around my feet" (*THG* 62). Ironically, the three stylists also do not view her as human until they wax her legs of hair (and a few layers of skin): "The three step back and admire their work, 'Excellent! You almost look like a human being now!'" (62). Waxing and polishing is what the stylists believe constitute her humanity, further demonstrating the society's utter focus on appearance. This dehumanization continues within the Arena, where Collins uses animal imagery to describe the tributes, specifically the Careers, who begin "closing in, just like a pack of wild dogs" (181). The tributes' figurative transformation into animals persists until their literal transformation into a pack of muttations that are part human, part wolf.

More significant than merely highlighting the Capitol's warped values is that the audience determines the success and failure of tributes while they are actually in the Arena by providing sponsorship to the tributes they find appealing, making physical prowess secondary to the ability to manipulate the audience's empathy and affection. However, this empathy is intimately connected with appearance and persona, as Katniss's mentor, Haymitch Abernathy, reveals when he grabs her shoulders after she argues about the truth of her and Peeta being star-crossed lovers: "Who cares? It's all a big show. It's all how you're perceived" (135). Altering public persona and physical appearance to an image that is more endearing, charming, and attractive to Capitol audiences is the surest way to win the Games. This insight poses an interesting psychological twist for Katniss and for us as readers, in that qualities we tend to associate with the superficial become the very aspects that enable survival, determining matters of life and death. Being remade into a "shiny thing" may result in demonization, but it is also necessary. With the help of her stylist, Cinna, and Haymitch's additional coaching on how to develop the appearance of a love relationship between her and Peeta at the end of *The Hunger Games* as the first novel in the trilogy, Katniss cultivates the ability to woo sponsors and thus secures several "gifts" while she is in the Arena, including burn medicine, broth, crescent bread, sleep syrup, and a container of the rich lamb dish she was fond of during her time at the Capitol. These simple "shiny objects" do, as Haymitch advises, greatly assist Katniss and Peeta in becoming the last two tributes standing.

Not only was the objectification of tributes problematic for students, but so were the ways in which tributes were paraded in front of the public before being thrown to their deaths. Student Katrina Hewitt notes, "There is nothing real about what happens in the Arena. [The Games are] manipulated by the Capitol [and] orchestrated without regard to how it affects those involved. The tributes are essentially pawns." There are two important aspects of the Capitol's orchestrated show: (1) it illustrates the Capitol's use of media to control and manipulate viewers as well as tributes, and (2) this manipulation allows for the further dehumanization of the tributues, or reality TV show stars in the real world.

The government wields the most power over the Hunger Games, using media and Gamemakers to manipulate the citizens of Panem as well as the physical environment within the Arena. The government's overt use of power and its complete disregard for human life are evidenced not only by the Games themselves, but in the Capitol's control of the food supply, which is also used as a way to ensure that a revolution of the districts against the Capitol would never happen again. The threat of starvation propels the Capitol's dominance over human life in Panem, distracting citizens from rebellion and maintaining their oppression: "Since she was eleven years old, Katniss has spent every day preoccupied with how to feed her family.... The Capitol uses food, or lack thereof, as a weapon. One of the goals of the Games is to remind the oppressed districts that a full stomach is synonymous with power" (Egan 69). By keeping the twelve districts in poverty, the Capitol preserves supreme power, relying on citizens' primeval natures to wipe out compassion and civil unity. The Games are then used in conjunction with starvation to this same end, as Katniss reflects that the Games are treated "as a festivity, a sporting event pitting every district against the other," thus adding to the humiliation and sense of control the Capitol is able to wield over the citizens (*THG* 19).

The Capitol relies heavily on Gamemakers to provide the entertainment necessary to keep the audience enthralled and, therefore, abstracted, for "an entertained populace is a docile populace" (Bartlett 10). Games that are deemed the most successful are especially primitive and bloody, keeping the audience on the edge of its seat: "they like to see the tributes draw blood personally" (*THG* 219). Therefore, the Head Gamemaker is expected to keep the Games going when action lulls; they may set the forest on fire, plunge temperatures to bitter cold, or unleash muttations to change-up and re-intensify the Games. However, the psychological damage is as important as the physical violence, as illustrated by the following excerpt: "The Gamemakers don't want me dead. Not yet anyway. Everyone knows they could destroy us all within seconds of the opening gong. The real sport of the Hunger Games is watching the tributes kill one another" (*THG* 177). As this passage demonstrates, the Capitol depends on both the Gamemaker's manipulation of the environment and the audience in asserting power. Without an audience, televising the Games would be futile and the government impotent.

One way in which the government controls the audience, as well as the tributes, is through sensational media interviews. Mallory Kessen addresses the "glitzy interviews the tributes must give," observing that Collins warns against this garish sensationalism, relating this dehumanization of Katniss and other tributes to the popular reality show, *Jersey Shore*: "As seen in people's reactions to someone like Snooki, it can be very easy to forget that someone is a human when the cameras let us judge them." As a way to combat viewers' propensity for judgment, students concluded that viewers must approach reality television with a more critical eye, a practice that translates well to the classroom. Additionally, one student, Clare Volz, observes that "Collins asks us not to forget that others are suffering while we lead our lives of extravagance and surplus." Collins expresses her caution through the gaudy representation of the shallow citizens of the Capitol and those citizens who have become so enthralled by the drama of the Hunger Games that they are desensitized to the poverty of the districts and death of children, surrendered to the sacrificial altar of the Arena. This reflection opens a critical dimension of thought in terms of how we operate as consumers of entertainment. Have we, like the citizens of the Capital, become so accustomed to viewing physical and emotional injury that we have lost touch with the reality of those whose lives are deeply impacted by these difficulties? As anyone who has been personally affected by an accident, the severing of a close relationship, an illness, or an addiction know, the effects of emotional and psychological suffering are often deep and long lasting, as Collins illustrates through various allusions and representations of mental illness and emotional scarring, including Haymitch's alcoholism and isolation, Katniss's mother's depression, the "madness" that overtakes Titus, who becomes cannibalistic (*THG* 143), Cato's rage and ripping of his hair (*THG* 224), and Katniss's own emotional struggles and periods of seclusion. Have we become, as Katrina Hewitt insists the Capitol audience is, mere pawns in media orchestrated spectacles?

Cultural Implications

"We obtain pleasure from the pain of others. *The Hunger Games* exaggerates this, but only slightly. We breed people to live their lives in pursuit of entertaining others as they seriously harm themselves... Perhaps they are not fighting a battle to death in an arena, but they're experiencing concussions on the field and a life of backstabbing family/friends who do not learn to [cultivate] healthy relationships."

—Clare Volz, student

As Collins prompts readers to reflect on public fascination with celebrity and image-making, it is worth considering the possibility that preteens and teens who demonstrably strive for popularity and physical attractiveness commiserate or identify with participants on reality-television programs (Patino, Kaltcheva, and Smith 2011). *Real to Me: Girls and Reality TV*, a 2011 study by the Girl Scout Research Institute, reveals some striking correlations between girls' self-image and viewing of reality television.[2] The study reported that girls who regularly view reality television are "more focused on the value of physical appearance" as evidenced by these findings: 72 percent of the study's participants say they spend a lot of time on their appearance, as opposed to the 42 percent of non-viewers; more than a third (38 percent) think that a girl's value is based on how she looks, as compared to 28 percent of non-viewers; and 28 percent say they would rather be recognized for their outer rather than their inner beauty, as compared to 18 percent of non-viewers. Student Paige Kerrigan echoes this idea more broadly. She states:

> Our obsession with media and reality television has forced us to become dependent on the doings of these celebrities instead of focusing on our own lives. [Collins's trilogy] cautions our obsession with perfection and beauty and the importance of changing our appearance [by asking] "at what cost?" Drug abuse? Eating disorders? Alcoholism? Surgery addiction?

Another student, Laura Risaliti, links this obsession with image to the reality show *Bridalplasty*, in which women compete for different plastic surgeries to perfect their appearances and have the "perfect wedding." The wedding-related competitions seem benign enough, but Risaliti raises ethical concerns regarding the show because it focuses on "working the system" in ways that cause the competitors to build alliances bent on manipulation. In a group discussion about the show's impact, students expressed serious concern about *Bridalplasty*'s messaging, raising the following questions: Why is appearance so important? What are these women going for? Do they really want the marriage, or do they just want the wedding? These are insightful questions that prove to be even more poignant when we consider that younger adolescents (i.e., middle and high school students) are some of the biggest consumers of reality television and may not be asking these questions. Herein lay the concern: viewing reality television without critical thought can gradually erode or at least shift the standard for what is important, since the consumption of reality shows without analyzing them diminishes the critical thinking skills of our students and alters their values and relationships.

Reality television's responsibility in the shifting morality and the normalizing of unhealthy behaviors, which Collins cautions against in her trilogy, is evident in the behavior of middle school students. One student, Tonya Atha, observes the impact these shows had on her students while she was doing her field work in a middle school, specifically regarding how the language of some reality shows has worked its way into middle-schoolers' vernacular. Atha states that students openly talk in the hallways about "smooshing," the term used in *Jersey Shore* for having sex. Tangentially, Risaliti discusses profanity, skimpy outfits, abusive relationships, binge drinking, fighting, and casual sex among the routine components of *Jersey Shore*, components that contribute to the loss of childhood wonder and rob the innocence of youth. As she puts it, "many teens who watch the show idolize the cast and want to follow in their footsteps, even though they may be five, ten, or fifteen years younger."

Adolescent engagement with reality television is also augmented by social pressure. As student Meghan McComb states: "Not watching these [reality TV] shows, in essence, can be detrimental to an adolescent's social standing. Without knowing what is going on in the latest episode of said television series, you feel out of touch with the social scene." Like the children of Panem who are given few options regarding their participation in the Hunger Games, adolescents struggle with the social expectations and pressures placed on them by peers and media, and reality television impacts the way they view themselves and interact with each other, to the point of altering their very language and behavior.

Conclusion

These pre-service teachers who look at this enormously popular trilogy with such a thoughtful, critical eye bode hope for our future. As a tool for addressing serious questions concerning socioeconomic stratification and poverty, government control, and the lengths to which we will go—at other people's expense—to be entertained, *The Hunger Games* is tremendously valuable. As future teacher Risaliti puts it, "*The Hunger Games* series makes every reader a President Snow. We are forced to ask ourselves, 'What am I willing to compromise for the sake of my own personal enjoyment?'"

Because of its popularity and literary value, *The Hunger Games* proves a fruitful text to use in an academic setting to engage students in critical discussion about the text itself as well as the American culture it boldly critiques. Issues pertinent to *The Hunger Games*, including the loss of childhood wonder and robbing the innocence of youth, socioeconomic stratification and poverty, government control and societal uprising, and the pains of adolescent emotional development, are critical to the text and understanding of our culture, particularly if examined as a series of warnings of excessive government control and consumerism. *The Hunger Games* provides not only a treatise on reality television, but also a critical lens for self-reflection and societal analysis of our insatiable thirst for entertainment that is built upon violence, conspiracy, and manipulation.

Enacted in a manufactured Arena before an audience, the life-or-death nature of *The Hunger Games* mirrors the sand and grit of the gladiator fights in ancient Rome and reveals our culture's continued embrace of human suffering as entertainment. Through a marriage of the ancient and the futuristic, Collins suggests we become a conscious, self-reflective audience, challenging us to consider to what degree we have evolved from the days of the gladiator and how distant the future is in which the Hunger Games await.

Notes

1. Also see Ann M. M. Childs's essay in this collection for more on the relationship between the Capitol audience and the reader.

2. As of now, a similar study has not been done to track correlations between boys' self-image and viewing of reality television.

Works Cited

American Idol. Prod. Ken Warwick. Fox. Los Angeles. 2002. Television.
Bartlett, Myke. "Appetite for Spectacle: Violence and Entertainment in *The Hunger Games*." *Screen Education* 66.1 (2012): 8–17. *Informit Humanities & Social Sciences Collection*. Web. 25 May 2013.
Big Brother. Prod. Marnie Sirota et. al. Channel 4. London. 2000. Television.
Bosman, Julie. "Amazon Crowns *Hunger Games* as Its Top Seller, Surpassing *Harry Potter* Series." *The New York Times*. 17 August 2012. Web. 25 May 2013.
Bridalplasty. Prod. Mark Cronin. E! Los Angeles. 2010. Television.
Bushman, B. J. "Does Venting Anger Feed or Extinguish the Flame? Catharsis, Rumination, Distraction, Anger, and Aggressive Responding." *Personality and Social Psychology Bulletin* 28.6 (2002): 724–31. Print.
Collins, Suzanne. *Catching Fire*. New York: Scholastic, 2009. Print.
_____. *The Hunger Games*. New York: Scholastic, 2008. Print.
_____. *Mockingjay*. New York: Scholastic, 2010. Print.
Coyne, Sarah M., Simon L. Robinson, and David A. Nelson. "Does Reality Backbite? Physical, Verbal, and Relational Aggression in Reality Television Programs." *Journal of Broadcasting & Electronic Media* 54.2 (2010): 282–98. Print.
Egan, Kate. *The World of the Hunger Games*. New York: Scholastic, 2012. Print.
Hewitt, Katrina. Questionnaire/Personal interview. 29 January 2013.
The Hunger Games. Dir. Gary Ross. Lionsgate, 2012. DVD.
Jersey Shore. Prod. SallyAnn Salsano. MTV. Burbank. 2009. Television.
Kerrigan, Paige. Questionnaire/Personal interview. 29 January 2013.
Kessen, Mallory. Questionnaire/Personal interview. 29 January 2013.

Patino, Anthony, Velitchka D. Kaltcheva, and Michael F. Smith. "The Appeal of Reality Television for Teen and Pre-Teen Audiences: The Power of 'Connectedness' and Psycho-Demographics." *Journal of Advertising Research* 51.1 (2011): 288–97. Print.
"Real to Me: Girls and Reality TV." *Girl Scout Research Institute*. Girl Scouts of the United States of America, 2011. Web. 25 February 2013.
Risaliti, Laura. Questionnaire/Personal interview. 29 January 2013.
Rittenberg, Rebekah. Questionnaire/Personal interview. 29 January 2013.
Volz, Clare. Questionnaire/Personal interview. 29 January 2013.

Part V
Envisioning Future Spaces

Outside the Seam
The Construction of and Relationship to Panem's Nature

CARISSA ANN BAKER

From the depictions of wilderness space outside District 12 to the depictions of manufactured "natural" space of the Arena, Suzanne Collins's *The Hunger Games* trilogy is rife with connections to and disconnections from the land. These texts break literary ground as their popularity coincides with obvious references to the environment. These references are especially timely and call on the young people of the present and future to think critically about the environmental destruction that is happening all over the world, and to connect their interests in "green" reading practices to "green" action. In this essay, I assert that society's relationship to earth is the primary, rather than secondary, theme for the trilogy, as this relationship enables Katniss's triumphs, serves as the basis of Panem's culture and politics, and provides the foundation for the trilogy's other important themes. Characters' lack of connection to the natural world causes individuals' strife, the government's oppressive power, a dichotomous society, and war. Because of these frightening images of what can happen when humans disconnect from nature, *The Hunger Games* trilogy is an important work of fiction that young adults should read and that scholars need to scrutinize from an ecocritical standpoint, in order that we all might understand the trilogy's profound (and prophetic) commentary on humanity's current and future place in the natural world.

Ecological criticism is an emerging field that investigates relationships between people, texts, and environments. Cheryl Glotfelty, an ecocritical scholar, describes "ecocriticism" in her text, *The Ecocriticism Reader: Landmarks in Literary Ecology*, as the "study of the relationship between literature and the physical environment" or an "earth-centered approach to literary studies" with *place* as a "new critical category" (xviii, xix). Place is a comprehensive category; it is not only physical, environmental space, but also a political, emotional, and theoretical designation. The late 1980's held the "birth of environmental literary studies," but ecological criticism has gone through noticeable phases, including investigations of literary depictions of nature, rediscovering nature writing, locating place in authorial identity, and aligning it with other literary theories (xvii, xxiii, xxiv). Although scholars in this field approach texts through multiple theoretical angles, it is important to note that "all ecological criticism shares the fundamental premise that human culture is connected to the physical world, affecting it and affected by it" (xix). In addition, ecocriticism explores the "interconnections between nature and culture," with scholars sharing a "common motivation"—dealing with the "troubling awareness that we have reached the age of environmental limits, a time when the consequences of human actions are damaging the planet's life support systems" (xix, xx). Glotfelty recognizes this crisis of awareness when she looks at the wider world of academia: "Although scholarship claims to have 'responded to contemporary pressures,' it has apparently ignored the most pressing contemporary issue of all, namely, the global environmental crisis" (xv). Over the years, the field has extended itself to many disciplines and texts; however, young adult literature has been noticeably absent from ecocritical study, and much of the current scholarship in this area is focused on children's literature—perhaps as a result of perceptions among critics that the genre of young adult literature does not lend itself to ecological study. YA literature's absence from ecocriticism means that it is a theoretical imperative to study the literature that the future generations, who must claim responsibility for repairing the earth, are actually reading.

The Hunger Games trilogy demonstrates this imperative, of course, with its depiction of the tension between humankind and environment, to the point that Panem's condition of environmental crisis conspicuously mimics and exaggerates that of the "real world." Thus, this essay investigates the vital connections to and disconnections from nature depicted throughout the series. Probing the deep connections to nature in these texts is a valuable exercise, as it can yield vital insight into the concept of place in narrative, for use by scholars of young adult literature and ecocriticism. One of Glotfelty's most compelling statements is her warning to literary scholars that, "as environmental problems compound, work as usual seems unconscionably frivolous" (xx). Texts like *The Hunger Games* give scholars the opportunity to participate in this essential conversation, in which young adults and scholars may consider Panem's condition as a warning about the destructive nature of some technology, apathy, and oppressive structures that eliminate natural relationships. I contend that *The Hunger Games*'s depiction of Panem functions as a cautionary tale and that examining the aforementioned themes enables young adult literature to participate in the global debate about the state of the environment.

In addition, such examinations demonstrate ecological criticism's relevance to the culture of young adults who are in a position to effect change in the ways we read literary texts, in the ways we treat our environment, and in the ways literature can call its readers to action.

In this essay, I will explore the novels' manifestations of nature: "real" nature as wilderness, the Capitol's artificial constructed spaces, and hybrid expressions of nature such as the mockingjay. In addition to discussing these manifestations, I argue that every character in the series can be understood in terms of his or her relationship to *place*, specifically natural and synthetic physical spaces. Katniss's bond with nature is so significant that her worldview and language are constructed in reference to the environment. Likewise, Panem itself, its language, and its worldview reflect a troubled relationship to the natural world. These relationships, I assert, actually illustrate a continuum of nature and culture, with Collins's work calling for balance. Finally, I will investigate some fundamental themes which call upon readers in the real world to cultivate a connection to authentic natural spaces. Drawing upon the work of other scholars, this essay will be an invitation to other ecocritics to consider young adult literature and to all readers to consider the significance of place in these works. I hope that this essay will also prompt young adults, critics, and other readers to reflect on their own relationships to the natural world.

Real Nature: The Meadow Oasis

In *The Hunger Games,* Collins's first novel in the trilogy, Katniss Everdeen's description of District 12's wilderness serves as a textual manifestation of nature as sustenance, and in all three novels, Katniss's identity as a hunter is vital to her narrative. Katniss and Gale feed their families on the greens and meat they gather and hunt from the woods. Sharon D. King's "(Im)Mutable Natures: Animal, Human and Hybrid Horror" problematizes this identity by reflecting on the relationship between humans and animals, with Katniss identifying more with the latter. Her identification with the wilderness is what makes Katniss a viable contender in the Arena, as she herself is aware, since her hunting and gathering skills enable her to obtain decent nutrition and the exercise strengthens her body, more so than some of the other tributes (*THG* 95). In this way, the wilderness forms her body, lifestyle, and self-knowledge. Even her familiarity with berries, enabling one of Katniss's more important gestures of rebellion at the end of the first novel, demonstrates her identification with wilderness as transgressive nature, rather than cultivated, nature. Countering the Capitol's perception of the supremacy of cultivated nature, Katniss proves that understanding the forest and what lies within can lead to subversion and power. After the Gamemakers announce that Peeta and Katniss, as the final two surviving tributes in the Games, cannot both win, Katniss and Peeta agree to swallow the berries. Although their motivations for swallowing the berries differ—with Katniss "only thinking of out-smarting the Gamemakers" (*THG* 358) and with Peeta acting out of love for Katniss and a refusal to be the Capitol's pawn—both tributes consider suicide the better alternative to following the tenuous rules of the Games, in which tributes are pawns and fight to the death. The Gamemakers, once they realize the two tributes' intentions to eat the poisonous berries, stop Katniss and Peeta mere seconds before they swallow the berries and hurriedly declare the tributes victors of the 74th Hunger Games. The tributes' act is dramatized in the Capitol's media as an act of love, but by more astute spectators in the Capitol, such as President Snow, this act is viewed as rebellion. In terms of Katniss's identity, this action of using her knowledge of the sustenance to be found in the woods asserts her rightful place in the wilderness and further establishes her transgressive function in the plot.

This form of transgression is not isolated to Katniss's "trick with the berries." Katniss uses the wilderness, its space and sustenance, and its proximity to her District, to subvert the Capitol both before and after the Games, considering that her "hunting in the woods surrounding District 12 violates at least a dozen laws and is punishable by death" (*CF* 9). Katniss knows that the Capitol's oppressive regime controls the districts by restricting food supplies and other necessities, but her skills in hunting and gathering and in selling her game in the Hob, District 12's black market, provide for her family and friends despite the restrictions inside the District; this further undermines the Capitol's power (*THG* 19). In an interview that appeared in the *Journal of Adolescent and Adult Literacy*, Suzanne Collins describes the "use of hunger as a weapon to control populations" as an act of tyrannical government (qtd. in Blasingame 726). The Capitol clearly uses this mechanism to subjugate entire populations. Yet one young woman defies this systematic starvation, and the forest is her co-conspirator. This is a potent instance of how the author uses bonds with nature to construct meaning.

The forest itself is a central character in these works, as it saves, destroys, and connects human characters to their world. It is because Katniss remembered, by seeing a dandelion, the time in the woods with her father that she learns how to avoid malnourishment and feed her family, declaring the woods as her "savior" (*THG* 32, 49, 51). Unlike other characters, such as Katniss's sister Prim, who would shun the wilderness because of the wildlife and hard-to-navigate terrain, Katniss embraces it. She does not understand the relationship the Capitol people have with food, which seems to appear on command with no effort on the part of consumers. The Capitol pretends that nature is obsolete or absent, despite the relationships between the outlying Districts, as suppliers to the Capitol and nature. In contrast, Katniss cannot imagine coming by food in any way other than by hunting or gathering it oneself, nor can she imagine life's patterns—or "the hours [she] now commit[s] to combing the woods for sustenance"—arranged in any other way (65). Scarcity and adversity are material realities to her, a part of her identity, and an aspect of living with the land. The forest is an example of the vital theme of connection to nature. Through Collins's use of the wilderness as a central character, readers are called to focus on the significance of environment to the story world.

In addition to its other advantageous aspects, the wilderness, the woods outside of District 12 in particular, represents safety, where Katniss and Gale can rant against the Capitol and where the Capitol cannot control the thoughts, expressions, or identities of Katniss and Gale. In her essay, "Communal Spectacle: Reshaping History and Memory through Violence," Gretchen Koenig concurs that with her actions, Katniss "escapes to the open wildness of the land beyond the fence to find a sense of autonomy" (39). The wilderness is thus not only a physical space but a symbolic one conducive to independence. For Gale, the environment of the woods is a rhetorical space, a space to formulate a critical voice, to contrive revolutions, and to condemn the Capitol's brutal Games. The forest is tied to their existence, and the land becomes the stage for speech-making, even though Gale's audience is not a public one, and is comprised only of himself and Katniss. Thus, culture and nature, so often presented as binary, are merged. Although these areas seem separate, and Katniss and Gale leave the town space for the green space, the woods provide symbolic sustenance for political subversion. Furthermore, for Katniss, prior knowledge and experience in the woods transfers to the "wilderness" of the Arena, where trees are Katniss's safe spaces when she is being pursued, where she is able to use her skills of managing the terrain of the woods. Katniss may have a limited traditional education, but she has schooled herself in the forest and its ways. In addition, when in the relative security of District 13, the forest represents for Katniss a mental distraction from the underground reality of the rebel District, "overrid[ing]" her concerns and thoughts about the Rebellion (*MJ* 51–2). Although District 13 is safer inside, she opts to flee to the woods whenever she possibly can. Truly, to Katniss, the wilderness is "the doorway to both sustenance and sanity" (127). This passage reveals that despite her society's best attempt to escape into an artificial world, Katniss possesses an innate tie to the natural one. Whether it is for physical, symbolic, or emotional nourishment, the woods are a focal point in the story and continuously sustain the protagonist.

No matter its different purposes, the wilderness, in its many expressions, is the tie that binds the Everdeen family. Katniss is uncomfortable in a healing role, and like her hunter father (deceased before the plot begins), lives for days in the woods, while her mother and sister are healers. Each uses nature to save or heal, be it hunger or illness. While Katniss quips that "[k]illing things is much easier than [healing others herself]," she marvels as she or Gale is steadily healed by organic remedies, usually as a result of the expertise of Katniss's mother, sister, and even Rue, who know how to mend patients with natural remedies, using "dried herbs" throughout the trilogy and rarely the artificial medications of the Capitol (*THG* 250, *CF* 111). Katniss implicitly trusts the medicinal value of the fruits of the forest, her mother's "herbal concoction[s]," while the efficacy of the mechanized, "high-tech medicine brewed up in the Capitol's labs" is suspect (*THG* 188). The relationships between characters and nature here seem to establish that bonds and roles within a family are still essentially tied to the greater natural world. Accordingly, it shatters Katniss when her family, and her woods, are destroyed. As the forest is devastated, her family is damaged, while renewal occurs simultaneously. The wilderness is thus intrinsically associated with the Everdeen family and once again provides a narrative fulcrum.

Imitation Nature: The Capitol Veneer

The Capitol seems to have a vestigial relationship to nature in its allusion to the season of harvest, by terming the selection of tributes "the reaping" and by placing an oversized Cornucopia in the Arena. However, the Capitol has severed all connections to actual wilderness and experiences it only through indirect means, including representations on television and products from outlying districts. Capitol citizens do not produce goods; they only consume them, so nature is a commodity and citizens have no connection to nature's raw state. Indeed, the Capitol is a place where culture has wholly supplanted nature. Instead of District 12's earth tones and the grime associated with its mining industry, the Capitol is an immaculate example of cultural wealth and power. Katniss's descriptions liken the Capitol to a garish, alien landscape, full of "glistening buildings ... shiny cars ... oddly dressed people with bizarre hair and painted faces ..." and "colors [that] seem artificial, ... like ... candy we can never afford to buy at the tiny sweet shop in District 12" (*THG* 59). Katniss deems this landscape foreign yet familiar, magnificent yet gaudy, and consequently, she compares it to the luxury candy only the richer residents of her district can buy, thus signaling that as gleaming as it may be, it will always be out of reach. Poverty has rendered Katniss resentful, and the difference in landscapes jars her sensibilities. For Katniss, the Capitol is understood in terms of bright colors and opulence. Reality and fantasy, nature and its imitation, are juxtaposed when war finally comes to the Capitol, severing its imposed barrier, or hierarchy, between nature and culture, and yet again emphasizing that the Capitol's culture is predicated on that barrier and hierarchy, which until the war, had been kept intact. Katniss, ever a representative of the green world, remains critical of the consumerist culture and the façade of freedom, or the "bread and circuses" that mollify the Capitol populace and encourage them to give up "responsibilities" and "power" (223).

The Capitol's citizens provide another interesting facet of Collins's depiction of the Capitol's artificiality, as citizens are just as artificial and have little or no connection to nature—from their treatment of their own bodies, to their eating practices, to their use of space, to their conception of what it means to suffer. Katniss's district is ruled by the Capitol, but only "tributes" are formally invited (before their slaughter in the Arena) to venture inside and experience first-hand its gleaming richness. Instead of being thrilled as Capitol citizens might expect from their poor District counterparts, Katniss reacts to the emptiness of Capitol culture with disgust. This reaction registers on the small scale when she meets Capitol citizens. During the Victory Tour in *Catching Fire,* a typical Capitol party leaves her stunned by the extreme disparity between her compatriots in District 12 and the citizens of Capitol; those at home are emaciated while Capitol citizens vomit "for the pleasure of filling their bellies again and again" (*CF* 80). She notices that although their lives are already cushy, they drug themselves with caffeine and "brightly colored pills" (48). When thinking about her own appearance, Katniss muses on the possibilities showcased by the Capitol residents and responds with irony and disgust at the "freakish" appearance of Capitol citizens—irony and disgust that registers on an individual scale as well as on a societal scale (49). Even during the rebellion, in a high-stakes raid, Katniss is so attentive to the freakish appearance of the woman she kills in a Capitol house that her impression of this woman is one that almost disassociates her from her humanity: "She wears a bright turquoise silk robe embroidered with exotic birds. Her magenta hair's fluffed up like a cloud and decorated with gilded butterflies. Grease from the half-eaten sausage she's holding smears her lipstick" (*MJ* 314). Here, Katniss's sense of the virtual inhumanity strengthens her disgust for Capitol culture; it is foreign because it is distant from real, raw, and earthy nature with which Katniss is familiar, and because it reconstructs natures as flashy, garish, and commercial.

Additionally, Katniss's disgust at the woman and the Capitol culture as a whole relates to her perception that Capitol citizens are oblivious to genuine suffering. When on the run from Capitol forces, Katniss speaks to, and is aided by, the Capitol citizen Tigris, a cosmetic hybrid with her pulled skin, whiskers and tiger stripes; she is "the embodiment of Capitol shallowness" despite her assistance (320). Tigris has been displaced from the showy world of the Games, so out of her resentment, she helps the rebels, yet Katniss still sees her as synthetic and strange. Although Katniss eventually learns to tolerate and even appreciate her stylists/prep team (the silly Flavius, Octavia, and Venia), Gamemaker-turned-rebel Plutarch to some extent, and even her handler Effie Trinket, she nevertheless notices the contrast between these individuals' Capitol-produced luxury and the reality of her upbringing in District 12. Katniss's most significant change of heart toward certain individuals from the Capitol takes the forms of empathy and compassion, when Katniss's prep team is imprisoned and tortured for taking extra bread in District 13. The empathy and compassion, Katniss rationalizes, comes from connecting her own experiences of upheaval with those of her prep team, whose sense of security is destroyed when they are thrust into District 13's sparse reality, much different from the simulated comfort of the Capitol. Cinna is the only Capitol resident from whom Katniss perceives genuine empathy, and likewise is the only one who seems aware of the reality of District suffering, and thus represents what is typically missing from the Capitol. Cinna's awareness prompts him to play an instrumental role in the rebellion, as Katniss's advocate and the designer of Katniss's most scandalous attire—her wedding dress that burns away into a mockingjay during the Quarter Quell's opening ceremony, and Katniss's Mockingjay suit intended for the rebellion. Cinna's role connects his comprehension of suffering to the art that he creates to give Katniss a chance at survival. Yet, Cinna's advocacy means that he pays for this role with his life, his "assault ... staged to unhinge [Katniss]," minutes before her entry into the Quarter Quell Arena (*CF* 267). Cinna's fate shows that under the Capitol's regime, actively connecting an awareness of nature, awareness of one's real situation, and awareness of suffering is not without danger and fatal consequences. This turn of events in the plot raises the narrative and philosophical question: would this story be different if more citizens were aware of and acted on such connections—more citizens than just Cinna and other isolated examples?

President Snow, throughout the books, registers Katniss's strongest sense of disgust at artificial nature and at the progenitor of Panem's suffering. To Katniss's senses, President Snow reeks of "conflicting scents of roses and blood" (*CF* 17). The rose he leaves her as a message is "cloying and artificial" (*MJ* 14). The muttations he later sends after the rebels are reminders of Snow's power to "control nature" and incite fear. Whereas Katniss's role as the Mockingjay demonstrates the use of unexpected hybrids to symbolize rebellion and the empowerment of oppressed Districts, Snow poignantly uses artificial nature to co-opt natural symbols with terrifying and destructive results. Roses, a common emblem of beauty, love, or nature, are used as a mental weapon. Berries will kill in the Arena. Animals are recreated as grotesque. Snow is perhaps a hybrid too, combining human, animal, and even monster-like traits, as Katniss commonly associates him with snakes. Snow has distorted nature; his representation of environment to his people, which creates a perverted perception of nature, is one that Katniss must subvert in order to triumph. This is a powerful example of the prominence of the nature arc in the novels; Katniss begins in natural wilderness but must fight in artificial environments and against Snow's distortion and simulation. At the conclusion, however, Katniss returns to nature and thus illustrates the perseverance of authentic nature's value.

In the Arena, Katniss observes the details of the replicated environs, which function for her as both salvation and downfall, since in nature there is variation and ways to memorize terrain, but in a simulated environment "nothing seems to change" (*THG* 165). The fire is imitated and ruthless, with the flames' "unnatural height, a uniformity that marks them as human-made, machine-made, Gamemaker-made" (173). There is disgust in all of her accounts of synthetic nature. Even the fog, "too uniform to be natural," is used as a killer (*CF* 297). Lightning and trees are equally counterfeit (360). The Capitol creates environmental characteristics with ease but not perfection. Katniss would undoubtedly propose in this space that authentic nature trumps the simulacrum. For one thing, Katniss can discern between the levels of danger and security in real and simulated environments. Although real, wild nature in Katniss's narrative is fraught with darkness, hungry carnivores, and other threats that produce fear, it offers some degree of safety. In contrast, the controlled, mechanical creations of the Capitol signify peril only, never safety. Katniss figures that the threat of the tracker jackers that appear in the Arena, "one of the Capitol's muttations, ... like the jabberjays," are spawned in a lab and "strategically placed, like land mines, around the districts during the war" (*THG* 185). The jabberjays are used as torture devices, mimicking the dying screams of loved ones (*CF* 340). The tracker jackers drive a person to madness with hallucinations if they don't kill the person with their poison first. Other "mutts," such as monkeys and rodents, are bloodthirsty (303, 289). Real nature is not necessarily idyllic, but it brings sustenance and shelter; artificial nature is only gruesome and ugly. This evidence serves to prove that the novels continue to interrogate the systematic deprecation and appropriation of the natural world.

The Capitol, with its destructive power, disfigures nature while attempting to recreate it—and achieves an irony that is horrific and twisted. The 50th Hunger Games, in which Haymitch gains his victory and his lifetime of heartbreak, demonstrate the ironic power of disfiguring nature. The façade of these

Games is aesthetically stunning—"the most breathtaking place imaginable" (162). But quickly, this beauty becomes the scene of bloodshed and dreadful imitation animals including homicidal "candy pink birds" and carnivorous "fluffy squirrels," by which the Gamemakers work the worst psychological and physical horrors (201). In "Coal Dust and Ballads: Appalachia and District 12," (2012), Tina Hanlon identifies the "artificial wilderness ... designed to cause injury and death, showing how sadistic humans can use technology to pervert nature" (64). Even the ability to see nature as beautiful is tainted by the Capitol's sadistic motives, which ensure that its citizens will fear nature and desire distance from it. This manipulation of humans' associations with nature showcases the control that is possible with this move; if the Capitol divorces its citizens from nature, they remain distant from creation, suffering, awareness, and power.

The most disturbing Capitol creations appear as human-animal hybrids. In the first book of the trilogy, mutts come after the three last-standing tributes in the Arena and appear as "no natural-born animals" with "unmistakably human eyes" (*THG* 331). In this scene, these malevolent mutts resemble all the tributes killed prior to the face-off between Katniss and Peeta and their opponent Cato; their purposes are to mock, unhinge, and terrorize the survivors, and ultimately to create carnage for the viewers. In *Mockingjay*, as Katniss and rebel troops infiltrate the Capitol, lizard-humans with rose scents pursue them through the sewer system (306). Similar to earlier "muttations," these lizard mutts taunt the rebels and their smell produces a visceral association with and dread of Snow. King finds that the "monstrosity of the hybrid creatures goes beyond even their carnate forms" as their venom brainwashes Peeta into perceiving Katniss as non-human (114). It is apparent that nature, or the appearance of nature, or sometimes the manipulation of real nature, is indeed the greatest weapon the Capitol uses. Bill Clemente, in his article "Panem in America: Crisis Economics and a Call for Political Engagement," describes the "technologies of menace" that create the Arena but also accidentally produces the "animal weapon" of the mockingjay (24). Despite the Capitol's cultivated detachment from nature and wilderness, Snow knows that nature holds power and uses it to control, terrify and maintain the citizens of Panem. The Capitol citizens are lost and drugged, which makes them easier to manage. Unaware of the power structures that contain them, they are complacent with the problematic dissociation from the natural world. Someone like Katniss, who appreciates the survival inherent in the natural world and who is aware of the consequences of dissociating from or tampering with nature, is a perpetual threat to the Capitol's peace. Indeed, as Valerie Frankel states in her article "Reflection in a Plastic Mirror," it is because of the Arena's "artificial nature" that Katniss helps to "[break] through the phoniness and [destroy] it" the second time she visits (56). There is literally a kink in the artificial armor of the Arena; when Katniss physically pierces the force field to escape in *Catching Fire*, she symbolically destroys the assertion that simulated nature is perfect or more powerful than the authentic.

Hybrid Rebellion: Mockingjay Songs

Not all hybrid creations in the book are threatening. Unlike the Capitol-created mutts, mockingjays are a species occurring as an accident of an attempt to control nature, merging the natural mockingbird and the Capitol-created jabberjay. As they represent nature's ultimate strength and superiority over engineering, Katniss and the rebellion consider mockingjays "a slap in the face to the Capitol" (*THG* 42). Becoming herself the symbol of rebellion in the third book, *Mockingjay*, it is appropriate that Katniss provides the history of the bird and comments on its significance: "A mockingjay is a creature the Capitol never intended to exist. They hadn't counted on the highly controlled jabberjay having the brains to adapt to the wild, to pass on its genetic code, to thrive in a new form. They hadn't anticipated its will to live" (*CF* 92). Katniss's commentary aptly describes what happens with the rebellion itself. The Capitol is surprised when the districts it had oppressed and controlled for so long rise up and have the will to fight for freedom. The mockingjay becomes the symbol for the rebellion throughout Panem, as Katniss rises to fame and becomes the physical embodiment of the mockingjay ideal, from first wearing a mockingjay pin in the 74th Hunger Games to wearing a mockingjay garment in the final stages of the rebellion. Through the foresight of her stylist Cinna, who designs the mockingjay outfit, Katniss is able to live out her role in publicity stunts and in combat. Plutarch later advises an apprehensive Katniss: "We had to save you because you're the mockingjay...While you live, the revolution lives" (386). Katniss has been transformed into this hybrid to become a symbol, and the revolution hinges on this symbol, one that is still connected to nature's inherent power, specifically its power to transform and persist.

Furthermore, Katniss's identity as the Mockingjay and man-made objects like her pin continue to signal her association with the woods, possibly one reason she immediately makes a connection to the piece: "My fingers trace the circle around the little gold mockingjay and I think of the woods" (*THG* 54). As I explored earlier, the woods are the site of survival, healing, and subversion, thus another significant feature of the mockingjay as hybrid and symbol. Although Katniss is hesitant about her role, she eventually resolves to function as the mockingjay: "The bird, the pin, the song, the berries, the watch, the cracker, the dress that burst into flames. I am the mockingjay. The one that survived despite the Capitol's plans. The symbol of the rebellion" (*CF* 386). While at the beginning of the narrative, Katniss's goal is to survive the Games, she changes her focus when she tries to save Peeta, as "[her] way to defy the Capitol, to subvert its terrible games" (338). In the introduction to *Of Bread, Blood and* The Hunger Games*: Critical Essays on the Suzanne Collins Trilogy*, Mary Pharr and Leisa Clark declare, "Katniss *is* the epic hero Mockingjay," a persona and symbol (13). At the end of the final novel, Katniss is burned like the flaming bird she represents; King believes she has a "fusion with the rebellious hybrid creature" (114). She truly becomes a hybrid herself at that point, like the mockingjay and like her shattered district. Phoenix-like, they will all try to rise out of the ashes together but retain their scars. Katniss as the hybrid, the mockingjay, and the combination of human and nature together represents, in this story, renewal, and functions to upgrade and thus complete this trilogy's major theme of society's relationship to nature; in these novels, the revolution is fueled by symbols of nature.

Although District 13 appears at first, in *Mockingjay*, to be a purely human-crafted wonder, Katniss's time there reveals it to be a hybrid space. While still very cold, sterile, claustrophobic, and rigid, there is yet an oasis. Katniss discovers and feels solace in a small semblance of nature:

> Inside is the first beautiful thing I've seen in the District 13 compound: a replication of a meadow, filled with real trees and flowering plants, and alive with humming-birds. Beetee sits motionless in a wheelchair at the center of the meadow, watching a spring-green bird hover in midair as it sips nectar from a large orange blossom [*MJ* 65].

Collins explores the possibility for humans to use technology to recreate beautiful nature, rather than the terrifying, macabre nature of the Arena, in her ambivalent depiction of District 13. Frankel deems District 13 to be even more artificial than the Capitol, and Katniss must "[seek] nature in small ways" (57). This assessment is accurate considering that Katniss subsists on the parts of the District she understands. Katniss is the character who enhances District 13's purpose as a space that sustains life and nurtures emotions, demonstrating a turn in the direction of making it an enjoyable place to live. When she discovers that the district is situated within the woods, she negotiates with District 13's officials to arrange for Gale and herself to hunt in the forest area and to offer their wild-caught meat to the kitchen staff to supplement the engineered rations. Even Prim's cat Buttercup, which Katniss rescues from the wreckage of District 12, is eventually allowed to reside in District 13 through Katniss's negotiations, to the delight of the residents who have been confined during the rebellion months. District 13, through accepting refugees, has become more diverse, and class does not seem to have the same distinction it does elsewhere.

Perhaps this is a symbol for the possibility of this science-based district. Although also culpable in war, the scientists of District 13 can represent the hope of peaceful coexistence, sustainable farming, healthy emotions, and a respectful relationship to nature. Indeed, this is one of the most profound connections to nature in the novels. District 13 is built in the ashes of its post-apocalyptic condition, is still in the process of developing itself as a society, and has not yet cultivated a moderate (rather than excessive) culture of pleasure and entertainment, but it is a symbol of opportunity. Some of that opportunity stems from an evolving relationship to the natural world.

Katniss and Her Language of Earth

Since *The Hunger Games* is Katniss's story, it is no surprise that the strongest relationship between language and the land is in her words; undeniably, she is fluent in the language of landscape. *The Hunger Games* trilogy is a first-person narrative throughout, often descriptive and surprisingly poetic, but much of Katniss's prose is noticeably sparse and cynical. She responds to the world's cruelty and chaos with occasional callousness and frequent emotional distance. The primary times these narrative features change are during her meditations on nature, when Katniss employs poetic language, pathos, and occasional affirmative expressions. Her descriptions of the Meadow are particularly descriptive and detailed: "We settle back in a nook in the rocks. From this place, we are invisible but have a clear view of the valley, which is teeming with summer life, greens to gather, roots to dig, fish iridescent in the sunlight. The day is glorious, with a blue sky and soft breeze" (9). Her prose shows awareness of nature, but even more, it diverges from her normally singular goal of survival when she notices the aesthetic properties of the landscape. Even seeing one of Peeta's paintings recalls the beauty of nature: "The alternate pattern of light and dark suggests sunlight falling through the leaves in the woods" (96). The novels are dotted with such literary descriptions of the land she describes as "*[n]othing but a place where I was happy*" (*MJ* 127). There is little joy in most of Katniss's recollections throughout the series, and she notes the "weighty existence" that "pressures" her; the woods experience is the exception (*CF* 365). While discussing nature, she seems to move from a position of documenting history to being a *writer of a story*. The narrative can be perceived as an organic exercise; connection to nature in this case may actually be the impetus for this story, especially as readers consider the correlation between her family history and nature. Katniss's authorial voice is laced with the voice of the wilderness that informs her.

Throughout the plot of the first novel, Katniss repeats a fantasy of running away and living in the woods; her vision beyond is always tied to the freedom and safety she finds in earth. She reflects, "For a moment, I yearn for something ... the idea of us leaving the district ... making our way in the woods" (*THG* 25). Katniss's fantasies continue in *Catching Fire* with several considerations of the consequences of escape. She asks, "What would they do if I simply vanished? Disappeared into the woods and never came out? Could I even manage to take everyone I love with me, start a new life deep in the wild?" (*CF* 46). In *Mockingjay*, Katniss's consideration of fleeing matures into questions of whether she would have had a happy life with Gale in the "wild" if they had "escaped ... into the woods and left 12 behind forever" (366). This would be one of the most frequent regrets in the series. Frankel calls this a fantasy and likens it to the desires of early American writers to "retreat into the forest" for its "simplicity, endless bounty and safety from the agendas of others" (56). The American literary tradition watched the concept of wilderness transform from that of the savage and fearful and distant to that of subsistence and integrality for humanity. Katniss continues this need for balance with nature. Her deepest dream to run away is never to a place unknown, a different land, District 13, or the Capitol splendor; it is always somewhere in *her woods*. Katniss, or possibly the entire series, posits that harmony with the natural is essential to human existence.

Even in the Arena, in the limited times she does not think of the simulation around her, Katniss finds comfort in nature. She notes the "hopeful smell of pine trees" or proclaims that "being in the woods is rejuvenating" (*THG* 148). She notices as she is "back on pine needles and the gentle incline of the forest floor" and "the woods come alive with animal sounds" (314, 216). Her longing erupts, even as she is in mortal danger during her second trip to the Arena: "I begin to ache for them, for my district, for my woods. A decent woods with sturdy hardwood trees, plentiful food, game that isn't creepy. Rushing streams. Cool breezes" (*CF* 293). When she is in the woods, she feels at home; when she is anywhere else, she longs for the comfort of home. Even *visions* of nature sustain her in dangerous situations and they establish her continual link with the wild.

Katniss's language is constructed from a natural standpoint, so when Katniss makes negative associations, they are nonetheless laden with nature metaphors. Her comparisons between humans and animals include observations that capture the dehumanization, violence, and brute force that characterize the rhythm of the Games. Katniss describes Haymitch as "prodding [the victors] like animals," and says that being in the Arena is "like [being] a plucked bird, ready for the roasting" and "easy prey," that others are trying to "corral [them]," or "prepare [them] for the slaughter" (*THG* 58, 61, 72, 73, 74, 117). Katniss concedes she must flee "like the wild, wounded creature" she is

(289). Enemy tributes are a "pack of wild dogs" in a "Career pack" and are the "Capitol's lapdogs" (181, 167, 161). It is obvious that she views the entire Games as a hunt with children as prey. It is not only her language, then, but Katniss's very worldview that relies on environmental understanding. Her perspective in life is as a member of a marginal space between wilderness and society. The Seam itself is closer to wilderness than are the Capitol or the more comfortable citizens of the District such as Peeta, yet it is still separated by fences and the culture of District citizens. There are boundaries in Katniss's world: between the Seam and other district inhabitants, between the Capitol and the districts, between districts, between District 12 and the Meadow, between Panem and wilderness. Seams, stitches, margins, borders, transitional and liminal spaces weave through this narrative; Katniss's community, identity, history, past, and future are influenced by both margins and green spaces.

Pointing out Katniss's less violent comparisons, Frankel argues that Katniss views the Capitol "prep team" in charge of making her look suitable for television as "incomprehensible twittering birds rather than people" (51). Negative and positive associations are still related to natural perception in some way. When being confounded with tracker jacker hallucinations of altered nature, her prose continues with descriptive characteristics that rely on senses to illustrate connection to nature:

> I drag myself over to the honeysuckle bush and pluck a flower. I gently pull the stamen through the blossom and set the drop of nectar on my tongue. The sweetness spread through my mouth, down my throat, warming my veins with memories of summer, and my home woods and Gale's presence beside me [*THG* 196].

Katniss is not in her own mind here, and yet enough clarity is achieved that visions of nature dance in her head. Her negative, positive and subconscious emotions are equally constructed in terms of nature. Her language is laden with nature imagery and metaphors. Katniss is so wholly informed by nature that she seems unique or at least uncommon in young adult fiction.

Nature is what draws Katniss to other people, and each of her close relationships is defined by the association. Katniss connects to fellow tribute Rue deeply, and the relationship is closer as they both literally cling to nature. Rue goes "leaping from tree to tree" in a way that shows she is attached to her family's heritage in the orchards (189). Katniss teases Rue about this: "Orchards, huh? That must be how you can fly around the trees like you've got wings" (200). She later continues this comparison by likening Rue's family to a "flock of small dark birds" (*CF* 58). As Rue is dying from her wounds, Katniss sings, continuing the connection her father had with mockingjays and singing the mountain airs of ancestors. The song brilliantly weaves together mourning and a connection to nature: "Deep in the meadow, under the willow / A bed of grass, a soft green pillow / Lay down your head, and close your sleepy eyes / And when again they open, the sun will rise. / Here it's safe, here it's warm / Here the daisies guard you from every harm" (*THG* 234). This scene is tied to one in *Mockingjay*, in which Katniss sings to mourn her dead district and the mockingjays sing along. In that scene, she is supposed to be filming a piece in her smoldering home, but an uncommon bout of emotion overtakes her. Music and nature are linked in her world, in a painful but therapeutic way.

One of the most beautiful scenes in the series occurs when Rue dies and Katniss gives her a burial ritual appropriate for children of the earth: "A few steps into the woods grows a bank of wildflowers.... Slowly, one stem at a time, I decorate her body in the flowers. ...Wreathing her face. Weaving her hair with bright colors.... She could really be asleep in that meadow after all" (*THG* 237). Katniss is detailed in her description, and she strongly conveys her love of nature. The only appropriate way for Rue to pass on is as close to the lovely things in nature as possible, until the moment the intrusive, grisly metal corpse collector takes her away. This very display is considered an assault on the Capitol's Games; children are supposed to rejoice in each other's deaths, and audiences feel entitled to be entertained by a brutal show. The Capitol surely resents her display of beauty, as the loveliness of this funeral is another disconnect from these viewers who have experienced the enculturation of distance from nature. For the viewers in the Capitol, at least, this must have been a quaint and strange display. Katniss has an awareness of audience and sensitivity to Rue's identity as tied to nature when she asserts that "there is a part of every tribute they can't own" (236). For her, and for Rue, that part is a deep link to the natural world.

There is no doubt that nature memories thread the long relationship between Katniss and Gale. They have known each other a long time, but jaunts in the wilderness define their relationship. Katniss explains:

> In the woods waits the only person with whom I can be myself. Gale. I can feel the muscles in my face relaxing, my pace quickening as I climb the hills to our place, a rock overlooking a valley. A thicket of berries protects it from unwanted eyes. The sight of him waiting there brings on a smile. Gale says I never smile except in the woods [6].

The presence of happiness, though infrequent, is likewise tied to their shared experience in nature. Katniss recalls, "Being out in the woods with Gale ... sometimes I was actually happy" (112). She perceives that Gale has a similar connection: "I think of Gale, who is only really alive in the woods, with its fresh air and sunlight and clean, flowing water" (*CF* 5). Although Gale and Katniss do not always talk when in the woods, their deepest and most revelatory conversations are there. One of the most disturbing metaphors to Katniss, but nonetheless showcasing Gale's similar understanding of the world, is when

Gale relates the hunting of people to the hunting of animals while not seeing much difference (*THG* 40). This idea shocks Katniss (though she later confirms the similarity "in execution"), but it certainly indicates his parallel connection to the land (241). Although her relationship with Gale is complicated, it is not extreme to say that her perception of him is uniformly colored by his association with the woods. This is yet another line of evidence that describes a worldview informed by the natural world.

Katniss's connection with her father is likewise built on the memories of being with him in the woods, characterized by experiencing "the smell of blossoms and greenery ... the blue sky, ... the chatter of the woods" (*CF* 33). These experiences in nature define Katniss's very family history, a history documented, even, by a naturalist's book kept by her father, her mother and then herself (*THG* 50). The book functions as a system of family records-keeping even though many relatives and friends pass away. Though the book was started with images of nature, it is sustained by intertwining memories of people. Again, this speaks of the bonds inherent between nature and humanity.

Katniss draws a metaphor with nature even in making her choice of a husband. Katniss's eventual choice of Peeta over Gale to be her life partner is connected to nature. She chooses Peeta because he represents the beautiful, gentle part of nature, "the dandelion in the spring, ... rebirth instead of destruction" (*MJ* 388). Here she discerns Peeta's dissimilarity to her while marking Gale's resemblance to her with his representation of the moody, fierce part of nature. Though she has been in the wilderness with Gale more than Peeta, Peeta understands nature and humanity (both tenderness and brutality) through his art. Each engages with nature in a different way, and this balance is precisely what she would have lacked with Gale. They both watch as their world changes, but for Katniss, the history of her environment is closely tied to the history of her life. Peeta also represents his environment, one that, as Max Despain clarifies in "The 'Fine Reality of Hunger Satisfied': Food as Cultural Metaphor in Panem," is closely connected to bread, a "symbol of cultivation and community," and by extension human culture (71). Thus Katniss and Peeta end up in a world that is inclusive of both nature and culture, which seems to be the ideal state in Collins's Panem. Perhaps this is the very lesson that the entire series asks us to ponder.

A Primary Imperative: Seeking Authentic Connections with Nature

Although the themes of government oppression and a glorification of violence and reality television by the affluent members of society function as obvious focal points in the trilogy, the theme of characters' and societies' relationships to earth are more subtly and ubiquitously woven into the narrative. Indeed, the frequency of passages related to the earth is likely greater than many examples of dystopian or post-apocalyptic fiction. A close examination of *The Hunger Games, Catching Fire,* and *Mockingjay* reveals more references to nature than can be explored in a single piece of scholarship; Katniss's language of earth alone could fill a chapter. Still, the careful descriptions of Panem's natural world and its opposite, the Capitol's simulacra of city and Arena, as well as the connections between characters and the land, lead to the trilogy's primary imperative to seek authentic connections to nature. Hanlon, while focusing on the depiction of Appalachia, finds that the trilogy "[demonstrates] from beginning to end that living with nature is a basic human right and necessity" (64). This is the true end of the revolution: the right of connection to sustaining nature. Each of the characters that the reader is guided to empathize with is tied to the land in some way. The villains, whether in the Capitol or District 13, are cut off from the land. Collins presents a continuum, with nature on one end and culture on the other; one's awareness of the importance of the earth is an important criterion of life in Panem. The synthetic Capitol world would reel with the introduction of nature, while Katniss's nature-driven world must accept the reality of human culture. Balance, as represented by the relationship between Peeta and Katniss, is a key to living and accepting the world as it is. Collins's continuum has implications for other young adult books and for ecocritics who want to examine how much this spectrum is expressed in the real world.

The novels mourn the loss not only of a more connected nation with shared resources; they strongly lament the lack of union with the land. Nature has become controlled and inauthentic in many districts. Katniss's disdain for District 8's lifestyle would be applicable in many of today's urban areas: "I remember District 8, an ugly urban place stinking of industrial fumes, the people housed in run-down tenements. Barely a blade of grass in sight. No opportunity, ever, to learn the ways of nature" (*CF* 142). Katniss views lack of interaction with nature as a real failing, one that seems to strip humanity from those who live this way. In addition to experiencing the Capitol's control of their resources, these districts are imprisoned away from nature and handicapped by being made incapable of producing many goods for themselves. Katniss looks at both The Capitol and District 13 with aversion because of their detachment from the natural. In Katniss's worldview, it is a bond with nature that sustains humanity.

As noted, Peeta is more accepting of humanity's role in the earth's future. The more philosophical of the two, Peeta brings up profound questions of war, environmental destruction and the possible fate of humanity: "Our conditions are more tenuous. Is this really what we want to do? Kill ourselves off completely? In the hopes that—what? Some decent species will inherit the smoking remains of the earth?" (*MJ* 29). He pleads for a different way to live and immediately links the ruin of earth to the ruin of man. Katniss chastises herself for her lapses in awareness of disconnections from nature—which are usually very keen: "Was I simply too out of it before to register the loss of my world?" (120). Yet when she describes a better world, it is with nature in mind: "As I drift off, I try to imagine that world, somewhere in the future, with no Games, no Capitol. A place like the meadow in the song I sang to Rue as she died" (*CF* 354). Unlike common ideas of the future, filled with technology or luxury, her vision of the future is filled with images of embracing the natural world. Peeta and Katniss, united at the conclusion of the trilogy, can combine these ideas for the necessary balance that is so obviously lacking throughout pre–Rebellion Panem.

The themes of *The Hunger Games* were intended to be overt. As Collins explains, "The sociopolitical overtones of *The Hunger Games* were very intentionally created to characterize current and past world events" (qtd. in Blasingame 726). Environmental crisis is no doubt a current world event, and its regulation or conservation is closely tied to government. Collins continues, "Tyrannical governments have also used the techniques of geographical containment of certain populations, as well as the nearly complete elimination of the rights of the individual" (726). The author specifies that controlling the environment of a population is a crucial step in possessing power and suppressing a society. The Games assist with this goal: "In the book, the annual Hunger Games themselves are a power tool used as a reminder of who is in charge and what will happen to citizens who don't capitulate" (726). When citizens do dissent, the result is not always affirmative, as Collins discusses: "District 13 essentially is a wasteland because the people there had tried to revolt against the Capitol and suffered gruesome consequences" (727). This uprising led to decades of strife and a land scarred. Future upheavals, like the one in District 12, lead to similar disfiguration of people and lands. Pharr and Clark's Introduction explains that Panem, with its "inhabitable land drastically reduced through a cascade of natural and man-made disasters," is "painfully easy to imagine" (9). As this series is intended for young adults, these weighty themes may be pondered by the young, who will necessarily inherit similar dilemmas to those depicted in the story.

True to her word about her future desires for the renewal of nature in Panem and renewal of hope for herself and loved ones, Katniss returns home even when there is nothing left. Her mother has too many painful memories to stay, and yet Katniss chooses to witness a rebirth of her Meadow home. The Meadow is very literally a graveyard in the beginning of *Mockingjay* as

Katniss steps on a human skull (5). The green has even then been destroyed by the Capitol when their war made it a mass grave. Yet eventually, as is the penchant of real nature, there is restoration. Katniss finds comfort and hope in nature's re-greening, particularly in the Meadow, where years later, Katniss and Peeta's children play (388–389). This is a lesson in connection to nature; at least a third generation in the Everdeen family plays in the wilderness. The beginning and end of the series find the characters in the Meadow. Young adults reading the novels can draw conclusions about the importance of ties to nature. They can ask if their own society is becoming more disconnected from nature as it becomes more connected to technology. They can recognize technology even as something that can be conducive to nature's preservation. They can locate an authentic bond with nature in this series and explore their own relationships with the natural world. They can plot themselves on the continuum of nature and culture and reconcile themselves to the need for balance.

One possible connection to the continuum being represented in *The Hunger Games* comes from the ecofeminist work of Maria Mies and Vandana Shiva. They explain the estrangement from nature common to theory and derived from Enlightenment values where humanity's ideal was "emancipation from nature" (335). Mies and Shiva describe societal structures that might mimic Clemente's assertion of people in *The Hunger Games* as "capital" and "a commodity harvested for the Capitol's appetite" (Clemente 25). Mies and Shiva define the "subsistence perspective," where societies act on "direct satisfaction of human needs," a humane way to exist beyond political and economic structures. Though this perspective seems to shun technologies, it recognizes the "shared concern" of people worldwide when they are faced with environmental crisis, a concern that "override[s]...differences" (Mies and Shiva 335). Importantly for *The Hunger Games*, the subsistence perspective finds that the privileged few reside outside of nature, while the majority and the marginal live within nature and necessity (336). Equally vital, nature should not be "transcended" because it too must subsist. Katniss's life seems set on such survival. As Pharr and Clark argue in their Introduction, she is "always more comfortable with her role as survivor than hero" (12). At the end of the series, Panem will likely share the subsistence perspective, which would clearly be based on a balanced part of the continuum as it is neither fully anthropocentric or fully ecocentric. Their rebuilding will need to include a balance between nature and culture (and within culture, technology) to be successful. Scholars that work on the subsistence perspective have gone into much more depth than this one paragraph, and I am reminded once again how many avenues of theoretical and environmental discovery are achievable in these texts.

Further Outside the Seam

This essay has only scratched the surface of ecocritical possibility. Further studies can focus more deeply on specific environmental aspects of the books such as the nature-based language or the relationship between region and connection to earth. There are already many articles on gender in *The Hunger Games,* so it would be a logical extension to perform more in depth ecofeminist analyses of the works. Ecofeminism, generally concerned with societal structures that simultaneously subjugate women and the land, would be an informative discourse, though it seems that class is a more important distinction than gender in the series. Scholars should explore other young adult literature for these themes to see if there is a general presence of environmental awareness in texts geared towards future protectors. I would like to see ecocriticism take a prominent role in examining the literature of young adults, especially because of the need for that group of readers to gain agency and figure into the process of renewing the earth. There is no doubt that some dystopian, post-apocalyptic literature realizes a fatal disconnect from the environment, so researching these connections, especially in fiction geared towards youth, would be valuable. Moreover, it would be beneficial for other writers of young adult literature to take an active role in interrogating the genre and adding to the conversation. Literature that allows young adults to empathize with and review their own world is an essential way to combat apathy and encourage education and activism.

The Hunger Games trilogy is filled with the language of the earth, a call for a deeper societal connection with the land and importantly, an awareness of our growing disconnection even in a time that is filled with "green" rhetoric. Clemente notes that these novels "argue for the necessity of increased awareness, despite the uncertainties and often painful consequences that engagement brings" (21). Environmental awareness, political awareness, and self-awareness are all explored in Collins's work. The trilogy identifies, through the example of Panem, some of the issues that young adults can recognize in their own world. In their Introduction, Pharr and Clark discern that the series "posits Panem as the future of all that once was North America, if not the world" (12). Panem, like our world, has real nature, artificial nature, hybrid nature, language that includes or excludes nature, environmental crisis, poverty, warfare, and a continuum of relationships to and recognition of nature. As new audiences continue to approach the series, this investigation of authenticity and relationships between society and manmade or real natural spaces can continue. The world of the trilogy, while fictional, is timely and impactful. Young adults reading the books can similarly go beyond the Seam to discover their own Meadows. With such reflection, we can only hope that young people will fight for the earth with the same degree of fervor with which Katniss fought.

Works Cited

Blasingame, James. "An Interview with Suzanne Collins." *Journal of Adolescent and Adult Literacy* 52.8 (2009): 726–7. Print.
Clemente, Bill. "Panem in America: Crisis Economics and a Call for Political Engagement." Pharr and Clark, 20–29.
Collins, Suzanne. *Catching Fire*. New York: Scholastic, 2009. Print.
_____. *The Hunger Games*. New York: Scholastic, 2008. Print.
_____. *Mockingjay*. New York: Scholastic, 2010. Print.
Despain, Max. "The 'Fine Reality of Hunger Satisfied': Food as Cultural Metaphor in Panem." Pharr and Clark, 69–78.
Frankel, Valerie. "Reflection in a Plastic Mirror." Pharr and Clark, 49–58.
Glotfelty, Cheryll. "Introduction: Literary Studies in an Age of Environmental Crisis." *The Ecocriticism Reader: Landmarks in Literary Ecocology*. Eds. Cheryll Glotfelty and Harold Fromm. Athens: University of Georgia Press, 1996. xv-xxxvii. Print.
Hanlon, Tina. "Coal Dust and Ballads: Appalachia and District 12." Pharr and Clark, 59–68.
King, Sharon. "(Im)Mutable Natures: Animal, Human and Hybrid Horror." Pharr and Clark, 108–117.
Koenig, Gretchen. "Communal Spectacle: Reshaping History and Memory through Violence." Pharr and Clark, 39–48.
Mies, Maria. "The Subsistence Perspective." Cologne, Germany. 2005. Trans. Lisa Rosenblatt. *Republicart*. 8 February 2013. Web.
_____, and Vandana Shiva. "The Subsistence Perspective." *The Feminist Standpoint Theory Reader: Intellectual & Political Controversies*. Ed. Sandra Harding. New York: Routledge, 2004. 333–37. Print.
Pharr, Mary, and Leisa Clark, eds. *Of Bread, Blood and* The Hunger Games*: Critical Essays on the Suzanne Collins Trilogy*. Jefferson, NC: McFarland, 2012. Print.

Political Muttations
"Real or Not Real?"

Bruce Martin

> "There is tenderness only in the coarsest demand; that no-one shall go hungry anymore."
> —Theodor Adorno (1991, 156)

Suzanne Collins's *The Hunger Games* trilogy offers readers a story about a futuristic world of genetically and psychologically engineered mutations of human and non-human nature, a world where political power is consecrated through ritual child sacrifice. These novels contain a multidimensional critique of war and violence underpinning an exploration of self-transformation and political revolution. Keeping with the long tradition of dystopian speculative fiction, Collins creates an imaginary future in which science and technology transform society and nature into exaggerated images of the present—horrors of natural and political "muttations." The relevance for real world politics, like the trilogy's parallel paths of personal transformation and political evolution, can be clarified with the help of early Frankfurt School critical theory, which explored the relationships between individual identity and political ideology. The critical theorists' development of the concept of *mimesis* in relation to sacrifice and identity can help illuminate the specifically political content of the trilogy.[1] Collins's creative treatment of the role of sacrifice in both the imposition of political domination and the successful subversion of this domination through rebellion is most visible in the trilogy's details, and can be seen as an insightful addendum to critical theory's understanding of sacrifice and political domination.[2]

The trilogy offers lessons for its readers about the limits of control and domination, revealing how even the strongest powers attempting to control nature and human nature can be resisted and overthrown. Collins observed that Katniss Everdeen is "a girl who should never have existed ... this new creature evolved, which is the mockingjay, which is Katniss" (Margulis par. 10–

12). The "mockingjay" represents the existence of the impossible, a hybrid between natural and man-made, surviving and flourishing despite the ruling powers' plans. The mutations that occur through natural evolution are transformed in the futuristic North American nation of Panem through the technological interventions of those holding economic and political power. These technologically engineered "muttations" include genetically modified organisms that distort and disfigure nature into weapons for domination. However, like the mockingjay bird (the unanticipated offspring of the Capitol's jabber jay "muttation" and nature's mockingbird), and Katniss's emergence from the Arena as the "Mockingjay" (the symbol of rebellion), the trilogy also unveils in its details an "impossible" politics, a radical "political muttation" that subverts the logic of domination. Within Panem's system of total domination it was outside its self-understanding, its reason or logic, for either the bird or the symbol to come into existence—yet they did. Like the unanticipated consequences of these muttations, the details of the novels, of any work of art, may expose or betray the best intentions of the writer or artist. The details always have the potential to reveal what escapes the work, as Adorno indicates in *Aesthetic Theory*:

> Details, and this is one of their defining qualities, seek to transcend themselves in some overarching synthesis.... In any event, a detail will always be a posited, and therefore deficient, kind of entity. Disintegration dwells amid integration, manifesting itself in it [421].

Katniss Everdeen travels on a journey from the immediacy of individual survival to increasing self-awareness, including discovery of her unique role in the larger political and cultural arena of her world. Her journey feels like a high-speed train ride through a carnivalesque house of distortion mirrors, a maze of starts and stops where kindly, compassionate Peeta—the boy with the bread—becomes a Capitol-created homicidal muttation, and where Katniss eventually views even herself as a muttation, a "fire-mutt" (*MJ* 352). However, Katniss's father reminds her when she is young, "if you can find yourself you will never go hungry," pragmatically referring to the cattail root for which she is named (*THG* 52). It is through her repeated willingness to sacrifice herself that she finally finds her new identity, one of self-creation and self-governance, rising from the process of political "muttation."

Collins not only uses the process and products of muttation to dramatize the nightmarish biological aspects of *The Hunger Games*, she also turns it into a technique for tapping into the rich literary history of dystopian speculative fiction, especially its political aspects. This process of "literary muttation," the transformation of themes and images inherited from earlier dystopian speculative fiction, not only continues the dystopian tradition of critiquing war and violence, but also generates a new allegory of contemporary American culture containing its own radical political and cultural critique. Real world political ideologies, past and present, inhabit the trilogy as modifications of the "genre DNA" found in earlier dystopian speculative/science fiction, a mimetic re-creation and transformation of the political critiques at the core of this literature.[3] Panem's political muttations contain reincarnated strands of literary genetic material found in twentieth-century dystopian classics such as George Orwell's *1984* Aldous Huxley's *Brave New World*, and Ray Bradbury's *Fahrenheit 451*. This "dystopian DNA" incubates in a swirl of references to Greek myths, Roman history, and American politics and culture, resulting in a literary mutation, or "muttation," in the form of an allegorical vision of a future reflecting exaggerated and distorted features of the present. The trilogy's political muttations appear as a constellation of ghostly dystopian voices that speak to one another, sometimes exposing truths beyond the author's intentions, like the unexpected emergence of the Mockingjay.[4]

Collins cites as the first or primary inspiration for *The Hunger Games* the classic Greek myth of "Theseus and the Minotaur" ("A Conversation"). The myth's theme of political punishment revolves around the story of a conquered Athens which must submit "seven youths and seven maidens" in tribute to the more powerful Crete where the children are thrown into a labyrinth containing the Minotaur waiting to devour them. Tracking the complex, radical political content within the trilogy requires the reader to attend to the trail left by the details, in the way that Theseus follows Ariadne's thread that marked the path of escape from the labyrinth that contained the Minotaur. In addition to this Greek myth, inspiration for the Hunger Games Arena came from ancient Roman gladiator games requiring a "fight to the death," with the story of Spartacus guiding the details of the gladiators' rebellion. Contemporary inspirations include "reality" television,[5] but Collins also cites the literature that influenced her as a young reader, including William Golding's *Lord of the Flies*, Emile Zola's *Germinal*, and works by Kurt Vonnegut, as well as those of Orwell and Bradbury. The political critiques underlying these works of dystopian speculative fiction provide sources for some of the specific plot components of Collins's trilogy, as well as provide the overall perspective on contemporary politics, couched in an exaggerated and distorted image of a futuristic political nightmare.

The resonance of these myths, history and dystopian literature for contemporary audiences results in the trilogy's political content initially resembling Katniss's "trick with the berries," producing different meanings for different people (*MJ* 75). However, unraveling the influences woven into the details of the trilogy reveals a consistently radical political vision tying it all together. *The Hunger Games* trilogy is not simply a political Rorschach test, a neutral field for the projection of existing political identities. Rather, it expounds a consistent, even radical, politics—embedded within its story of self-transformation and political revolution. Critical examination of the trilogy unearths not a simple retelling of the ancient story of sacrificial ritual, but a guide for overturning the "logic of sacrifice" itself. How could Katniss's "trick with the berries," the threatened double-suicide that would leave the Capitol without its exemplary victor, lead to the downfall of an empire?

Guidance for answering this question can be found in the work of early Frankfurt School critical theory, which developed critical orientations not only toward German fascism and Soviet totalitarianism, but also toward American consumer capitalism.[6] The critical theorists' concern for the ongoing domination of human and non-human nature parallels the critique of war, violence, and politics contained in the trilogy. The early critical theorists based their comprehensive critique largely on their understanding of the anthropological and psychological implications of the concept of *mimesis* as it relates to sacrifice and identity. The basic outlines of the critique will be shown below, first in an overview of critical theory's understanding of the psychological and cultural sources of political domination, and then by drawing on these key critical concepts to examine the specific political images and ideologies found in the trilogy, most notably in the descriptions of the cultures and citizens of the Districts and the Capitol. The issues of racism that emerged around the film adaptation of the first book of the trilogy will highlight the differences in interpretation that readers and audiences have of the trilogy's political and cultural meaning. Details of the political "models" found in the trilogy provide suggestions for a politics that might help in avoiding a "real world" future that resembles that of Panem.

Like the earlier dystopian works Collins cites as important influences on her own personal and professional development, *The Hunger Games* trilogy can best be understood as a warning about deeply troubling cultural and political problems in the present. A compelling interpretation of that ominous message from the fictional future can be found in the consistency of the story's details which contain a subtle yet elaborately layered deep critique of the present. Those details can be found in the allusions to Greek myths, Roman history, and the literary inheritance from classic dystopian speculative fiction. *The Hunger Games* is a literary work of art, but like all art it has its political implications. In his essay on Charles Dickens, George Orwell connected the relationship of art to politics, in its details: "But every writer, especially every novelist, *has* a 'message,' whether he admits it or not, and the minutest details of his work are influenced by it. All art is propaganda" ("All Art" 47).

The Games, Political Domination, and Critical Theory

Katniss Everdeen travels a path that leads to the transformation of her personal identity, and to her leadership of a nation in a time of political revolution. This story of simultaneous change in individual self-awareness and political revolution is also a parable of contemporary conditions that can be more fully understood with the help of early Frankfurt School critical theory's insights concerning individual identity and political ideology. The critical theorists used the key concept of *mimesis* to better understand the relationships between sacrifice, identity, and political ideology. Their critical analysis can clarify the trilogy's implications for contemporary politics, and help explain the sometimes contradictory interpretations and reactions to the novels and their film adaptations.

As with Suzanne Collins's reliance on the Myth of Theseus as an inspiration for the Hunger Games, the critical theorists began exploring individual identity and political ideology with discussion of the transition of archaic myth into modern enlightenment, and the subsequent reversal of enlightened reason back into a mythic structure. This critical analysis initially establishes the relationship between *mimesis*—a word of Greek origins usually translated as "representation" or "appearance"—and sacrifice.[7] Western Enlightenment's development of reason, argue the critical theorists, made possible the escape from mythic nature, from the fateful necessity of nature's domination of humanity. However, with Enlightenment's reversal, reason is made as oppressive and dominating as the mythic nature it first sought to escape.

Horkheimer and Adorno link ritual sacrifice with the development of rationality, detailing how the "impulse of *mimesis*" is used to establish control over nature, including human nature. They explain how *mimesis* departs from its basic "liberatory" form which enables development of individual self-identity into a "perverse" form underlying anti–Semitism and racism (168–208). In the trilogy, distorted and disfigured creatures of the Capitol's muttations are used to torture and terrify the Arena tributes. Likewise, the perverse form of *mimesis* is used by fascists to intensify the social and psychological persecution of their victims. Critical theory's analysis of *mimesis* and identity also sheds light on the use of propaganda and sacrifice by the government of Panem, epitomized in the Arena during the annual Hunger Games. The Capitol uses the ritual sacrifice of the tributes to reinforce its power to dominate the districts. The Capitol's control is not simply over resources and territory, but also over Panem's inhabitants' ability to think critically about alternative possibilities beyond their current conditions.

Critical theory's use of the term *mimesis* is related to the words mime, mimicry, and imitation, and differs from other interpretations that are primarily guided by its early Greek understandings (McDonald 8–25). In Plato's *Republic, mimesis* plays a central role in the "true and good" constitution of the just political system—as the principle of exclusion. In Book 10 of the *Republic,* Plato claims poets and similar artists must be excluded from the ideal, "just" state because their representations excite the emotions, encouraging irrationality, thus undermining the basis of his utopian state: Reason. Poets, painters, and others who evoke an emotional response from fellow citizens set a bad example for those who love truth, those who should rely solely on reason if they are to gain access to the "true knowledge" necessary for the properly run *polis,* the Greek city-state. Plato insists the poets must be banned, not for *mimesis* itself, but specifically for *what* is represented: suffering, irrationality, and the instinctual desires that lead those of good character away from knowledge and truth. Collins's trilogy would have trouble getting past the censors and guardians of Plato's republic, with its displays of murder, betrayal and deceit overshadowing the rare instances of the good, beautiful and reasonable. The Capitol's use of the Hunger Games to elicit brutal behavior from tributes and to perpetuate a culture of hedonistic excess, deceit, and political corruption constitutes a reversal of Plato's political ideal.

In contrast to the aesthetic tradition inherited from the Greeks, critical theory's largely anthropological understanding of *mimesis* follows Walter Benjamin's short essay "On the Mimetic Faculty." This essay begins not with an appeal to Greek aesthetic philosophy, but to Nature, to suggest that nature itself produces similarities. For Benjamin, the mimetic faculty is a subterranean force within even the most developed forms of human activity, including language. The very ability to perceive similarities or resemblances is a manifestation of "the powerful compulsion in former times to become and behave like something else" (333). This compulsion to imitate, to be like the other, is exhibited in the earliest of human behavior, including children's play, when the child not only imitates adults, in language and in play-acting social roles such as doctor, teacher or warrior, but also as objects such as a train or windmill. The mimetic faculty is one of the most basic of human activities, and is present in nature generally. According to Benjamin, this "gift" of recognizing and producing similarities has changed historically. It is initially found in language, dance and ritual magic, while more recent manifestations include technological reproduction.

With respect to analysis of *The Hunger Games* trilogy, *mimesis* has its most important implications in its relation to sacrifice and political domination. Critical theory's anthropological understanding of *mimesis* connects practices of ritual sacrifice to the development of human reason. Discussion of the shaman's use of the powers of *mimesis* during acts of ritual sacrifice emphasizes the "ruse" at the heart of sacrificial ritual, where an object or living being of lesser value is exchanged for something of greater value. In return for sacrificial victims, the shaman obtains god-like power over nature. Applying this system of exchange to the trilogy, the ritual sacrifice of tributes grants Panem's rulers the power to control the nation.

For the critical theorists, the earliest conversion of mythic reason from simple explanation of the world to its potential control and use took the form of ritual magic—the precursor to science—which does not organize nature conceptually as science does through example, but instead operates through *mimesis*. The specificity or uniqueness of the object of shamanistic magic is at the heart of the priest's or shaman's attempts to influence events. In ritual magic, the unique characteristic of the sacrificial victim is what gives the priest or shaman access to the greater power for which the ritual is designed. However, this ability to represent something in common between the victim and the greater power begins the movement toward a logical discourse that culminates in science and math and their progeny—technology. *The Hunger Games* brings together the power of sacrificial ritual with all the brutal potential of perverse *mimesis* available in advanced technology. The combination of sacrificial ritual and mandatory television viewing of the brutality in the Arena, as "reality" entertainment, is intended to reinforce acceptance of the Capitol's power to dominate the districts, but it also creates the opportunity for the subversion of the logic of sacrifice and domination on which that power depends. As President Snow observed, "Katniss Everdeen, the girl who was on fire, ... provided a spark that, left unattended, may grow to an inferno that destroys Panem" (*CF* 23).

The Capitol presents the history of Panem as one of progress, interrupted historically by the rebellious districts whose children become sacrificial victims as tribute to those who see themselves as more advanced and culturally developed. However, the people of the districts have a contrary view of this history, one similar to critical theory's judgment of the process of Western Enlightenment. The critical theorists argued that although shamanistic magic honors the uniqueness of the individual, in its attempt to influence the mythic or fated character of the world (the endless repetition of nature), this process of ritual substitution initiates the conceptual process that reduces nature to category and example. Science later extends this demythologizing or "disenchantment" of the world, but at the expense of individual uniqueness. Historical "progress" from magic to science, myth to enlightenment, is therefore also a story of regression, of return into the mythic, of renewed confrontation with fateful necessity, but now in the form of society rather than mere nature—as political domination of the individual. Enlightenment's self-history of human reason relies on the core concept of progress, often stated as the gradual extension of control over nature for the purpose of human self-preservation. Critical theory's contrasting view of Enlightenment is exemplified in Walter Benjamin's discussion of Klee's painting named "Angelus Novalis." Benjamin describes this angel, which is pushed backwards by a wind from Paradise, as the "angel of history" looking to the past: "Where we perceive a chain of events, he sees one single catastrophe which keeps piling wreckage upon wreckage...This storm irresistibly propels him into the future to which his back is turned, while the pile of debris before him grows skyward. This storm is what we call progress" (*Illuminations* 257–258).

Throughout the trilogy, Katniss constantly reflects on the damage and deaths she seems to leave in her wake. Her reflection includes the ongoing catastrophe that is Panem, and it is this history of political and ecological disaster that sets the "dystopian" tone of her journey. The potential for dystopian fiction to provide glimpses of alternatives to existing political systems, even utopian political possibilities, are circumscribed in the contemporary setting by environmental/ecological limits that were little recognized before the 1960s. Gone are the times when endless material wealth and consumption were unquestioned. Earlier utopian science fiction often envisioned a future cornucopia of happiness, achieved simply by a greater application of technology. The implied warning of *The Hunger Games* trilogy is two-fold: (1) the current environmental and technological path is leading to catastrophe, and (2) the politics underpinning this path are inadequate to address the problem. "Reaping Day" always commences with the recitation of the history of Panem's emergence out of the "ashes of North America," the inherited remains of "[t]he disasters, the droughts, the storms, the fires, the encroaching seas that swallowed up so much of the land, the brutal war for what little sustenance remained" (*THG* 18).

After Panem emerges from the remnants of ecological collapse and warfare, the Capitol imposes an economic and political system on the people of the outlying districts that includes both physical and psychological domination. In its analysis of society, critical theory argues that the ever increasing domination of nature has gone beyond that of external nature to include psychological or internal "human nature" as well. Adorno critiqued this as "identity thinking," where even the potentials of critical thought are reduced or sacrificed, limited to the rational calculation of an "instrumental" reason, humans becoming both the means of domination as well as the material for domination. Breaking the spell of this logic of domination requires awareness that repressed fragments of *mimesis* hold possibilities for hope and potential alternative thought:

> The point which thinking aims at its material is not solely a spiritualized control of nature...Our thinking heeds a potential that waits in the object, and it unconsciously obeys the idea of making amends to the pieces for what it has done....

Accompanying irreconcilable thoughts is the hope for reconcilement [*Negative Dialectics* 19].

For critical theory, *mimesis* is at the heart of the relationship between self-preservation and identity formation. The abstracting, identifying "self" internalizes its impressions of the world as the human organism struggles for survival, eventually resulting in the formation of the "individual." For Katniss Everdeen, her personal identity initially revolves around her daily struggle for survival. Our protagonist's journey leads simultaneously to both personal and political self-discovery, her survival instincts and ability to think outside the box lead Katniss to her "roots" and her radical personal and political identity. When she volunteers to take her sister's place in the Games, Katniss chooses the "radical thing," a willingness to sacrifice herself for her sister, the one person she loves enough to die for (*THG* 25). It is Katniss's willingness to sacrifice herself for her sister that opens the possibility for overturning the logic of sacrifice on which the Capitol's power and political domination depend. Katniss subverts the logic of sacrifice again with the "trick with the berries," and then again when she assassinates Panem's post-rebellion leader, President Coin. Katniss Everdeen challenges Panem's political muttation with her own personal and political transformation. Collins's trilogy challenges contemporary politics and culture by providing a glimpse of an alternative, radically different, future.

Future Reflections on Contemporary Politics

Collins's dystopian political world is also a vision of a radical political possibility. The trilogy is an exaggerated depiction of current political and cultural tendencies that if not addressed could lead to a catastrophe like that which gave birth to Panem. The values needed for avoiding this negative future are revealed during Katniss's revolutionary struggle. Collins's vision also can be understood as an indictment of prevailing political spectacles parading as a choice between what are merely "two sides of the same coin."[8] The popular appeal of this political vision can be seen in reactions to the film adaptation of Collins's first novel in the trilogy, reviews which included interpretations supporting the respective politics of both Tea Party supporters and Occupy Wall Street sympathizers (Bond par. 1–2). Collins herself observed that reactions to the trilogy are unusually strongly based on the personal experiences each reader brings to the books ("Responses"). A critical examination of the trilogy must help clarify its broader political implications while still acknowledging its deeply personal resonance for individual readers.

The trilogy's complex characters and extended publication timeframe, along with the movie's blockbuster opening, continue to inspire a broad spectrum of political interpretations. Comments have included the crude and bigoted, plus blanket condemnation—"it was mostly a load of crap—though entertaining" (Harrison par. 3), but also the subtle and challenging, and even enthusiastic attempts at appropriation—"happens to be an ambitious, timely political parable" (Allan par. 3). In interviews, Collins indicated she hoped the novels' readers would become more reflective about the war and violence they see on television ("Responses"). The critical reflection the books have set in motion, however, has often been contradictory and limited, most obviously on fan websites.[9] Untangling the "dystopian DNA" of the trilogy's political muttations may help identify the origins of the contradictory reactions, and reveal reasons for the often limited critical reflection found in popular culture generally.

The Capitol exploits the Hunger Games Arena as a metaphor for Panem society, reinforcing its ideology of domination. If readers' political understandings stop here, at the level of Capitol propaganda, the world of the trilogy may appear simply to mirror their own ideological belief in a reality of competition for individual survival. This radically conservative interpretation asserts that the world always has been and will be this way, society and nature consisting of an inescapable (mythic) world of Darwinian competition.[10] In this simplistic interpretation, the dystopian world of the Capitol's Hunger Games is understood as an allegory that seems to obviously mirror and affirm our own. Blind to the trilogy's overt language, not to mention its subtle details, this crude reading embraces the Social Darwinism of the Games and the Capitol citizens themselves, a "survival-of-the-fittest" ideology of kill-or-be-killed. Politically producing a Hobbesian "war of all-against-all," this reading easily accommodates fascism and racism, legitimizing systems of domination where the other is quickly labeled as less than fully human.[11] This type of reading was evident in the racist Twittered reactions to the movie casting of a young African-American actress in the role of Rue (Bull par. 6).[12] This reaction to Rue as Katniss's substitute sister in the Arena and pivotal character in the development of both Katniss's self-identity and political awakening came despite Rue being clearly identified in *The Hunger Games* as having "bright dark eyes and satiny brown skin" (58) and despite descriptions of Rue and Thresh as having the same "dark skin" (126).

A contrasting reaction, again based partly on movie castings, viewed the characters played by African-American actors simply as examples of stereotypically racist "Magical Negro" roles (Hughey). This term describes characters embodying black stereotypes that merely function as the means for the white protagonist's spiritual enlightenment, rather than being important in themselves. However, *The Hunger Games* trilogy enables a more persuasive, alternative reading of these characters, traceable in the trilogy's many details. This alternative reading searches out the narrative's less obvious influences and pathways, gradually leading to a more complex and consistent political understanding.

More important than the racist reactions to the film's casting, Rue's function as character is primarily to embody and transfer into the Arena Katniss's fears for Prim, as Rue suffers the fate Prim would have suffered if Katniss had not volunteered to take her place. In addition to the personal implications for Katniss, an alternative "political alliance" reading of the trilogy not only addresses issues of sisterhood, but has implications for race and class alliances as well, most notably in the interaction between the citizens of Districts 11 and 12.[13] Rue's *death* is thus better understood as a moment in Katniss's enhanced political awareness, as she begins to empathize with Peeta's earlier declared desire to be more than a piece in others' games (*THG* 142). Katniss acknowledges this understanding when she realizes that her vow to Rue to win the Games seems, after Rue's death, "even more important" than the similar vow she gave to Prim (242). Katniss better understands Peeta's desire to maintain his identity against the Games' design to reduce all to barbarism. In *The Hunger Games* portion of the trilogy, the gift of bread from District 11, Rue's home district, strengthens this political tie further, even though this detail is omitted from the film. In restitution for this omission, the film's editing directly connects Katniss's alliance with and care for Rue in death to scenes of an immediate uprising in District 11 (borrowing material that appears later in the trilogy, during the Victory Tour depicted in *Catching Fire*). Beyond the Arena of the 74th Hunger Games, especially in *Catching Fire*, additional connections form between the two districts as the rebellion unfolds, not the least of which is the execution of the old man that Katniss witnesses in District 11 during her Victory Tour (*CF* 62). This reading of the trilogy, focusing on its political aspects, provides greater insights into Collins's critique of contemporary politics, but it is in the more explicitly political details of the trilogy that the potentials of its "political muttations" become most visible, as explored in the next sections.

Panem's Political Muttations

The different political systems outlined in the trilogy represent multiple political ideologies, including those discussed here as: (1) the "oligarchic competitivism" of the Capitol/capital, (2) the "scientific socialism" of District 13, (3) the "anarchic" structure of District 12 under the Capitol, and (4) Plutarch's "centralized republic" of post-revolutionary Panem. These political systems emphasize content similar to that found in past speculative dystopias, including the key political component of its "genre DNA"—the repression of dissent—as explored in Bradbury's *Fahrenheit 451* or Orwell's *1984*. Dystopian political fiction has also explored the more indirect, sophisticated repression and political domination carried out by what critical theorist Herbert Marcuse analyzed as "repressive desublimation." This concept describes how socially approved forms of release of both sexuality and aggressiveness are used as a means of promoting individual and social conformism and to facilitate further manipulation.[14] Aldous Huxley, a pacifist, extensively explored the political deployment of erotic and destructive instincts for the purpose of controlling populations in his 1932 classic *Brave New World*. Collins imaginatively draws on the multiple sources of dystopian inheritance in her creation of the world of Panem with its distorted and disfigured creatures and politics. These transformations are explored in the following section on the political systems found in the trilogy. The trilogy's subtle descriptions of these inherited "political muttations" include not only the forms of government and political ideologies they embody, but also their impact on individuals and their self-identity.

Capitol/al Phantoms

The Capitol's citizens are imprisoned in a politics of pleasure, a culture of narcissistic consumption regulated through a system of sado-masochistic punishment of others as well as themselves, a political system whose survival is based on corruption and the strategy of *panem et circenses* pioneered by Ancient Rome. As victor of the "Dark Days" war, the Capitol is able to enjoy this hedonistic lifestyle because of its continued exploitation of the outlying districts, whose slave-like residents produce the food, minerals, and industrial goods that the Capitol consumes. The "Treaty of Treason" institutionalized this domination and oppression by creating the sacrificial ritual called the Hunger Games, a celebratory pageant designed to remind the districts of their defeat in the country's historic battle for political survival. District children annually perform in the televised spectacle of death for the Capitol's entertainment, whose citizens bet on tributes' deaths and, if rich enough, are provided with opportunities for purchasing the sexual services of the Games' victors. The Capitol's political and economic powers are combined to sadistic perfection in Collins's exaggerated representation of contemporary casino capitalism, revealing the consequences of a society living for the pleasures of the current moment yet engulfed in corruption and exploitation.

Many elements of Capitol society resemble those of Huxley's *Brave New World*, except for *The Hunger Games* trilogy's elimination of the stronger visions of endless technological progress found in much of twentieth-century speculative fiction. The new realities of the current century are reflected in the origins of Panem: ecological collapse and global war. The "dystopian DNA" legacy of George Orwell (Eric Blair), a socialist, also haunts the Capitol in its surveillance systems and its ironic euphemisms, where Peacekeepers make war and suppress dissent. In both Panem and *1984* the television/telescreen is mandatory viewing. Like *1984*'s Ministry of Truth, the Capitol rewrites history with the claim that District 13 does not exist, the "news" footage of its destruction a frequently repeated reminder of the annihilation awaiting those who rebel. Specters of Orwellian torture also roam the Capitol's dark backstreets. In *1984*, torture was carried out in Room 101 of the Ministry of Love, in which rebels' minds and emotions were permanently changed through fear of "the worst thing in the world."[15] The Capitol's technologically advanced torture methods also convert love into hate through the power of fear, summoned with greater efficiency by means of chemical injection of tracker jacker venom, reflecting the increasingly sophisticated literary application of science and technology to the field of torture since Orwell's time.

Whereas many other dystopias, such as *1984*, depict the authoritarians' eventual triumph, *The Hunger Games* trilogy depicts the successful defeat of the powers of control and oppression. Public reversal of the meaning of sacrifice undercuts Panem's rulers' ability to control and manipulate its people. Sacrifice of individual tributes during the Games is intended to reinforce the power of the Capitol, humiliating the Districts, forcing them to acknowledge their own powerlessness. However, Katniss and Peeta, as District 12 tributes, end the game with their "trick with the berries"—breaking the rules on which Capitol power depends, thus threatening it with a gesture of self-sacrifice, a move unanticipated by the normal reasoning of the Capitol's game. Katniss's gamble was to bet that the Capitol valued the symbol of hope represented by *two* victors more than the symbol of fear represented by their death as simply two more sacrificial tributes. The Head Gamemaker, Seneca Crane, lost his life for folding. President Snow believed he should have "blown [Katniss and Peeta] to dust" (*CF* 20). On one level, Katniss understood the gamble with the berries as a last ditch effort at survival for herself and Peeta, as she herself confesses: "I was only thinking of out-smarting the Gamemakers" (*THG* 358). Her gamble was a refusal to live by the arbitrary imposition of rules that would force the sacrifice of one for the other, of choosing to value one life above another. Her refusal also reveals the "chink" in the Capitol's ideological armor, just as the rebels' ability to see the "vibration" in the force field makes destruction of the Arena possible in the Quarter Quell, as depicted in *Catching Fire* (378). For those still under the spell of Capitol propaganda, the "'trick with the berries" can be interpreted sentimentally as the act of star-crossed lovers, willing to commit mutual suicide. However, those who are disenchanted see instead an act of rebellion, a victory of the weak over the powerful, and the creation of a symbol of hope for the end of suffering. For Katniss, the primary motivation behind the "trick with the berries" ultimately remained unclear even to herself. Later, qualifying her initial self-understanding in this regard, she further confesses: "The trouble is, I don't know exactly what was going on inside me at that moment" (*CF* 118). However, there was only one motivation that indicated to her that she was someone of worth—the one that defied the Capitol (118).

Underground Oppositions

In contrast to the hedonistic, corrupt Capitol, District 13 is the hyper-rational, zero tolerance, underground society forced to use its expertise in nuclear weaponry and military training to allocate, in a scientific and systematic fashion, scarce resources simply to survive. Its political system is reminiscent of Orwell's *1984*, perhaps even informed by (fictitious) Emmanuel Goldstein's "The Theory and Practice of Oligarchical Collectivism," the guiding principles of the government in Orwell's novel (191). District 13's citizens lead lives that are mirror opposites of their Capitol cousins' flamboyance and endless self-indulgent consumption. The underground citizens inhabit a gray, joyless, government-issue lifestyle, where "waste is practically a criminal activity" (*MJ* 18). Newly arrived political refugees receive a government-issued apartment, furniture, and clothing consisting of unisex gray pants and shirts, expected to be tucked in. This society is a self-sufficient citizen army, its soldiers over-programmed, lacking a sense of humor, exhibiting little evidence of compassion (*MJ* 29) All citizens' schedules, including their ID numbers, are tattooed daily on their arms, a sharp contrast to the Capitol's cosmetic and fashionable tattoo displays—providing yet another inverse or reverse mirroring found in the trilogy.

This joyless hyper-rationalism includes food rationing, with each citizen receiving only enough calories to fulfill pre-programmed duties before his or her next meal. Zero-tolerance policies are most visible in the ways in which District 13 treats its violators of the rules of consumption, as defined by scientifically-determined nutritional necessity. In *Mockingjay*, Katniss finds her prep team in the District's dungeons, imprisoned for taking a piece of bread out of the common dining area. Collins clearly references the atrocities of Abu Ghraib as she describes Katniss finding her prep team half-naked, bruised, shackled to the wall, whimpering like a "cowed dog," sounds she found to be "all too human and familiar" (43). This description deploys words made famous by American prisons and torture centers, where prisoners were found "forced into cramped body positions" and who had trouble walking (49). Katniss sees for herself that "[t]his is the sort of thing that goes on in District 13 as well" as the Capitol (49), an early indication that while the two governments may appear to be polar opposites, what they have in common is ultimately most important.

In addition to the cuisine being similar to that in *1984*, the District's leadership also resembles Big Brother. Alma Coin is a cold, power hungry "Big Sister," her Capitol adversary's opposite in many ways, except that she and President Snow both lust for power and are willing to sacrifice others for their ambition. The presidents represent two sides of the same political coin of domination, common descendants of the politics that earlier led to catastrophe. Coin's totalitarian scientific socialism contrasts with Snow's authoritarian consumerist corporatism, only one example of Collins's repetition of character opposites, providing texture and nuance to her fundamental critique of war and violence.

In aligning with the rebels to defeat the Capitol, Coin mirrors Snow's willingness to use any means to achieve their common desire—control of Panem. Recognizing this, Katniss terminates Coin's proposal of a "final" Hunger Games by assassinating, or rather sacrificing, Coin, and by attempting suicide, blocked at the last moment by Peeta. In addition, Snow's timely coincidental death ensures that Panem has played its last Hunger Games. Katniss's nationally televised trial for assassination ends without her conviction, having been represented as a "hopeless, shell-shocked lunatic" before the eyes of Panem (*MJ* 378). Not guilty by reason of insanity must be the verdict. After all, her behavior resides outside Panem's version of reason—the logic of domination.

Plutarch's Republic

As victory over the Capitol appears increasingly likely, the rebels question whether post-revolution political structures will be adequate to address the challenges of war and violence inherited from the past. Panem's governance through "bread and circuses" arose because, in Head Gamemaker Plutarch Heavensbee's final retelling of history, "people had given up their political responsibilities and therefore their power" (*MJ* 223). Plutarch describes the anticipated post-revolution republic as a centralized government with a system of representation. Rebels' suspicions about this new system run deep, but Plutarch reminds them that the republic form of government has worked before, and asserts, "if our ancestors could do it why can't we?" However, Katniss remains unconvinced by the historical argument: "Frankly, our ancestors don't seem much to brag about (*MJ* 84)." Like Benjamin's "angel of history," she only sees wars and a broken planet, evidence those ancestors cared little about later generations, but in resignation, she thinks even this republic idea would be an "improvement on what we have now." Following the successful revolution, Plutarch later offers additional consolation that this time political prospects might be different: "Maybe we are witnessing the evolution of the human race" (*MJ* 379).

Katniss has good reason to distrust the rebels as well. Whether they are victors from other districts, defectors from the Capitol, or soldiers from District 13, the rebels also use her as a pawn in the rebellion, both inside and outside the Arena. Like the tortured Peeta, Katniss is challenged to sort truth from lies, coming even from the "allies" surrounding her. She also has difficulty separating "real" from "not real" in situations for which meanings are unexpectedly reversed and inverted (*MJ* 282), like the Orwellian "Ignorance is Strength," "War is Peace," "Freedom is Slavery," and love is hate. Ultimately, rebel military forces fighting the Capitol even become so intently focused on the most effective means to destroy their enemy that they also cynically choose to adopt the spectacle of the death of innocent children to secure their own claim to power. Katniss clearly understands her difference from Coin, and even from Gale, whose reasoning leads to the acceptance of the fundamental immorality of resorting to killing children intentionally for political advantage. Katniss rejects this "ends justify the means" mentality shared by Capitol and rebels, choosing to assassinate Coin in an attempt to prevent its continuation. At that moment she abandons hope of seeing a future free of the sacrifice of children for power. If the story were to end here, as with Orwell's *1984*, the reader would be left with a conclusion of endless hopelessness, but Katniss survives even her own attempts at self-destruction, eventually returning home to a new life.

Homeland Insecurities

District 12 exists in the margins of Panem as the trilogy begins, small and poor, with a starving population that poses little threat to the Capitol. In the interview "A Conversation," Collins says that Emile Zola's *Germinal* influenced her characterization when creating District 12, particularly in situating District 12 alongside a coal mine, but more anarchism appears in the home of the girl on fire than just a coal mine. At best, the laws of Panem are minimally enforced in this district, with many openly flaunted, not the least of which are those prohibiting hunting. Tolerance for law breakers is widespread, including those conducting business in the Hob, where outlaws and law enforcers alike can share camaraderie over bowls of wild dog stew.

Although Gale, as a refugee from the fire-bombed District 12, suggests to Katniss that their hosts in District 13 are "us with nuclear weapons," District 12 before it was reduced to dust and ashes had contained as much of the Capitol's seamy underside as District 13's survivalism. When former Capitol citizen and Head Gamemaker, Plutarch, first joins the rebels in the District 13 underground hideout, he expects a little more side action, at least some high-ranking access to hard-to-obtain commodities like coffee. Plutarch questions how a little black market activity like that found in District 12's Hob could undermine the rebellion. Exasperated at the restrictions under the Coin regime, he observes, addressing Katniss and Gale, "Look how moral you two are! Virtually incorruptible!" (*MJ* 42). Ironically, in the world of Panem, political culture seems to have little bearing on individual ethics. The District 12 tributes' behavior did not reflect the lawlessness of their home district, and neither was the strict legal code of District 13 an assurance of ethical behavior by its leadership. At least within the trilogy, individual ethical choices are not fated to reflect muttations of political ideology.

Post-revolution District 12 is profoundly different less than two years after Prim is originally selected for the Hunger Games, with nearly all of its former residents killed, reduced to bones and ashes, and buried beneath the Meadow. The destruction of ninety percent of the population is reminiscent of what Billy Pilgrim witnesses in Vonnegut's *Slaughterhouse-Five*, another detail containing that inherited "genre DNA" of dystopian speculative fiction. A few refugees gradually return to begin life anew, including Katniss and Peeta, whose home eventually includes their two children. The willingness to bring children into this world happens slowly—"it took five, ten, fifteen years"—and it is still unclear to their parents how to teach them the history of Panem's Hunger Games (*MJ* 389), not unlike the issues Adorno grappled with in his essay on "Education after Auschwitz" (*Can One Live After Auschwitz?* 19). The former tributes never forget past horrors, yet slowly embrace the future with cautious—but renewed—hope. The indirect referencing of the bombing of Dresden during World War II (Vonnegut's "dystopian DNA"), as well as the Holocaust imagery, remind audiences of the "real world" catastrophic consequences of war and violence. The challenge is to always remember those consequences and create a future that will never again witness such horrors.

Conclusion

The "political muttations" contained within *The Hunger Games* trilogy take the form of both imaginative re-combinations of its inheritance from dystopian fiction and an overall critique of war and violence, with implications for current politics. It is all too easy to see why this vision of failed politics and corrupted social and cultural values has made *The Hunger Games* story so attractive to its audience. Katniss's ultimate victory over the forces of domination in the future North America offers a glimpse of hope to offset the overwhelming evidence of current and future catastrophe.

The Hunger Games trilogy offers a negative image of the future, a distorting mirror reflecting contemporary conditions. The trilogy's critical content has the potential for further development as part of the conversation surrounding forthcoming film adaptations; this ongoing critical effort may perhaps help prevent the films themselves from being reduced to mere examples of the "bread and circuses" at the heart of Collins's critique. Early Frankfurt School critical theory offers support in this ongoing effort, especially Adorno's extensive writings on aesthetics and emancipatory political theory, including his attempts to find avenues of hope during hopeless times.[16] The films' producers and directors have a tremendous challenge to create works that honor the depth of critique contained within the trilogy while still meeting the standards of the entertainment industry. Critics are challenged to reveal the inadequacies of even the sincerest cinematic efforts to remain loyal to the spirit of Collins's critique.

Although mentioned only briefly in this essay, the trilogy's various "sister" figures and their relationships to sacrifice should be examined in fuller detail. In addition to Frankfurt School-inspired feminists and eco-feminists who have re-examined critical theory's early writings on sacrifice, recent work by other political philosophy-oriented authors could bring additional helpful insights as well.[17] The similarities of Katniss's perspectives to that of eco-feminism could also be extended using many of the same categories of analysis found in this essay, while relating them back to the tradition of critical theory.[18]

Addressing the worldwide political actions during and following the "Arab Spring" of 2011, political philosopher Slavoj Žižek speaks to the difficulty of interpreting the current historical moment:

> We should turn around the historicist perspective of understanding an event through its context and genesis. Radical emancipatory outbursts cannot be understood in this way: instead of analyzing them as part of the continuum of past and present, we should bring in the perspective of the future, taking them as limited, distorted (sometimes even perverted) fragments of a utopian future that lies dormant in the present as its hidden potential [128].

Even with Katniss's eventual freedom, her ability to pursue happiness appears almost impossible when coupled with remembrance of so much past suffering. The beautiful grass and flowers of the Meadow are fed by the ashes of the dead. Her children's freedom and safety in the present exist as a result of the sacrifices of those in the past. The lessons from dystopian political fiction, including *The Hunger Games* trilogy's twisted muttations on this inheritance, can inform a "real world" politics, one sufficient to honor past sacrifices, built on a foundation other than the continued use of power for dominating others. It would be a radical departure from past or present politics, something that has never existed before.

Political muttations like the Mockingjay exist. Real, or not real? Real. Just not yet.

Notes

1. This essay relies on the idea of *mimesis* as developed by early Frankfurt School critical theory for understanding the use of sacrifice in creation of the political identities and subjects found in systems of economic and political domination. The concept of *mimesis* has been developed by others, outside of the Frankfurt School theorists' framework, as well, to examine its implications in relation to sacrifice, politics, and literature. These developments often are rooted in the work of Rene Girard, most notably in *Violence and the Sacred*, but also in a number of his other works (*Mimesis and Theory*). Others have taken Girard's ideas and applied them to natural science (Garrels).

2. Development of this "supplement" to critical theory's understanding of the logic of sacrifice and domination would require further "interpretation, commentary and criticism" as set out by Adorno, for example, in his *Aesthetic Theory* (277).

3. The phrase "genre DNA" is introduced here as a metaphor related to *mimesis*. Although not originating in the work of Frankfurt School critical theory, the concept of *mimesis* was also drawn upon by Richard Dawkins' in relation to his theory of cultural evolution and its basic unit of transmission, the *meme* (*Selfish Gene* 192). For Dawkins "cultural transmission can be seen as analogous to genetic transmission" (189). Others have further developed this idea of the *meme* as a means of cultural evolution, as found in Kate Distin's *The Selfish Meme*, and Robert Aunger's *The Electric Meme: A New Theory of How We Think*. Reflections on the implications of Frankfurt School understandings of *mimesis* in contrast to the concept's development by those inspired by Girard or Dawkins are outside the scope of this paper, but present clear opportunities for further exploration. Outside the framework of *mimesis*, Tom Henthorne has looked at Collins's use of themes from the dystopian genre as part of a "digital age reading" of texts under the heading of "Sampling, Remix and Intertextuality" (Henthorne 151).

4. Adorno's development of Benjamin's idea of philosophic "constellations" is discussed at length by Lambert Zuidervaart in Adorno's *Aesthetic Theory*, as well as Susan Buck-Morss in *The Origin of Negative Dialectics*.

5. For an extended discussion of reality television in relation to *The Hunger Games* see Tom Henthorne's *Approaching the Hunger Games Trilogy* (95–107).

6. There is a very extensive secondary literature about Frankfurt School critical theory, especially concerning the group's social and cultural philosophers who initially developed it, including Max Horkheimer, Theodor Adorno, Walter Benjamin and Herbert Marcuse. Some of the better overviews of their work include *Introduction to Critical Theory: Horkheimer to Habermas* (Held); *The Dialectical Imagination: A History of the Frankfurt School and the Institute of Social Research, 1923–1950* (Jay); *The Frankfurt School: Its History, Theories, and Political Significance* (Wiggershaus). An excellent collection of key essays from the group can be found in *The Essential Frankfurt School Reader* (Arrato and Gebhardt).

7. This discussion of *mimesis* in the work of early Frankfurt School critical theory can be found in an earlier more detailed treatment in "Mimetic Moments: Adorno and Ecofeminism"

(Martin), which focuses more closely on the biological and psychoanalytic aspects of the term. For an examination of many of the anthropological implications of *mimesis* see Michael Taussig. An extended discussion of the relationships between *mimesis*, sacrifice and identity, from a "green" critical theory perspective, can be found in "Sacred Identity and the Sacrificial Spirit" (Martin).

8. Many observers have commented on the "two sides of the same coin" metaphor within the trilogy. This pairing of opposites throughout the story occurs at multiple levels, ideologically, in character descriptions, and in subplots. V. Arrow has highlighted some of the possible "parallelisms," or what is treated here as "mirroring" effects that result from the properties of *mimesis*. For example, Arrow notes the similar roles of Cinna and Boggs and their respective support teams (165).

9. The conflicting and contradictory interpretations are most evident on the trilogy's fan websites, easily found with a simple internet search. Tom Henthorne has explored the impact of these fansites in a book chapter, "Make of It What You Will (Remix): *The* Hunger Games *Trilogy as Digital Text*" (Henthorne 139). Although occasionally appearing within fan forums, more nuanced differences of interpretation can be found in the growing secondary literature about the trilogy, including *The Hunger Games and Philosophy* (Dunn and Michaud),*The Panem Companion* (Arrow*), The Girl Who Was on Fire* (Wilson), and *Of Bread, Blood and* The Hunger Games (Pharr and Clark).

10. Abigail Mann has examined the relationships between "Competition and Kindness" within the philosophical context of Social Darwinism as an aspect of *The Hunger Games*. (Dunn and Michaud 104–120).

11. Joseph J. Foy has provided a detailed examination of the Hobbesian idea of a "war of all-against-all" as an aspect of *The Hunger Games* (206–221).

12. Some of the tweets included, "I was pumped about the Hunger Games. Until I learned that a black girl was playing Rue," ... "Kk call me racist but when I found out rue was black her death wasn't as sad #ihatemyself," ... "Cinna and Rue weren't supposed to be black... Why did the producer make all the good characters black?" and "EWW, rue is black?? I'm not watching" (Bull). See Deidre Anne Evans Garriott's essay in this collection, "Performing the Capitol in Digital Spaces: The Punitive Gaze of the Panopticon Among Fans and Critics," for an extended study of these tweets.

13. The role of socioeconomic class in the structure of Panem, including its relationship to race and gender, can be found in V. Arrow's *The Panem Companion*, especially chapter 4, "The Socioeconomics of Tessarae" (43).

14. Herbert Marcuse developed aspects of critical theory along slightly different directions from that of Horkheimer and Adorno. This was especially true in relation to their respective extensions of psychoanalytic theory. In addition to *One-Dimensional Man,* Marcuse's other major work on psychological repression and the desublimation of the instincts was *Eros and Civilization: A Philosophical Inquiry into Freud.*

15. For Winston Smith in *1984,* "the worst thing in the world" was his fear of rats (297), which was used by Big Brother to force him to betray his love.

16. Adorno's work as a whole can be seen as an attempt to hold onto hope against overwhelming evidence of hopelessness in the face of advancing domination of humans and nature. In all of his work, he presents an extended meditation on the increasing closure of hope. The philosophical justifications for his mode of presentation can be found in *Negative Dialectics.* An extended discussion of the relationship between critical consciousness and works of art can be found in *Aesthetic theory*, and masterful examples of the almost aphoristic writing he preferred can be found in *Minima Moralia.* The relationship between happiness, hope and utopia are discussed by Adorno and Ernst Bloch ("Something's Missing: A Discussion between Ernst Bloch and Theodor W. Adorno on the Contradictions of Utopian Longing") in *The Utopian Function of Art and Literature.*

17. Bonnie Honig recently re-examined "sororal sacrifice" in the context of the Greek play *Antigone*. An immanent critique of Horkheimer and Adorno's analysis of sacrifice in *Antigone*, from a feminist critical perspective, can be found in Patricia J. Mills' *Woman, Nature, and Psyche*.

18. Many of the trilogy's details provide grounds for further analysis of its "deep green" currents as well. Similarities between Katniss's life before she becomes a tribute, and that which is urged by those who follow the path of "deep green resistance" are not likely to be accidental, especially the relationship between ecological catastrophe and the need for extensive "survival" skills (McBay). A few of the trilogy's smallest details are especially interesting; Katniss's favorite color is green, and her first fashion statement as a tribute concerns how good the "mockingjay pin" looks against the "deep green" background of her shirt and pants (*THG* 42). The pin itself also would be important as the basis for a further examination of the trilogy's many examples of "sororal sacrifice." The pin's history encompasses not only the story of loss of sisters to the Games, but the deeper symbolism of the rebellion found in the living "mockingjay," including the human Mockingjay.

Works Cited

Adorno, Theodor W. *Aesthetic Theory*. Trans. C. Lenhardt. Eds. Gretel Adorno and Rolf Tiedemann. London: Routledge and Kegan Paul, 1970. Print.
_____. "Education After Auschwitz." *Can One Live after Auschwitz?: A Philosophical Reader*. Ed. Rolf Tiedemann. Stanford: Stanford University Press, 2003. Print.
_____. *Minima Moralia: Reflections from Damaged Life*. Trans. E. F. N. Jephcott. New York: Verso, 1991. Print.
_____. *Negative Dialectics*. Trans. E. B. Ashton. New York: Continuum, 1966. Print.
Allan, Nicole. "*The Hunger Games* Crosses Child Warfare with Class Warfare." Atlantic.com. 23 March 2012. Web. 9 February 2013.
Arrato, Andrew, and Eike Gebhardt, eds. *The Essential Frankfurt School Reader*. New York: Continuum, 1990. Print.
Arrow, V. *The Panem Companion: From Mellark Bakery to Mockingjays*. Dallas: BenBella Books, 2012. Print.
Aunger, Robert. *The Electric Meme: A New Theory of How We Think*. New York: Free Press, 2002. Print.
Benjamin, Walter. *Illuminations: Essays and Reflections*. Trans. Harry Zohn. Ed. Hannah Arendt. New York: Schocken Books, 1969. Print.
_____. "On the Mimetic Faculty." 1933. *Reflections*. Trans. Edmund Jephcott. Ed. Peter Demetz. New York: Schocken Books, 1978. Print.
Bloch, Ernst. *The Utopian Function of Art and Literature: Selected Essays*. 1988. Trans. Jack Zipes and Frank Mecklenburg. Cambridge, MA: MIT Press, 1993. Print.
Bond, Paul. "The Politics of *The Hunger Games*." Hollywoodreporter.com. 23 March 2012. Web. 8 February 2013.
Bradbury, Ray. *Fahrenheit 451*. 1951. New York: Simon & Schuster, 2012. Print.
Buck-Morss, Susan. *The Origin of Negative Dialectics*. New York: Free Press, 1977. Print.
Bull, Sarah. "*The Hunger Games* Hit by Racism Row as Movie Fans Tweet Vile Slurs over Casting of Black Teen Actress as Heroine Rue." Dailymail.com. 30 March 2012. Web. 9 February 2013.
Collins, Suzanne. *Catching Fire*. New York: Scholastic, 2009. Print.
_____. "A Conversation." Scholastic.com. Scholastic, n.d. Web. 18 November 2012.
_____. *The Hunger Games*. New York: Scholastic, 2008. Print.
_____. *The Hunger Games*: Suzanne Collins Video Clips: Responses to Book. Scholastic.com. n.d. Web. 9 February 2013.

_____. *Mockingjay*. New York: Scholastic, 2010. Print.
_____. "Suzanne Collins Answers Questions about the Hunger Games Trilogy." YouTube.com. 2 September 2010. Web. 18 November 2012.
Dawkins, Richard. *The Selfish Gene*. 1976. Oxford: Oxford University Press, 2006. Print.
Distin, Kate. *The Selfish Meme: A Critical Reassessment*. Cambridge; Cambridge University Press, 2005. Print.
Dunn, George A., and Nicolas Michaud, eds. *The Hunger Games and Philosophy: A Critique of Pure Treason*. Hoboken: John Wiley & Sons, 2012. Print.
Foy, Joseph J. "'Safe to Do What?': Morality and the War of All against All in the Arena." *The Hunger Games and Philosophy: A Critique of Pure Treason*. Eds. George A. Dunn and Nicolas Michaud. Hoboken: John Wiley & Sons, 2012. 206–221. Print.
Garrels, Scott R. *Mimesis and Science: Empirical Research on Imitation and the Mimetic Theory of Culture and Religion*. East Lansing: Michigan State University Press, 2011. Print.
Girard, Rene. *Mimesis and Theory: Essays on Literature and Criticism, 1953–2005*. Ed. Robert Doran. Stanford: Stanford University Press, 2008. Print.
_____. *Violence and the Sacred*. 1972. Trans. Patrick Gregory. Baltimore: Johns Hopkins University Press, 1977. Print.
Golding, William. *Lord of the Flies*. 1954. New York: Berkley, 2003. Print.
Harrison. "*The Hunger Games*: Political Parable or Just Mindless Crap?" Capitolcommentary.com. 6 April 2012. Web. 9 February 2013.
Held, David. *Introduction to Critical Theory: Horkheimer to Habermas*. Berkeley: University of California Press, 1980. Print.
Henthrone, Tom. *Approaching* The Hunger Games *Trilogy*. Jefferson, NC: McFarland, 2012. Print.
Honig, Bonnie. "Ismene's Forced Choice: Sacrifice and Sorority in Sophocles' *Antigone*." *Arethusa* 44 (2011): 29–68. Print.
Horkheimer, Max, and Theodor W. Adorno. *Dialectic of Enlightenment*. 1944. Trans. John Cumming. New York: Continuum, 1987. Print.
Hughey, Matthew W. "Cinethetic Racism: White Redemption and Black Stereotypes in 'Magical Negro' Films." *Social Problems* 56.3 (2009): 543–577. Print.
Huxley, Aldous. *Brave New World*. 1932. New York: HarperCollins, 2004. Print.
Jay, Martin. *The Dialectical Imagination: A History of the Frankfurt School and the Institute of Social Research, 1923–1950*. Boston: Little Brown, 1973. Print.
Mann, Abigail. "Competition and Kindness: The Darwinian World of the Hunger Games." *The Hunger Games and Philosophy: A Critique of Pure Treason*. Eds. George A. Dunn and Nicolas Michaud. Hoboken: John Wiley & Sons, 2012. 104–120. Print.
Marcuse, Herbert. *Eros and Civilization: A Philosophical Inquiry into Freud*. 1955. Boston: Beacon Press, 1966. Print.
_____. *One-Dimensional Man: Studies in the Ideology of Advanced Industrial Society*. Boston: Beacon Press, 1964. Print.
Margolis, Rick. "The Last Battle: With 'Mockingjay' on Its Way, Suzanne Collins Weighs in on Katniss and the Capitol." scholarlylibraryjournalwww. Scholarly Library Journal. Media Source. August 2010. Web. 1 August 2012.
Martin, D. Bruce. "Mimetic Moments: Adorno and Ecofeminism." *Feminist Interpretations of Theodor Adorno*. Ed. Renee Heberle. University Park: Pennsylvania State University Press, 2006. Print.
_____. "Sacred Identity and the Sacrificial Spirit." *Critical Ecologies*. Ed. Andrew Biro. Toronto: Toronto University Press, 2011. Print.
McBay, Aric, Lierre Keith, and Derrick Jensen. *Deep Green Resistance: Strategy to Save the Planet*. New York: Seven Stories Press, 2011. Print.
McDonald, Brian. "The Final Word in Entertainment: Mimetic and Monstrous Art in the

Hunger Games." *The Hunger Games and Philosophy: A Critique of Pure Treason*. Eds. George A. Dunn and Nicolas Michaud. Hoboken: John Wiley & Sons, 2012. 8–25. Print.
Mills, Patricia Jagentowicz. *Woman, Nature, and Psyche*. New Haven: Yale University Press, 1987. Print.
Orwell, George. *1984*. 1949. New York: Everyman's Library, 1992. Print.
_____. *All Art Is Propaganda: Critical Essays*. 2008. Boston: Mariner Books, 2009. Print.
Pharr, Mary F., and Leisa A. Clark, eds. *Of Bread, Blood and* The Hunger Games*: Critical Essays on the Suzanne Collins Trilogy*. Jefferson, NC: McFarland, 2012. Print.
Taussig, Michael. *Mimesis and Alterity*. New York: Routledge, 1993. Print.
Vonnegut, Kurt. *Slaughterhouse-Five, or The Children's Crusade: A Duty-Dance with Death*. 1969. New York: Dell, 1991. Print.
Wiggershaus, Rolf. *The Frankfurt School: Its History, Theories, and Political Significance*. Trans. Michael Robertson. Cambridge, MA: MIT Press, 1994. Print.
Wilson, Leah, ed. *The Girl Who Was on Fire*. Dallas: BamBella Books, 2011. Print.
Žižek, Slavoj. *The Year of Dreaming Dangerously*. London: Verso, 2012. Print.
Zola, Emile. *Germinal*. 1885. Trans. Peter Collier. Oxford: Oxford University Press, 2008. Print.
Zuidervaart, Lambert. *Adorno's Aesthetic Theory: The Redemption of Illusion*. Cambridge, MA: MIT Press, 1991. Print.

Conclusion: Where Can We Go and What Can We Disrupt from Here?

We hope that it has not escaped readers' notice that the titles of the first and last essays of this collection invoke one of the most salient questions of *The Hunger Games*—Peeta and Katniss's question about what is "Real or Not Real?" in their memories of their experiences of the Games. Several of the essays extend Peeta's question to investigations into the nature of narratives and storytelling, political possibilities, the future, the present, and even our processes as scholars. In questioning the "real," this collection participates in the disruption that the trilogy calls for. It situates *The Hunger Games* directly within the blurry distinctions and complex relationship between fiction and reality, to examine discursive relationships among the novels, politics, social discourse, gender discourse, literary scholarship, and popular responses. In addition, it disrupts familiar critical territories to map out newer and more appropriate ones. In these new territories, more complications, more transgressions, and more responses to the trilogy and other such texts are possible.

Just as the "Real or Not Real?" question frames our scholarly processes and approaches to the trilogy, the implied question at the end of Katniss's Epilogue—of what she must she do and how she must proceed into her own future—extends to our relationship with the critical spaces and places we have entered. Where do we go from here? What can we disrupt? Or, should we? After all, *The Hunger Games* trilogy and scholarship on it come with *real* consequences, positive or negative. Thus, compiling a collection of essays on fiction such as *The Hunger Games* does not come without a certain mindfulness of how our enthusiasm and creativity as normally positive traits could very well morph into a colonizing spirit, or the competitive and cut-throat spirit of the Hunger Games themselves. With this mindfulness, we are wary of putting out the very fire that Katniss started, the fire whose flames this collection has fanned. Rather than usurping critical space, critically performing the Capitol, or appropriating critical narratives, we hope that this conclusion can serve as a space to reflect on the work of this collection, to take a step back instead of proceeding forth into newer territory. This posture of self-imposed moderation can then allow our successors to disrupt our claims, tell their own stories, and create their own critical spaces. Indeed, as some of our essays have claimed, the Capitol tries to close down district citizens' possibilities and choices for directing their own lives, while the essays in this collection pick up on Katniss's accomplishments in making more choices available to readers. *The Hunger Games* and this collection celebrate choices in narratives, choices in gender, choices in discourses, critical readings, and research approaches. As the initial hype of *The Hunger Games* mellows to a more sustainable critical interest, we look forward to witnessing the choices that the trilogy's scholars will make in the coming decades.

Still, even in this posture of humility and anticipation of others' contributions to existing criticism, we can make the general claim that *The Hunger Games* scholarship will likely continue raising more questions than it answers, as does Katniss's Epilogue. Certainly, given the release of *Catching Fire* in November of 2013 and news of a two-part release of *Mockingjay*, such scholarship will be timely and exciting, right in the thick of things, and thus will occupy a unique position for examining the immediate and continued impact of Collins's work on the "real" world. Will pockets of *The Hunger Games*-inspired social activism arise, beyond the wearing of Mockingjay pins? Will the trilogy garner the status of "classic" YA or dystopian literature like some of those mentioned in our essays, such as *Catcher in the Rye* or *Lord of the Flies*, or will it continue in the ranks of popular fiction? Will it help to blur the boundaries between "classic" literature and "pop" fiction, occupying or creating a status all its own? Readers, scholars, teachers, publishers, filmmakers all have a stake in answering these questions.

As we question the trilogy's place in critical conversations, and its oscillation between classic and popular distinctions, we can examine the ways in which readers have sought to bind *The Hunger Games* to one classification and the ways in which readers have sought to resist singular classifications. As one installation in a growing body of *The Hunger Games* scholarship, this book questions, as does Collins, the trilogy's place within dystopian and YA categories. In so doing, we acknowledge that it intersects with both, but should be strictly bound to neither. For instance, several authors contributing to this collection, such as Arosteguy, Jones, and Martin, all view *The Hunger Games* as creating spaces for utopian possibilities, fictional and real. And as other contributors to this collection imply, these texts appeal to a much more inclusive audience than simply readers within the "adolescent" or "young adult" age brackets. These texts are enjoyed by teachers as much as they are by students, by parents as well as children, by grade school and university students, and by scholarly critics and book clubs alike. Perhaps it is the very breaking down of the boundaries between audiences that initiates this utopian impulse. If dystopia divides to conquer, then utopia relishes in the unity of diverse communities and peoples.

These attempts to create boundaries—"classic" versus "popular" literature, dystopian versus utopian literature, age restricted versus age-inclusive literature—are methods of turning *The Hunger Games* into a place. As a place, it is known and defined by a set of rules, by classifications and conventions, and by audiences. We argue that *The Hunger Games* cannot be so easily classified and bounded. Thus, we treat *The Hunger Games* as a textual space that destabilizes boundaries to create additional spaces for more conversations.

Because we are considering the trilogy as "space," we want to consider, briefly, a very physical place—the YA section of the local bookstore. Bookstores are, from necessity, divided places. The shelves an individual frequents mark them, define readers' tastes as science fiction lovers, romance addicts, biography fiends, or in our cases, dedicated adult readers of YA texts. Fellow patrons come to know things about us as we cordon ourselves off in particular sections. These sections divide; however, the YA section seems, often, to overcome this division, attracting readers from all ages, genders, and backgrounds. Yet, YA texts have become so popular for readers who do not identify as young adults, that popular YA texts are often republished with "adult" covers. This rearrangement of the physical space of the book makes such texts navigable across boundaries, but curiously, continues to emphasize the either/or status of the young adult and adult, revealing our culture's reliance on easy categories.

This book, authored and edited by a group of citizens, scholars, and readers, as dissolving boundaries and divisions in order to open up space in popular, critical, or real spheres, participates in what we feel is necessary critical work. If we are to dissociate ourselves from the metaphorical Capitol, its technology, its promises and provisions of beauty and comfort, and its price of warfare, oppression, and violence, and if we are to avoid counteracting the disruptive work we see *The Hunger Games* doing, then this collection and other works that follow will do well to stimulate more conversations about Panem, Katniss, her boys, and the Hunger Games. We do not posit a final and definitive word about genre, space, literary scholarship, and civic discourse. We seek to be *a* voice, perhaps one ember to fan the flame of activism and scholarship that emerge from this trilogy.

About the Contributors

Katie **Arosteguy** teaches advanced composition and English for the University Writing Program at UC Davis. She received a Ph.D. from Washington State University and her published works focus on the construction of masculinity and motherhood in American fiction and popular culture. She published an essay in the book *Mad Men, Women and Children* (2012) and has published articles in *Atenea*, *Women's Studies* and *Western American Literature*.

Carissa Ann **Baker** is a doctoral student at the University of Central Florida and a professor of English at Seminole State College of Florida. She is also involved with diversity and community engagement initiatives. Her primary research focus is literature and environment, particularly environmental education, ecofeminism, technology and the environment, and manmade "natural" spaces.

Anne M. **Canavan** holds a Ph.D. in English from Northern Illinois University. Some of her research interests include narratology and gothic literature. She is a longstanding member and area chair in the Midwest Popular Culture Association/American Culture Association.

Ann M. M. **Childs** reviews young adult and children's literature for *Kirkus Reviews*. Her research and writing focus on middle-grade and young adult fantasy and science fiction. An essay is upcoming in an anthology on female rebellion in dystopian fiction. She is a dual-degree graduate of the Simmons College's Center for the Study of Children's Literature.

Deidre Anne Evans **Garriott** received a Ph.D. in English from the University of Tennessee, Knoxville. She is the acting director of the Writing Center at the University of Tennessee, Knoxville, and researches the intersection of material rhetorics, rhetorics of space and place, and rhetorical identity. She is also working on a study of sites of historical memory.

Whitney Elaine **Jones** is a doctoral candidate in English at the University of Tennessee, Knoxville. Her research interests include British and children's literature. She published an essay in *Teaching with Harry Potter: Essays on Classroom Wizardry from Elementary School to College* (2013) and is working on projects about the use of dolls in the works of Frances Hodgson Burnett and the place of the artistic child in children's literature and the Victorian and Modernist *Bildungsroman*.

Adam **Levin** is a Ph.D. candidate in English literature at the University of Pretoria, South Africa. His research examines the tensions between testimonies of Holocaust survivors and those of Apartheid victims and perpetrators. He holds a master's degree from the University of the Witwatersrand and teaches critical thinking courses in various disciplines there. He created the blog *Pop Junkie*, where he writes about popular culture.

Bruce **Martin** is an administrator at New Mexico State University Alamogordo. He teaches political science courses and has been a long-time environmental, antinuclear, and peace activist in New Mexico. He earned a Ph.D. at the University of Massachusetts–Amherst. He has published essays on ecology and ecofeminism in *Critical Ecologies* (2011) and *Feminist Interpretations of Theodore Adorno* (2006).

Sarah N. **Petrovic** received a Ph.D. from Northern Illinois University and is an assistant professor at Oklahoma Wesleyan University. Among her research interests are film and literature intersections and contemporary British fiction. She is a longstanding member and area chair in the Midwest Popular Culture Association/American Culture Association.

Linda J. **Rice**, Ph.D., is an associate professor in the department of English at Ohio University where she teaches language arts methods and young adult literature. She is the author of *What Was It Like? Teaching History and Culture Through Young Adult Literature* (2006) and has published articles in several journals, including *The Journal of Research in Education*. She has also authored nine essays in five edited books.

Susan Shau Ming **Tan** is a Ph.D. student at the University of Cambridge. Her dissertation focuses on violence in young adult literature with an emphasis on YA dystopias. She has published and presented work on *The Hunger Games* and is a Dr. Herchel-Smith Fellow and a recipient of the Mellon-Mays Undergraduate Research Fellowship.

Julie Elizabeth **Tyler** is a Ph.D. candidate at the University of Tennessee, Knoxville. In addition to her activist work in the community and teaching courses in composition and literature at UT, she combines theoretical and qualitative research on topics related to academia and the "real" world, in the areas of contemporary literature, community literacy, and English as a second language. Her dissertation project is an empirical study of book clubs as social pedagogy.

Katie **Wrabel** is a graduate student at Ohio University pursuing a master's degree in literary history with a focus on Southern gothic literature and New Woman fiction. Her thesis project blends literary analysis with pedagogy in a study of selected works by Flannery O'Connor, Joyce Carol Oates, and Shirley Jackson. She was previously a high school English teacher.

Index

Abel, Elizabeth 173
adolescence 1, 5–8, 11–13, 16–20, 22–39, 41, 43, 43n2, 43n3, 67, 75, 81n21, 83–84, 90–98, 102–103, 105, 150, 178, 185, 187–188, 192–194, 200–201, 216–218, 244, 245; liminal 8, 12, 91, 105; literature 6, 106, 119, 121 (*see also* young adult literature); narrative 18, 25, 28; voice 3, 6, 18–19, 23, 28, 39, 41, 43n3
Adorno, Theodor 221, 224, 227, 237, 238n2, 238n4, 238n7, 239n14, 239n16, 240n17
adult 6, 17–24, 30–34, 36, 38, 40–41, 43n3, 44n5, 75, 83–98, 104, 128–129, 133, 137, 139, 182, 185, 225, 245
Agency 4, 6–8, 31, 34, 43–44n5, 45–47, 49–52, 57–58, 86–88, 90, 95, 122, 147, 154, 156, 165, 172, 182n3, 218
"anarchic structure" 230
arena 30–31, 33, 35–36, 40, 48–51, 54, 56, 86, 88–91, 93, 97, 102–103, 113, 131–132, 152, 163, 167, 178, 184, 187, 189–191, 194, 198, 200, 202–209, 211, 215, 221–222, 224, 226, 229–230, 232, 235
audience(s) 4, 6–8, 11, 13, 17, 20, 22, 31, 35, 43n3, 47, 50–51, 54–57, 66, 72, 84, 96, 98n5, 102–104, 107–110, 160–161, 171, 175–181, 182n1, 184–191, 194, 202, 213, 218, 222–223, 236–237, 244–245; Capitol 22, 47, 52, 54, 102–104, 107, 110, 122, 135, 187, 189, 191; district 11; intended 185–186
authenticity 3, 6–7, 9, 13, 17–19, 21–25, 30–31, 34–42, 43n3, 44n5, 126, 132–134, 140–141, 147, 154, 169, 171, 182n1, 200, 206, 208, 214–215, 217–218; voice 39, 41
author 4, 6, 18–31, 34, 36, 38, 40–41, 43n1, 43n4, 43–44n5, 46, 50, 53, 67, 78, 80n9, 104, 117, 121, 150, 162, 175, 199, 201, 210, 216, 222; implied 44n5
avoxes 18, 92, 115

Battle Royale 22; *see also* Takami, Koushun
Beetee 36, 69, 209
Benjamin, Walter 225, 227, 234, 238n6
berries 35–36, 40, 70, 90, 94, 200–201, 206, 208, 222–223, 228, 232–233
blog 3, 10–11, 124, 147–150, 156, 161–162, 165–170, 174, 176, 179, 181
Booth, Wayne 43–44n5
The Boy with the Bread 1, 65, 221
Bradbury, Ray 222
Buttercup 209

Capitol 1–2, 11, 16–22, 31, 34–38, 40, 42–43, 43n2, 47–50, 52, 54–57, 63–65, 70, 79n2, 83–86, 88–95, 102–105
Caruth, Cathy 125–126, 138, 142n2
child 1–3, 6–8, 10–11, 13, 16, 18, 20–22, 24, 26, 29, 32–33, 39–42, 61, 66–67, 76–78, 84–89, 91, 93, 96–97, 105, 108, 127–129, 133–137, 139, 146–151, 153, 155–157, 161, 163, 193, 213, 217, 225, 235–237, 245; evil 88–90, 92; literature 6, 19–21, 30, 61, 68, 75, 78–79, 81n21, 95–96, 104–106, 117, 129, 199; sacrifice 48, 83–85, 87–88, 90–91, 95–97, 117, 120, 163, 191, 220, 226, 231, 235; violence 83, 86, 88–89, 96–97, 119, 147–148, 163, 178, 185, 212, 222; vulnerable 83, 86–88, 90, 95
citizen 11, 16, 34, 55, 79n2, 83–85, 87–88, 92–93, 95–98, 98n4, 102–103, 105–108, 110–113, 115, 117, 119, 121, 122n3, 131, 137, 160, 163–164, 166, 169, 174, 177–180, 184, 186, 188, 190–191, 203–205, 207, 212, 216, 223, 225, 229–231, 233, 236, 244–245
Collins, Suzanne 111, 117, 130, 182n1, 201, 216, 220, 222–223, 228; *Catching Fire* 14, 35–40, 70, 90–91, 93, 106–107, 113, 116, 134–135, 157, 178, 204–205, 208, 211, 230, 232; *The Hunger Game* 14,

249

34–35, 37, 40, 45–52, 57, 60, 83, 86–88, 90, 102, 105–107, 111–113, 116, 135, 151–152, 155–156, 163, 169–170, 174, 179, 184, 188–189, 200, 229–230; interview 13, 117, 160, 201, 229, 235; *Mockingjay* 14, 16, 37–39, 55, 63, 115, 117–118, 134–136, 153, 156, 205, 208–209, 213, 221
coming of age 83–84
community 2, 8–9, 11–12, 25–26, 29, 38, 42, 53, 61, 73, 75, 77–78, 84–87, 89–91, 93, 96, 127, 135, 161, 164, 168–169, 175–177, 180–181, 185, 188, 212, 214, 245
Coontz, Stephanie 149
Cornucopia 203

Dargis, Manhola 11, 171–172, 178
daughter 47, 147–148, 150–154, 157
Deleuze, Gilles 18–19
dystopia 5, 8, 13, 61–62, 66, 72–78, 79n5, 108, 120–121, 245; didacticism 104, 119, 121, 132; literature 22–23, 73, 75, 77–78, 81n20, 84, 91, 95–97, 98n5, 104, 118–121, 129–130, 154, 171, 182, 215, 218, 220–223, 227–232, 236–237, 238n3, 244–245

ecocriticism 12, 198–199, 218
enlightenment 217, 224, 226–227
epilogue 5–6, 10, 13, 16–43, 75–76, 94, 132–137, 139, 150, 243–244

faith 9, 128, 132–141
father 49, 53, 65, 68–69, 78, 91, 132, 134, 137, 142n8, 147, 149, 151–153, 155, 201, 203, 212, 214, 221
femininity 8, 61–62, 64, 66, 71–72, 77, 80n9, 80–81n19
feminism 61; ecofeminism 217–218, 238–239n7
film 3, 6–7, 11, 22, 45–47, 52–58, 60, 109–110, 121, 148, 162, 165–169, 171–174, 176, 185, 223–224, 228, 230, 237; filmmakers 162, 167, 170, 172, 176–177, 181, 244
Foucault, Michel 46, 160, 162–164, 168–169, 177–178, 181; *Discipline and Punish: The Birth of the Prison* 160, 163–164, 177–178; "The Order of Discourse" 46
Frank, Anne 9, 131–132
Frankfurt School 12, 220, 223–224, 237, 238n1, 238n3, 238n6, 238–239n7
futuristic 130, 185, 194, 220–222

Gale 1–2, 37–38, 47, 54, 60, 62–67, 69–77, 79–80n7, 80n8, 80n16, 95, 107–108, 111, 115, 120, 138, 155, 169–170, 172, 174, 178, 184, 200, 202–203, 209, 211–214, 235–236
Gamemakers 36, 40, 48, 54, 56–57, 111, 113, 180, 187, 190, 201, 207, 232
gender 3–4, 7–8, 13, 43n1, 60–62, 64, 67–78, 79n2, 80n9, 80n15, 80n16, 80–81n19, 81n21, 148, 154, 171, 182–183n4, 218, 239n13, 243–245; female 6–8, 13, 45, 60–61, 64, 66, 68–69, 71–75, 78, 79n2, 79–80n7, 80n8, 80n10, 146, 167, 169, 172; femininity 8, 61–62, 64–66, 71–72, 74, 77, 79, 80n9, 80n10, 80–81n19, 169; male 7–8, 60–69, 72–73, 78, 79n2, 79–80n7, 80n10, 147, 154; masculinity 8, 60–75, 77–79, 80n8, 80n10, 80n14, 80n15, 80n16, 80–81n19, 81n21; traits 8, 61–65, 67–68, 72, 75, 78–79
Genette, Girard 43n4; paratext 43n4
genre 3, 5–6, 9, 20–23, 30, 46, 73–74, 77, 79n2, 80n10, 84, 91, 95–97, 98n5, 104–105, 118–119, 121, 125, 129, 140, 147, 160, 182n1, 199, 218, 238n3, 245; DNA 12, 222, 231, 236, 238n3
Germinal 222, 235
Girard, Réne 83–85, 93, 238n1, 238n3
the Girl on Fire 1, 47, 49, 73, 79, 235
Golding, William 22, 222
grassroots 3, 20
green 12, 204, 217–218, 238–239n7, 240n18; action 198; reading 198; space 202, 212, 217
Guattari, Félix 18–19
guilt 23, 26–27, 85, 106, 147, 149, 154, 158, 175, 234; guilty pleasure 148

Haymitch 17, 35, 38, 40, 47–51, 54–57, 64, 69, 87–88, 118–119, 158n1, 169, 179, 189–191, 206, 211
Helm, Janet 103, 112–114, 116, 122, 122n3; autonomy 115 -116; contact 112; disintegration 112–113; immersion/emmersion 115–116; model of racial development 112; pseudo-independence 112–114;
heterodiegetic level 46
Holocaust 4, 9, 124–141; literature 9, 124–130, 132, 139–141, 142n5; survivors 9, 124–126, 128, 133–134, 136, 138, 140–141; trauma 9, 124–129, 132, 139–141
The Hob 151, 201, 235–236

Horkheimer, Max 224, 238n6, 239n14
Huxley, Aldous 222, 231

identification 1–2, 9, 11, 23, 79–80n7, 102, 104, 106–107, 111–112, 114, 117–118, 121, 164, 175–176, 181, 200
identity 1, 7–8, 10, 28, 46, 48, 51, 57, 60, 62, 64, 66–67, 70, 72–75, 78, 79–80n7, 84–86, 88–95, 98n4, 103–105, 109, 110, 113–118, 120, 122, 122–123n3, 146, 150–151, 156–157, 199–202, 208, 212–213, 220–221, 223–224, 227–231, 238–239n7; feminine 64, 68; masculine 61–62, 66, 68, 72
implied author 43–44n5
implied reader 111
innocence 24, 86–87, 89, 97, 193
Internet 4, 11, 161–162, 165, 167, 169, 175–177, 180

Jabberjays 31, 206
Janet, Pierre 126
Jezebel 11, 166–170, 173–174, 176, 181
Journal of Adolescent and Adult Literacy 201
Juzwiak, Rich 169–170

Lange, Dorothea 53
Language of Earth 210, 215
Lord of the Flies 22, 222, 244
Lubavitch Girls 127

Magical Negro 229
Marcuse, Herbert 231, 238n6, 239n14
maternity 153–154, 156
maturation 8, 16, 28, 34, 67, 83–84, 88, 92, 94–97; of genre 23
McEwan, Ian 25, 27, 42; *Atonement* 25, 27
The Meadow 78, 133, 200, 210, 212, 216–217, 236–237
mimesis 12, 220, 223–228, 238n1, 238n3, 238–239n7, 239n8
misunderstanding 93–94
Mockingjay 30, 37–38, 55, 63, 93, 95, 106, 116, 118, 156, 200, 205, 207–209, 212–213, 220–222, 238; pin 3, 13, 53, 75, 240n18, 244
Morrison, Toni 25–27, 42, 173–174; *The Bluest Eye* 25–27, 42; *Playing in the Dark: Whiteness and the Literary Imagination* 174
mother 10, 49–50, 53, 69, 71–72, 76, 78, 87, 91, 95, 131, 146–158, 170, 174, 191, 203, 214, 216; motherline 151–152

mutation 12, 18, 31, 41, 187, 189–190, 205–208, 220–222, 224, 228–231, 236, 238

narrative 3–10, 13, 16–42, 44n5, 45–57, 63, 67, 69, 76, 95–97, 102–122, 124–141, 146–147, 150–151, 154, 167, 178, 199–200, 203, 205–206, 209–210, 212, 215, 230, 243–244; adolescent 17, 19–21, 24–25, 28, 33, 35–36, 46, 67, 95, 97, 150–154; adult 19, 25, 30, 33, 40–41, 96; control 6, 30, 38, 45–48, 51–54, 56–57, 117, 121–122; extra narrative 32–33; family provider 48; first person 7, 23, 27–28, 55, 67, 102–104, 106, 117, 210; inter narrative 33; intra narrative 32; matrilineal 146, 152, 155; memory 126, 137, 139–140; narrative proper 17, 20, 23, 25–27, 30–35, 38–40, 42; narrator 3, 6, 9, 16, 18, 22–23, 25, 27–31, 33–37, 43–44n5, 46, 66, 106, 129, 136–137, 170; paratext 43n4; post-narrative 17, 23–35, 39–42; pre-narrative 32–33; questionable 23–24, 28; as safe space 2, 4, 7–9, 102, 104–105, 122, 124, 129; star-crossed lovers 47–48, 50–52, 56, 179, 187, 189, 232; third person 7, 26, 30; tribute 47–49, 51
nature 12, 18–19, 31, 66, 198–218, 220–221, 224–227, 229
Nazi 128, 131, 139
The New York Times 11, 122n1, 166, 169, 171–172, 178

"Oligarchic competitivism" 230, 233,
oppression 5, 102–105, 109, 111–122, 139, 150, 162, 171, 190, 214, 231–232, 245
O'Reilly, Andrea 10, 146–147, 154–155, 157
Orwell, George 222–223, 231–233, 235; Big Brother 234; *1984* 222, 231–235
the Other 2, 4, 8–9, 18, 85–86, 89, 102–115, 117–122
othermother 10, 147, 154–156, 158n1

Panem et circenses 87, 120, 184, 231,
Panopticon 4, 10, 160, 162–164, 168–169, 176–182
parasocial relationship 186–187
Peeta 1, 16–17, 35–36, 38–39, 47–52, 54–57, 60, 62–67, 69–78, 79–80n7, 80n8, 80n9, 86, 90–91, 94, 108, 114–116, 131, 133–135, 152–153, 155, 157, 169–170, 174, 177–179, 187, 189–190, 201, 207,

209–210, 212, 214–217, 221, 230, 232, 234–236, 243
pharmakos 84, 88–90, 98n4
Phelan, James 6, 45
place 1–5, 9, 12, 81n21, 104, 153, 154, 177, 198–200, 203, 210–211, 243–245; displacement 84–85, 93; "new critical category" 198
Plato 225; *Republic* 225
Podnieks, Elizabeth 146–147, 154–155, 157
politics 1–5, 7–8, 12–13, 17–23, 26–31, 34, 37–38, 43n1, 54–55, 74–76, 78, 89–91, 93–95, 98n4, 116, 129, 132, 146, 149, 155–157, 161–162, 165, 170, 173, 175, 179, 181–182, 184, 198–199, 207, 216–218, 220–221, 223–236, 243; of maturation 8, 83–84, 87–88, 92, 94–98; real world 12, 220, 222–223, 225, 227–230, 236–238, 238n1
power 1, 6–8, 10, 12–13, 17, 28, 34, 45–47, 49, 52, 55–58, 63, 68–69, 72, 74, 77–79, 84–87, 90–97, 104, 105, 112, 117–122, 154–155, 163–164, 171, 177–178, 180–181, 182n3, 190–191, 198, 201, 203–208, 216, 220–221, 224, 226, 228, 231–233, 235, 238
Prim 16, 34, 47–49, 53, 63, 65, 69, 76, 83, 86–92, 94, 97, 118, 120, 133–134, 137, 152, 155–156, 163, 167, 170, 174, 187, 201, 209, 230, 236
privilege 4, 8–9, 26, 47, 63, 88, 102–122, 147, 170, 178, 217
punish 2, 11, 47, 83, 85, 89, 91–92, 94, 107, 114–115, 120, 160, 162–164, 168, 176–180, 182, 201, 222, 231
punitive gaze 4, 10–11, 160, 162–163

Quarter Quell 16, 31, 36, 40, 42, 91, 113, 205, 232

race 13, 43n1, 103, 109–110, 121, 122n3, 162, 165, 167–171, 173–177, 183n5, 230, 235
racism 11, 25, 105, 167–168, 174, 176, 178–179, 191, 223–224, 229
radical adolescence 8, 90, 92, 94, 96
reader 2–5, 7–13, 17–24, 27, 29–32, 34–35, 37–42, 43n3, 43–44n5, 46–48, 50, 57, 60–63, 67–69, 72–73, 78–79, 96–97, 102–122, 124–141, 142n5, 148–150, 161, 173–177, 185–186, 189, 193, 200, 218, 228–229, 244–245; female 61, 78, 80n8; implied 43–44n5, 96, 111, 122;

male 8, 7–8, 60–79; mother 146–150; privileged 4, 8–9, 102–122; young Jewish 4, 9, 124–141, 142n5
real world 3–4, 9, 12, 20, 29, 32, 34, 39–40, 84–85, 89, 104, 107, 109–110, 112–113, 115, 127, 130, 132, 147, 154, 156–157, 160, 162, 174, 188, 190, 199–200, 215, 220, 222–223, 236, 238, 244
reality television 1, 11, 54, 160, 162, 164, 170, 182n1, 184–194, 194n2, 214, 222; *Bridalplasty* 192; *Jersey Shore* 191, 193
The Reaping 34–36, 47–48, 56, 70, 83, 85–87, 105, 155–156, 163, 203, 227
rebellion 16, 20, 31, 33, 35–37, 39–40, 42, 57, 64, 70, 75, 77, 80n9, 88, 116, 152, 156, 162–163, 184, 190, 200–202, 204–205, 208–209, 216, 220–222, 228, 230, 233, 235–236, 240n18; adolescent 83–98; political 20
relationships 12, 67, 69, 107, 156, 178, 186–187, 192–193, 198, 199, 202–203, 212, 215, 217–218, 220, 224, 237, 243; love triangle 7–8, 60–79; mother/daughter 150–154
"repressive desublimation" 231
Republic 225; *see also* Plato
Reynolds, Kimberly 21, 40, 81n21
rhetoric 1, 3–4, 11, 43n5, 46, 83, 149, 161–162, 165, 167, 169, 174, 177, 202, 218
romanticism 86
Rorschach test 104, 117–118, 120–121, 223
Rose, Jacqueline 20–21, 24, 30
Rosenfeld, Alvin 125,
Roskies, David G. 125
Rowling, J.K. 25, 30; *Harry Potter and the Deathly Hallows* 25, 28–30
Rue 11, 30, 36, 52, 55–56, 86, 91, 110, 121, 155–156, 166–167, 172–175, 177, 183n5, 203, 212–213, 229–230, 239n12

sacrifice 12, 76, 77, 83–98, 98n4, 106, 154, 156, 220–238, 238n1, 238n2, 239–239n7, 240n17, 240n18
safe space 2, 4–9, 70, 102–122, 124–141, 202
Said, Edward 103
Salinger, J.D. 23; *The Catcher in the Rye* 23, 40; Holden Caulfield 23–25, 40, 42; "phonies" 23–24
scapegoat 7–8, 83–98
"scientific socialism" 230, 234
Seltzer, Sarah 166, 168–172, 181

silence 8, 18, 34, 39, 42, 88, 92–94, 115, 117–118; adult's 88, 92; child's 185; Katniss's 117–118
Slaughterhouse-Five 236
social media 11, 162, 165–166, 173, 177–178, 178
space 1–13, 21, 26–28, 31–32, 34–35, 39, 65, 89–90, 104–105, 107, 111, 114, 131, 147, 154, 158, 160–182, 198–218, 243–245; liminal 105, 212; neutral 149
speculative fiction 220–223, 232, 236
speech 46, 202; control of 18, 34, 46, 88, 92
Spivak, Gayatri Chakravorty 18; "Can the Subaltern Speak?" 43n1
Stewart, Dodai 174, 176–177, 179–181
storytelling 4, 8, 19–20, 23–24, 36, 38–42, 243; co-storytelling 38
subaltern 18, 43n1
subjectivity 61, 75, 77, 98n4
sympathy 4, 8, 70, 76, 102–122

Takami, Koushun 22; *see also Battle Royale*
teacher education 11, 187
Theseus and the Minotaur 130, 222, 224
tracker jackers 206
transgression 8, 11, 16, 20, 30–32, 35, 37–43; extra-narrative 32–33; intra-narrative 32; narrative 17–20, 29, 31–32; political 31; textual 20, 32, 34, 39, 41, 74, 80n9

trauma 4–5, 7–9, 16, 23, 26, 29–30, 32, 38, 72, 83–98, 102–122, 124–141
tribute 22, 34, 36, 38, 47–51, 53–56, 63, 71, 83–90, 92–94, 98n4, 103, 105, 108–110, 113–114, 131, 133, 163, 165, 167, 174–175, 178–180, 186–191, 193, 200–201, 203–204, 207, 212–213, 222, 224–226, 231–232, 236
Twitter 3, 11, 43n2, 110, 161–162, 166–181, 182n2, 229, 239n12

utopia 8, 61–62, 72–79, 79n5, 96, 130–134, 137–138, 142n7, 225, 227, 237, 239n16, 244–245; literature 60–81, 245

victim 83–95, 119–121, 125–127, 131, 224, 226
violence 10, 61, 63–66, 72, 76, 78, 83–85, 88–90, 92–97, 102, 148, 150, 154, 182, 185, 188, 190, 194, 211–212, 214, 221–223, 229, 234, 236, 245

West, Lindy 176–177, 179, 181

young adult literature 6, 19–20, 22, 25, 36, 39, 61, 79, 103–105, 119, 150, 153–155, 157, 169, 182, 199–200, 218

Žižek, Slavoj 237
Zola, Émile 222, 235

www.ingramcontent.com/pod-product-compliance
Ingram Content Group UK Ltd.
Pitfield, Milton Keynes, MK11 3LW, UK
UKHW041935140426
5217IPUK00014B/488